4

英语词汇速记大全
同义同类
归纳法

俞敏洪。著

群言出版社

图书在版编目(CIP)数据

英语词汇速记大全.4,同义同类归纳法 / 俞敏洪编
著. —北京:群言出版社,2006
ISBN 7-80080-590-5

Ⅰ.英... Ⅱ.俞... Ⅲ.英语—词汇—记忆术

Ⅳ.H313

中国版本图书馆 CIP 数据核字(2006)第 068725 号

责任编辑	王 超
封面设计	王 琳
出版发行	群言出版社
地 址	北京东城区东厂胡同北巷1号
邮政编码	100006
联系电话	65263345 65265404
电子信箱	qunyancbs@dem-league.org.cn
印 刷	北京朝阳新艺印刷有限公司
经 销	全国新华书店
版 次	2006 年 8 月第 1 版 2006 年 10 月第 2 次印刷
开 本	880×1230 1/32
印 张	12.5
字 数	286 千字
书 号	ISBN 7-80080-590-5
定 价	28.00 元

前　言

　　1991 年到 1999 年的八年，是我生活中最快乐的八年，因为我每天都和学生们在一起。不管创办新东方的过程受过多少挫折，不管个人生活遇到多少痛苦和不幸，只要一走进课堂，我就能看到学生灿烂的笑容，感受到学生为了前途而日夜奋斗的精神。学生的笑容让我兴奋，学生的精神让我感动。这些笑容和精神支撑着我枯燥的日常生活，使我渡过了很多难关。我也不断地把学生们感人的故事和我自己奋斗的故事讲给大家听。我们一起分享着学习、工作、生活的痛苦和快乐。我和学生们融为一体，尽管我叫不出大多数学生的名字，但他们成了我生活中真正的朋友和精神支柱。

　　1999 年以后，新东方越来越大，如果我每天继续走进教室教书，新东方就会在缺乏管理和秩序的混乱中崩溃。为了让新东方有序地存在并发展，为了让新东方成为优秀人才的聚集地，我忍痛割爱地放弃了每天站在讲台上的痛快，进入了枯燥而琐碎的日常管理之中。转眼六年过去了，在这六年中，新东方得到了长足的发展，新东方优秀教师越来越多，有很多教师在英语教学尤其是英语词汇教学中已经远远超过了我的水平。我感到欣慰，因为我的放弃，新东方越来越强大；我也感到遗憾，因为六年没有走上讲台，我自己的教学水平和词汇水平越来越低。我最大的愿望是有一天，当新东方的日常管理不需要我再操心时，我能够重新踏踏实实地研究我所爱好的英语词汇词源学，踏踏实实地写出一些有关词汇记忆和英语学习的书籍，并且踏踏实实地走进课堂，面对一张张可爱的笑脸，向他们讲述词汇的故事、学习的故事、生活的故事。那时候，我也许已经白发苍苍，但面对无数向往未来的面孔，我一定会回忆起我自己的无数青春往事，并再次点燃我自己的青春激情和火焰。

《英语词汇速记大全1——词根＋词缀记忆法》是我六年前的一部作品。当时我想写三到四部有关英语词汇记忆的书籍，其中第二本书《从熟悉的单词记生词》，在2000年时我已经在电脑中完成了，但不幸的是，有一次我的手提电脑掉到了地上，结果电脑和电脑中的文字全部被摧毁，同时被摧毁的还有我重新写书的勇气。后来我懂得了机器的不可靠，学会了随时把电脑中的文字拷贝到另一个硬盘上，但书还是没有写出来。我为自己的懒惰找了很多的理由，比如太忙啦，比如有更重要的事情啦，比如要陪很多人喝酒应酬啦，但最后发现永远丢失的不仅仅是作品，还有自己的成就感，最后把自己也给丢了，惟一留下的是反复出现在心头的遗憾。

也许这样的遗憾还要出现很多次，因为新东方还有很多事情没有做完，因为我个人生活中还有很多事情要用心去完善。但我知道时间不会等我，我也知道自己不能落在地球旋转速度的后面。因此，我会在未来的岁月里，挤出时间来继续我的研究工作。书籍是惟一能够表明我曾经努力的物证，书籍也是惟一能够化解我对自己期待的良药。一切都需要重新开始，我惟一需要的就是重新开始的勇气。

《英语词汇速记大全1——词根＋词缀记忆法》是一个很好的开始。单词记忆是英语学习者的必经之路，我的任务是把这条路铺得更加平坦和科学一点。几经周折，终于有了大家手里的英语词汇速记大全系列，本书是这一系列的第四本《英语词汇速记大全4——同义同类归纳法》。本书的最大特点就是高效、实用。说其高效，是因为这两种记忆法是快速积累词汇量的不二法门，毕竟，对大多数人来说，记忆一组相关词汇要比记忆无关词汇容易得多；说其实用，是因为本书不仅可以用于背单词，而且在大家阅读和写作时，完全可以当作词典查用。

在这里，感谢新东方大愚文化传播有限公司的全体人员，正是他们的努力，使新东方一本本优秀书籍的出版成为可能。一个人的力量成不了大事，只有有着共同的志向和目标的一群人在一起努力，才能取得成功。新东方的今天就是证明。

2006 年 6 月

目 录

第一部分 同类词汇归纳记忆

第二部分　同义词汇归纳记忆

第一部分　同类词汇归纳记忆

Education 教育

Schooling 学校教育

kindergarten	[ˈkɪndəˌgɑːtən]	n. 幼儿园 a. 幼儿园的，初级的
primary	[ˈpraɪməri]	a. 初级的，初步的
primary school		小学
elementary	[ˌeliˈmentəri]	a. 基础的，初步的
elementary school		小学
secondary	[ˈsekəndəri]	a. 次要的，中级的
secondary school		中学
university	[ˌjuːniˈvəːsəti]	n. 大学，综合性大学
college	[ˈkɔlidʒ]	n. 学院，大学
normal university		师范大学
key university		重点大学

comprehensive	[ˌkɔmpriˈhensiv]	a. 综合性的，全面的
comprehensive university	综合性大学	
technical	[ˈteknikəl]	a. 技术的，技巧方面的
technical school	工业学校	
vocational	[vəˈkeiʃənəl]	a. 职业的
vocational certificate	职业证书	
organization	[ˌɔːgənaiˈzeiʃən; ˌɔːgəniˈzeiʃən]	n. 组织，机构
union	[ˈjuːnjən]	n. 联合，协会
the Students' Union	学生会	
canteen	[kænˈtiːn]	n. 小卖部
University Medical Service	大学医疗服务	
campus	[ˈkæmpəs]	n. 校园
campus clinic	校园诊所	
auditorium	[ˌɔːdiˈtɔːriəm]	n. 礼堂，会堂
library	[ˈlaibrəri]	n. 图书馆
laundry	[ˈlɔːndri]	n. 洗衣店，洗衣房
dormitory	[ˈdɔːmitəri]	n. 宿舍
laboratory	[ˈlæbərətɔːri; ləˈbɔrətəri]	n. 实验室
semester	[səˈmestə]	n. 学期
option	[ˈɔpʃən]	n. 选择；选课
course	[kɔːs]	n. 过程；课程
counsel	[ˈkaunsəl]	n. 讨论，商讨 v. 咨询
counseling center	辅导中心	
remediation	[riˌmiːdiˈeiʃən]	n. 补习，辅导
classmate	[ˈklɑːsmeit]	n. 同班同学
monitor	[ˈmɔnitə]	n. 班长
genial	[ˈdʒiːnjəl]	a. 亲切的，和蔼的
fatherly	[ˈfɑːðəli]	a. 父亲般的；慈祥的
supervise	[ˈsjuːpəvaiz]	v. 监督；指导

exalt	[ig'zɔːlt] *v.* 提升；（高度）赞扬
praise	[preiz] *v./n.* 赞扬，表扬
supplicated	['sʌplikeitid] *a.* 恳求的
follow	['fɔləu] *v.* 跟随；遵照；听懂
imitate	['imiteit] *v.* 模仿，仿效
exhibit	[ig'zibit] *v.* 显示
attend	[ə'tend] *v.* 参加（会议等），上（学等）
administrate	[əd'ministreit] *v.* 管理，支配
graduate	['grædjueit] *v.* 毕业 *n.* 毕业生
postgraduate	[,pəust'grædjuit] *n.* 研究生 *a.* 大学毕业后进行的
doctor	['dɔktə] *n.* 博士
specialized	['speʃəlaizd] *a.* 专门的，专业的
principle	['prinsəpl] *n.* 法则，原理
textbook	['tekstbuk] *n.* 教科书，书本
video	['vidiəu] *n.* 电视，录像
lecture	['lektʃə] *n./v.* 演讲
recite	[ri'sait] *v.* 背诵，朗读
pronounce	[prə'nauns] *v.* 发音
repetition	[,repi'tiʃən] *n.* 重复
imitation	[,imi'teiʃən] *n.* 模仿
compose	[kəm'pəuz] *v.* 写作
repeat	[ri'piːt] *v.* 重复 *n.* 重复，反复

Subjects 学科分类

compulsory	[kəm'pʌlsəri] *a.* 必修的，被强迫的
compulsory course	必修课
mandatory	['mændətəri；'mændə,tɔːri] *a.* 强制的
mandatory subject	必修科目
mathematics	[,mæθə'mætiks] *n.* 数学
physics	['fiziks] *n.* 物理

chemistry	['kemistri]	*n.* 化学
biology	[bai'ɔlədʒi]	*n.* 生物
politics	['pɔlitiks]	*n.* 政治
history	['histəri]	*n.* 历史
geography	[dʒi'ɔgrəfi]	*n.* 地理
P.E.	体育	
geology	[dʒi'ɔlədʒi]	*n.* 地质学
literature	['litərətʃə]	*n.* 文学
science	['saiəns]	*n.* 自然科学，理科
sociology	[,səusi'ɔlədʒi]	*n.* 社会学
philosophy	[fi'lɔsəfi]	*n.* 哲学
psychology	[(p)sai'kɔlədʒi]	*n.* 心理学
engineering	[,endʒi'niəriŋ]	*n.* 工程学
medicine	['medisin]	*n.* 医学，内科学
astronomy	[ə'strɔnəmi]	*n.* 天文学
economics	[ekə'nɔmiks]	*n.* 经济学
law	[lɔː]	*n.* 法学
finance	[fai'næns]	*n.* 财政学
architecture	['ɑːkitektʃə]	*n.* 建筑学
ethnology	[eθ'nɔlədʒi]	*n.* 民族学
botany	['bɔtəni]	*n.* 植物学
zoology	[zəu'ɔlədʒi]	*n.* 动物学

Mathematics 数学

mathematician	[,mæθəmə'tiʃən]	*n.* 数学家
arithmetic	[ə'riθmətik]	*n.* 算术
calculation	[,kælkju'leiʃən]	*n.* 计算
calculator	['kælkjuleitə]	*n.* 计算器
abacus	['æbəkəs]	*n.* 算盘
numeral	['njuːmərəl]	*n.* 数字

sum	[sʌm] *n.* 总数，总和
aggregate	['æɡriɡeit] *v.* 总计
fraction	['frækʃən] *n.* 分数，小数
decimal	['desəməl] *a.* 十进位的；小数的 *n.* 小数；十进制
decimal fraction	小数
decimal point	小数点
digit	['didʒit] *n.* 数字
percentage	[pə'sentidʒ] *n.* 百分比，百分率
addition	[ə'diʃən] *n.* 加，加法
plus	[plʌs] *a.* 零上的，正的 *n.* 加号，正号
subtraction	[səb'trækʃən] *n.* 减，减法
minus	['mainəs] *a.* 负的；减去的 *n.* 负数；减号
minus sign	减号，负号
multiplication	[ˌmʌltipli'keiʃən] *n.* 乘法
multiplication table	乘法表
multiply	['mʌltiplai] *v.* 乘以
power	['pauə] *n.* 幂，乘方
square	[skweə] *a.* 正方形的；平方的；直角的 *n.* 正方形；平方
division	[di'viʒən] *n.* 除法
divide	[di'vaid] *v.* 除以
algebra	['ældʒibrə] *n.* 代数，代数学
equation	[i'kweiʃən] *n.* 方程式，等式
formula	['fɔ:mjulə] *n.* 公式
root	[ru:t] *n.* 根
geometry	[dʒi'ɔmitri] *n.* 几何（学）
geometric	[ˌdʒiəu'metrik] *a.* 几何的，几何学的
dimension	[di'menʃən] *n.* 维
parallel	['pærəlel] *a.* 平行的 *n.* 平行线
parallel lines	平行线
quadrilateral	[ˌkwɔdri'lætərəl] *n./a.* 四边形（的）

area	[ˈeəriə] *n.* 面积	
rectangle	[ˈrekˌtæŋgl] *n.* 长方形，矩形	
polygon	[ˈpɔligən] *n.* 多边形	
cube	[kjuːb] *n.* 立方体；立方，三次幂	
volume	[ˈvɔljuːm] *n.* 体积	
circle	[ˈsəːkl] *n.* 圆形	
ellipse	[iˈlips] *n.* 椭圆形	
oval	[ˈəuvəl] *n./a.* 椭圆形（的）	
cone	[kəun] *n.* 圆锥形	
circumference	[səˈkʌmfərəns] *n.* 圆周，周长	
diameter	[daiˈæmitə] *n.* 直径	
radius	[ˈreidiəs] *n.* 半径	
triangle	[ˈtraiæŋgl] *n.* 三角，三角形	
angle	[ˈæŋgl] *n.* 角	
degree	[diˈgriː] *n.* 度，度数	
differential	[ˌdifəˈrenʃəl] *a.* 微分的	
calculus	[ˈkælkjuləs] *n.* 微积分学	
integral	[ˈintigrəl] *n.* 积分	
differential calculus	微分学	
integral calculus	积分学	
function	[ˈfʌŋkʃən] *n.* 函数	
probability	[ˌprɔbəˈbiləti] *n.* 概率	
statistics	[stəˈtistiks] *n.* 统计，统计学	
quantitative	[ˈkwɔntitətiv] *a.* （数）量的，（定）量的	
deduction	[diˈdʌkʃən] *n.* 演绎，推论	
inference	[ˈinfərəns] *n.* 推论，演绎	
induction	[inˈdʌkʃən] *n.* 归纳	

Physics 物理

mechanics	[miˈkæniks] *n.* 力学

acoustics	[əˈkuːstiks] *n.* 声学
electromagnetism	[ilektrəuˈmægnitizəm] *n.* 电磁学
optics	[ˈɔptiks] *n.* 光学
dynamics	[daiˈnæmiks] *n.* 动力学
force	[fɔːs] *n.* 力
velocity	[viˈlɔsəti] *n.* 速度
acceleration	[ækˌseləˈreiʃən] *n.* 加速度
equilibrium	[ˌiːkwiˈlibriəm] *n.* 平衡
motion	[ˈməuʃən] *n.* 运动
inertia	[iˈnəːʃjə] *n.* 惯性
gravitation	[ˌgræviˈteiʃən] *n.* 万有引力
relativity	[ˌreləˈtiviti] *n.* 相对论；相对
gravity	[ˈgrævəti] *n.* 重力，地心引力
vibration	[vaiˈbreiʃən] *n.* 振动
media	[ˈmiːdiə] *n.* 媒质
frequency	[ˈfriːkwənsi] *n.* 频率
wavelength	[ˈweivleŋθ] *n.* 波长
pitch	[pitʃ] *n.* 音高
intensity	[inˈtensəti] *n.* 强度
echo	[ˈekəu] *n./v.* 回声
resonance	[ˈrezənəns] *n.* 回声，洪亮
sonar	[ˈsəunɑː] *n.* 声呐
electricity	[ˌilekˈtrisiti] *n.* 电
static	[ˈstætik] *a.* 静止的，静态的 *n.* 静电
static electricity	静电
magnetism	[ˈmægnitizəm] *n.* 磁，磁性
magnet	[ˈmægnit] *n.* 磁体
electromagnet	[iˌlektrəuˈmægnit] *n.* 电磁铁，电磁体
magnetic	[mægˈnetik] *a.* 磁的，有磁性的
magnetic field	磁场
electric current	电流

direct current	直流电
alternating current	交流电
electric circuit	电路
electric charge	电荷
electric voltage	电压
electric shock	触电
electric appliance	电器
conductor	[kən'dʌktə] n. 导体
insulator	['insjuleitə; 'insəleitə] n. 绝缘体
semiconductor	[ˌsemikən'dʌktə] n. 半导体
battery	['bætəri] n. 电池(组)，蓄电池(组)
cell	[sel] n. 电池
dry battery	干电池
storage battery	蓄电池
electronics	[ˌilek'trɔniks] n. 电子学
electronic	[ˌilek'trɔnik] a. 电子的
electronic component	电子零件
integrated	['intigreitid] a. 综合的，完整的
circuit	['sə:kit] n. 电路，线路
integrated circuit	集成电路
chip	[tʃip] n. 集成电器片，集成块
electron tube	电子管
vacuum	['vækjuəm] n. 真空
vacuum tube	真空管
transistor	[træn'sistə] n. 晶体管
amplification	[ˌæmplifi'keiʃən] n. 放大
amplify	['æmplifai] v. 放大
oscillation	[ˌɔsi'leiʃən] n. 振动
optical	['ɔptikəl] a. 光(学)的
optical fiber	光学纤维
lens	[lenz] n. 透镜；镜头；镜片

convex	[kɔn'veks] *a.* 凸出的
concave	[kɔn'keiv] *a.* 凹的
microscope	['maikrəskəup] *n.* 显微镜
telescope	['teliskəup] *n.* 望远镜
magnifier	['mægnifaiə] *n.* 放大镜
spectrum	['spektrəm] *n.* 谱，光谱
ultraviolet	[ˌʌltrə'vaiələt] *n.* 紫外线
X rays	X 射线
Gamma rays	γ 射线
infrared rays	红外线
microwaves	微波
transparent	[træns'peərənt] *a.* 透明的
translucent	[trænz'lju:sənt] *a.* 半透明的
opaque	[əu'peik] *a.* 不透明的

Chemistry 化学

chemical	['kemikəl] *a.* 化学的 *n.* 化学制品
property	['prɔpəti] *n.* 性质，特性
chemical property	化学特性，化学性质
chemical composition	化学成分
chemical makeup	化学成分
agent	['eidʒənt] *n.* 动因，作用物，剂
chemical agent	化学试剂
chemical reaction	化学反应
chemical change	化学变化
bond	[bɔnd] *n.* 联结，联系
chemical bond	化学键
apparatus	[ˌæpə'reitəs] *n.* 器械，器具，仪器
chemical apparatus	化学器械
substance	['sʌbstəns] *n.* 物质

matter	['mætə] *n.* 物质
material	[mə'tiəriəl] *n.* 物质
element	['elimənt] *n.* 元素
periodic	[ˌpiəri'ɔdik] *a.* 周期的，定期的
periodic table	周期表
hydrogen	['haidrədʒən] *n.* 氢
oxygen	['ɔksidʒən] *n.* 氧
nitrogen	['naitrədʒən] *n.* 氮
helium	['hi:liəm] *n.* 氦
carbon	['kɑːbən] *n.* 碳
calcium	['kælsiəm] *n.* 钙
silicon	['silikən] *n.* 硅
sulfur	['sʌlfə] *n.* 硫
iodine	['aiədain] *n.* 碘
compound	['kɔmpaund] *n.* 化合物
hydrocarbon	[ˌhaidrəu'kɑːbən] *n.* 碳氢化合物
derivative	[di'rivətiv] *n.* 衍生物
alchemy	['ælkəmi] *n.* 炼金术
petroleum	[pi'trəuliəm] *n.* 石油
petroleum products	石油产品
crude oil	原油
refine	[ri'fain] *v.* 提炼，精炼
gasoline	['gæsəli:n] *n.* 汽油
methane	['meθein] *n.* 甲烷
solution	[sə'l(j)u:ʃən] *n.* 溶液
dissolve	[di'zɔlv] *v.* 溶解
solvent	['sɔlvənt] *n.* 溶剂
solubility	[ˌsɔlju'biliti] *n.* 可溶性
cohesion	[kəu'hi:ʒən] *n.* 聚合(性)
adhesion	[əd'hi:ʒən] *n.* 粘附
atom	['ætəm] *n.* 原子，微粒，微量

nucleus	['nju:kliəs] *n*. 核子，原子核
electron	[i'lektrɔn] *n*. 电子
neutron	['nju:trɔn] *n*. 中子
proton	['prəutɔn] *n*. 质子
molecule	['mɔlikju:l] *n*. 分子
particle	['pɑ:tikl] *n*. 粒子
particle accelerator	粒子加速器
ion	['aiən] *n*. 离子
catalysis	[kə'tælisis] *n*. 催化作用
catalyst	['kætəlist] *n*. 催化剂
artificial	[,ɑ:ti'fiʃəl] *a*. 人造的
synthetic	[sin'θetik] *a*. 合成的
synthetic fiber	合成纤维
polymer	['pɔlimə] *n*. 聚合物
polymerization	[,pɔlimərai'zeiʃən] *n*. 聚合作用
plastic	['plæstik] *n*. 塑胶
dye	[dai] *n*. 染料 *v*. 给…染色

Infant Education 幼儿教育

infant	['infənt] *n*. 婴儿，幼儿 *a*. 婴儿的；幼稚的
immature	[,imə'tjuə] *a*. 不成熟的，未完全发育的
naive	[nɑ:'i:v] *a*. 天真的，幼稚的
curious	['kjuəriəs] *a*. 好奇的；求知的
inquisitive	[in'kwizətiv] *a*. 好奇的
emulate	['emjuleit] *n*. 仿效
slothful	['sləuθful] *a*. 偷懒的
ignorant	['ignərənt] *a*. 无知的
selfish	['selfiʃ] *a*. 自私的
shortsighted	['ʃɔ:t'saitid] *a*. 近视的，目光短浅的

self-centered	[ˌselfˈsentəd]	a. 以自我为中心的，利己主义的
bias	[ˈbaiəs]	n. 偏爱；偏见
naughty	[ˈnɔːti]	a. 顽皮的，淘气的
diffident	[ˈdifidənt]	a. 缺乏自信的；谦虚谨慎的
dependent	[diˈpendənt]	a. 依赖的，依靠的
self-respect	[ˌselfriˈspekt]	n. 自重
self-control	[ˌselfkənˈtrəul]	n. 克己，自制
allowance	[əˈlauəns]	n. 宽容
social	[ˈsəuʃəl]	a. 爱交际的，社交的
interpersonal	[ˌintəˈpəːsənəl]	a. 人与人之间的，人际的
rational	[ˈræʃənəl]	a. 理性的，合理的
moral	[ˈmɔrəl; ˈmɔːrəl]	n. 道德 a. 道德的
attain	[əˈtein]	v. 达到，获得
preference	[ˈprefərəns]	n. 偏爱，偏好
foster	[ˈfɔstə]	v. 养育；鼓励 n. 养育者；鼓励者
interact	[ˌintərˈækt]	v. 互相作用，互相影响
behavior	[biˈheivjə]	n. 行为，举止
blame	[bleim]	n. 指责，责备 v. 责备
mental	[ˈmentəl]	a. 精神的，智力的
intellectual	[ˌintəˈlektjuəl]	a. 智力的，需智力的
potential	[pəuˈtenʃəl]	a. 潜在的 n. 潜能，潜力
agile	[ˈædʒail]	a. 敏捷的，灵活的
creative	[kriːˈeitiv]	a. 创造性的
intellect	[ˈintəlekt]	n. 智力
imagination	[iˌmædʒiˈneiʃən]	n. 想像，想像力
activity	[ækˈtiviti]	n. 行为；活跃
clumsy	[ˈklʌmzi]	a. 笨拙的
stimulate	[ˈstimjuleit]	v. 刺激，激励
respond	[riˈspɔnd]	v. 回答，响应
puzzle	[ˈpʌzl]	n. 难题 v. 迷惑
distract	[disˈtrækt]	v. 转移

nature	['neitʃə]	n. 本性，天性
lead	[li:d]	v. 引导，领导　n. 引导

Living Organism 生物

Human Evolution 人类形成

era	['iərə]	n. 时代，纪元
Eolithic	[ˌi:əu'liθik]	a. 原始石器时代的
Neolithic	[ˌni:əu'liθik]	a. 新石器时代的
tribe	[traib]	n. 部落，宗族
hominid	['hɔminid]	n./a. 灵长目动物（的）
primate	['praimeit]	n. 灵长类（动物）
chimp	[tʃimp]	n. （非洲）黑猩猩
ape	[eip]	n. 猿
gorilla	[gə'rilə]	n. 大猩猩
anthropoid	['ænθrəpɔid]	n. 类人猿
caveman	['keivmæn]	n. 穴居人
dweller	['dwelə]	n. 居民
skeleton	['skelitən]	n. 骨架，骨骼
molar	['məulə]	n. 臼齿
intelligence	[in'telidʒəns]	n. 智力
transition	[træn'ziʃən]	n. 过渡；转变
mutation	[mju:'teiʃən]	n. 变异
resemble	[ri'zembl]	v. 类似于，像
capacity	[kə'pæsəti]	n. 能力；宽敞
capability	[ˌkeipə'biləti]	n. 能力；潜质
specimen	['spesimən]	n. 标本

coexist	[ˌkəuig'zist]	v. 共存
famine	['fæmin]	n. 饥荒
originate	[ə'ridʒineit]	v. 起源于；发生
homogeneous	[ˌhəumə'dʒiːniəs]	a. 同类的，相似的
clan	[klæn]	n. 宗族，氏族
Stone Age		石器时代
Bronze Age		（青）铜器时代
Iron Age		铁器时代
Paleolithic	[ˌpeiliəu'liθik；ˌpæliəu'liθik]	a. 旧石器时代的
Mesolithic	[ˌmezəu'liθik；ˌmesəu'liθik]	a. 中石器时代的
cranial	['kreiniəl]	a. 头颅的；头盖骨的；颅骨的

Laboring Activities 原始劳动

dig	[dig]	v. 挖
spade	[speid]	n. 锹，铲子
shovel	['ʃʌvəl]	n. 铲 v. 铲起
furrow	['fʌrəu]	v. 犁地
pluck	[plʌk]	v. 拔，摘
pioneer	[ˌpaiə'niə]	v. 开拓，开创
develop	[di'veləp]	v. 发展，开发
pick	[pik]	v. 采摘 n. 镐
cultivate	['kʌltiveit]	v. 种植
spear	[spiə]	n. 矛，梭镖
club	[klʌb]	n. 棍棒
defensive	[di'fensiv]	a. 自卫的
rough	[rʌf]	a. 未加工的，粗制的
sharpen	['ʃɑːpən]	v. 削尖
hunt	[hʌnt]	n./v. 打猎，猎取
grab	[græb]	n./v. 抓取，攫取
poultry	['pəultri]	n. 家禽

tame	[teim] *v.* 驯化	
domesticate	[də'mestikeit] *v.* 驯养	
slaughter	['slɔːtə] *v.* 屠宰	
fatigue	[fə'tiːg] *n./v.* 疲劳，劳累	
workable	['wəːkəbl] *a.* 行得通的	
inventive	[in'ventiv] *a.* 发明的，创造的	
facility	[fə'siləti] *n.* 技巧，技能	
tackle	['tækl] *n.* 滑轮，滑车(组)	
net	[net] *n.* 网，渔网	
handmade	['hænd'meid] *a.* 手工的	
maintain	[mein'tein] *v.* 赡养	
apprentice	[ə'prentis] *n./v.* (当)学徒	
blacksmith	['blæksmiθ] *n.* 铁匠	
silversmith	['silvəsmiθ] *n.* 银器匠	
repose	[ri'pəuz] *n./v.* 憩息；睡眠	

Human Body Structure 人体结构

skull	[skʌl] *n.* 颅骨，头骨	
brain	[brein] *n.* 脑，脑髓	
forehead	['fɔːhed; 'fɔrid] *n.* 额，前额	
eyebrow	['aibrau] *n.* 眉毛	
eyelid	['ailid] *n.* 眼睑，眼皮	
eyelash	['ailæʃ] *n.* 睫毛	
eye	[ai] *n.* 眼，眼睛；虹膜	
ear	[iə] *n.* 耳，耳朵	
cheek	[tʃiːk] *n.* 面颊，脸	
mouth	[mauθ] *n.* 嘴，口	
lip	[lip] *n.* 嘴唇	
tongue	[tʌŋ] *n.* 舌头	
tooth	[tuːθ] *n.* 牙齿	

chin	[tʃin]	*n.* 下巴，下颚
neck	[nek]	*n.* 颈，脖子
throat	[θrəut]	*n.* 咽喉，嗓子
shoulder	['ʃəuldə]	*n.* 肩（部）
wrist	[rist]	*n.* 腕，腕关节
elbow	['elbəu]	*n.* 肘部
finger	['fiŋgə]	*n.* 手指
thumb	[θʌm]	*n.* （大）拇指
chest	[tʃest]	*n.* 胸，胸腔
heart	[hɑːt]	*n.* 心，心脏
intestine	[in'testin]	肠
liver	['livə]	*n.* 肝脏
kidney	['kidni]	*n.* 肾，肾脏
stomach	['stʌmək]	*n.* 胃；胃口
lung	[lʌŋ]	*n.* 肺
belly	['beli]	*n.* 肚子，腹部
waist	[weist]	*n.* 腰，腰部
hip	[hip]	*n.* 臀部，髋部
spine	[spain]	*n.* 脊骨，脊柱，脊椎
knee	[niː]	*n.* 膝，膝盖
shin	[ʃin]	*n.* 胫，外胫，胫骨
heel	[hiːl]	*n.* 脚后跟，踵
toe	[təu]	*n.* 脚趾，足尖（部）
thigh	[θai]	*n.* 大腿
ankle	['æŋkl]	*n.* 踝，踝关节

Animal Species 动物种类

marine	[mə'riːn]	*a.* 海生的
aquatic	[ə'kwætik]	*a.* 水生的
dolphin	['dɔlfin]	*n.* 海豚

seal	[si:l] *n*. 海豹
shellfish	['ʃelfiʃ] *n*. 水生有壳动物（如牡蛎、蟹、虾及贝类等）
crab	[kræb] *n*. 螃蟹
prawn	[prɔ:n] *n*. 对虾
lobster	['lɔbstə] *n*. 龙虾
terrestrial	[ti'restriəl] *a*. 陆生的，陆栖的
mammal	['mæməl] *n*. 哺乳动物
chimpanzee	[ˌtʃimpən'zi:] *n*. 黑猩猩
reindeer	['rein,diə] *n*. 驯鹿
zebra	['zi:brə] *n*. 斑马
amphibian	[æm'fibiən] *n*. 两栖动物
bat	[bæt] *n*. 蝙蝠
bedbug	['bedbʌg] *n*. 臭虫
beetle	['bi:tl] *n*. 甲虫
spider	['spaidə] *n*. 蜘蛛
firefly	['faiəflai] *n*. 萤火虫
dragonfly	['drægənflai] *n*. 蜻蜓
rooster	['ru:stə] *n*.（＝cock）公鸡
dove	[dʌv] *n*. 鸽
kingfisher	['kiŋ,fiʃə] *n*. 翠鸟
swallow	['swɔləu] *n*. 燕子
eagle	['i:gl] *n*. 鹰
nightingale	['naitiŋgeil] *n*. 夜莺
peacock	['pi:kɔk] *n*. 孔雀
penguin	['peŋgwin] *n*. 企鹅
woodpecker	['wud,pekə] *n*. 啄木鸟

Body Structure of Animals 动物肢体

| beak | [bi:k] *n*. 鸟喙 |

wing	[wiŋ] *n.* 翼，翅膀
feather	['feðə] *n.* 羽毛，翎毛
limb	[lim] *n.* 肢，翼
talon	['tælən] *n.* 猛禽的锐爪
fell	[fel] *n.* 兽皮
fur	[fə:] *n.* 柔毛；毛皮
hoof	[hu:f] *n.* （牛马的）蹄
horn	[hɔ:n] *n.* （牛、羊、鹿等的）角
breast	[brest] *n.* 乳房
flank	[flæŋk] *n.* 肋，肋腹
paw	[pɔ:] *n.* 爪子
fin	[fin] *n.* 鳍
gill	[gil] *n.* [常用复] 鱼鳃
tentacle	['tentəkl] *n.* 触角，触须
antenna	[æn'tenə] *n.* 触角，触须
claw	[klɔ:] *n.* 爪，螯
ventral	['ventrəl] *a.* 腹部的
abdomen	['æbdəmen; æb'dəumen] *n.* 腹部

Inhabiting 栖息

habitat	['hæbitæt] *n.* （动物或植物的）栖息地，住处
continent	['kɔntinənt] *n.* 大陆
rainforest	['rein,fɔrist] *n.* 雨林
Antarctic	[æn'tɑ:ktik] *a.* 南极的
Arctic	['ɑ:ktik] *a.* 北极的
burrow	['bʌrəu; 'bə:rəu] *n.* 地洞
cave	[keiv] *n.* 山洞，洞穴
cavern	['kævən] *n.* 大洞穴
den	[den] *n.* 兽穴，窝
grassland	['grɑ:slænd; 'græslænd] *n.* 草原，草地

honeycomb	[ˈhʌnikəum]	n. 蜂巢
lair	[leə]	n. 野兽的巢穴
nest	[nest]	n. 巢，窝
nestle	[ˈnesl]	v. 筑巢
perch	[pəːtʃ]	n. (鸟类的)栖息处，栖枝
roost	[ruːst]	n. 栖木；鸟巢；鸡棚
menagerie	[miˈnædʒəri]	n. 动物园
pigpen	[ˈpigpen]	n. 猪舍
pigsty	[ˈpigstai]	n. 猪舍
pond	[pɔnd]	n. 池塘
fishbowl	[ˈfiʃbəul]	n. 玻璃鱼缸

Habits and Characteristics 性情习惯

truculent	[ˈtrʌkjulənt]	a. 残暴的，凶狠的
feral	[ˈfiərəl]	a. 凶猛的；野生的
ferocious	[fəˈrəuʃəs]	a. 凶猛的；残暴的
fiendish	[ˈfiːndiʃ]	a. 极凶猛的；残酷的
fierce	[fiəs]	a. 凶猛的
combative	[kəˈbætiv]	a. 好斗的
cultivated	[ˈkʌltiveitid]	a. 驯化的
meek	[miːk]	a. 温顺的；驯服的
tractable	[ˈtræktəbl]	a. 易于驾驭的，温顺的
docile	[ˈdəusail]	a. 驯服的，温顺的
timid	[ˈtimid]	a. 胆小的
cunning	[ˈkʌniŋ]	a. 狡猾的
gregarious	[griˈgeəriəs]	a. 合群的
hive	[haiv]	v. 群居
herbivorous	[həːˈbivərəs]	a. (动物)食草的，食草动物的
carnivorous	[kɑːˈnivərəs]	a. 食肉的

omnivorous	[ɔm'nivərəs] *a*. 杂食的
nocturnal	[nɔk'tə:nəl] *a*. 夜间活跃的
ecdysis	['ekdisis] *n*. (动物)蜕皮；换羽毛

Breeding and Migration 繁殖迁徙

inbreeding	['in,bri:diŋ] *n*. 同系繁殖
mate	[meit] *v*. 交配，配种
copulate	['kɔpjuleit] *v*. 交配，交媾
multiply	['mʌltiplai] *v*. 繁殖
propagate	['prɔpəgeit] *v*. 繁殖
reproduce	[,ri:prə'dju:s] *v*. 繁殖，生殖
crossbreed	['krɔsbri:d] *n*. 杂种 *v*. 培育杂种
thoroughbred	['θʌrəbred; 'θə:rəubred] *a*. 纯种的 *n*. 纯种动物
pregnant	['pregnənt] *a*. 怀孕的
childbearing	['tʃaild,beəriŋ] *n*. 分娩 *a*. 生育的
parturition	[,pɑ:tjuə'riʃən] *n*. 生产，分娩
calf	[kɑ:f; kæf] *n*. 牛犊；(鲸，象等大型哺乳动物的)幼崽
offspring	['ɔfspriŋ] *n*. (动物的)崽
whelp	[welp] *n*. 犬科的幼兽，幼子 *v*. 下崽
runt	[rʌnt] *n*. 发育不良的小动物
mature	[mə'tjuə] *a*. 成熟的
migrate	[mai'greit; 'maigreit] *v*. 迁移
immigrate	['imigreit] *v*. 移居(移入)

Plant Species 植物种类

| azalea | [ə'zeiljə] *n*. 杜鹃花 |
| peony | ['piəni] *n*. 芍药属植物；牡丹 |

lotus	['ləutəs] *n.* 莲，荷花	
orchid	['ɔːkid] *n.* 兰科植物，兰花	
daffodil	['dæfədil] *n.* 水仙花	
gardenia	[gɑːˈdiːnjə] *n.* 栀子花	
laurel	['lɔrəl; 'lɔːrəl] *n.* 月桂树	
bush	[buʃ] *n.* 灌木，灌木丛	
shrub	[ʃrʌb] *n.* 灌木	
evergreen	['evəgriːn] *a.* 常绿的 *n.* 常绿植物	
cypress	['saiprəs] *n.* 柏树	
willow	['wiləu] *n.* 柳，柳树	
holly	['hɔli] *n.* 冬青属植物；(圣诞节时装饰用的)冬青枝	
ivy	['aivi] *n.* 常春藤	
olive	['ɔliv] *n.* 橄榄树，橄榄	
scrub	[skrʌb] *n.* 矮树丛，灌木丛	
palm	[pɑːm] *n.* 棕榈树	
oak	[əuk] *n.* 橡树	
elm	[elm] *n.* 榆树	
aspen	['æspən] *n.* 白杨	
pine	[pain] *n.* 松树	
bamboo	[bæmˈbuː] *n.* 竹子	
cotton	['kɔtən] *n.* 棉花	
reed	[riːd] *n.* 芦苇	
straw	[strɔː] *n.* 稻草，麦秆	
hay	[hei] *n.* 干草	
tissue	['tiʃjuː] *n.* 组织	
spore	[spɔː] *n.* 孢子	
bean	[biːn] *n.* 豆	
cabbage	['kæbidʒ] *n.* 卷心菜，洋白菜	
carrot	['kærət] *n.* 胡萝卜	
cauliflower	['kɔli,flauə] *n.* 菜花，花椰菜	
cress	[kres] *n.* 水芹；十字花科的植物	

cucumber	[ˈkjuːkʌmbə] n. 黄瓜
eggplant	[ˈegplɑːnt; ˈegplænt] n. 茄子
garlic	[ˈgɑːlik] n. 大蒜
oat	[əut] n. 燕麦
onion	[ˈʌnjən] n. 洋葱
pea	[piː] n. 豌豆
peanut	[ˈpiːnʌt] n. 花生
potato	[pəˈteitəu] n. 土豆
pumpkin	[ˈpʌmpkin] n. 南瓜
radish	[ˈrædiʃ] n. 萝卜
tomato	[təˈmeitəu; təˈmɑːtəu] n. 西红柿
almond	[ˈɑːmənd] n. 杏
cherry	[ˈtʃeri] n. 樱桃（树）
coconut	[ˈkəukənʌt] n. 椰子
grape	[greip] n. 葡萄
lemon	[ˈlemən] n. 柠檬（树）
mango	[ˈmæŋgəu] n. 芒果
peach	[piːtʃ] n. 桃子
pear	[peə] n. 梨
pineapple	[ˈpainˌæpl] n. 凤梨，菠萝
strawberry	[ˈstrɔːbəri] n. 草莓
walnut	[ˈwɔːlnʌt] n. 胡桃，核桃
watermelon	[ˈwɔːtəˌmelən] n. 西瓜

Plant Cultivation 培育种植

green finger	园艺能手
gardener	[ˈgɑːdənə] n. 园丁
planter	[ˈplɑːntə; ˈplæntə] n. 农场的种植者或经管者；花盆（尤指室内的）

peasant	['pezənt]	n. 农民
crop	[krɔp]	n. 作物，庄稼 v. 收割；种植
breed	[briːd]	n. 品种 v. 养殖；养育
harrow	['hærəu]	n. 耙
plough	[plau]	n. 犁 v. 犁地
hoe	[həu]	v. 用锄整地 n. 锄头
graft	[grɑːft; græft]	n./v. 移植；嫁接
implantation	[ˌimplɑːn'teiʃən]	n. 移植
muck	[mʌk]	n. 堆肥 v. 施肥
manure	[mə'njuə]	n. 粪肥 v. 给…施肥
hose	[həuz]	n. (橡皮或帆布等制的)软管 v. 用软管淋浇(或冲洗)
irrigate	['irigeit]	v. 灌溉
drain	[drein]	n./v. 排水
scissor	['sizə]	n. 剪刀
trim	[trim]	n./v. 修剪，整理
weed	[wiːd]	n. 杂草，野草 v. 除草
mow	[məu]	v. 割(草等)
fertilize	['fəːtilaiz]	v. 使…受精；施肥于
pesticide	['pestisaid]	n. 杀虫剂，农药
harvest	['hɑːvist]	n. 收成 v. 收获
reap	[riːp]	v. 收割，收获

Plant Growth 植物生长

seed	[siːd]	n. 种子 v. 播种；结实
sprout	[spraut]	v. 萌芽；长出(叶、毛发等) n. 新芽，幼苗
bud	[bʌd]	n. 花蕾，叶芽 v. 发芽
germinate	['dʒəːmineit]	v. 发芽

bloom	[bluːm] *n.* 花；开花（期）*v.* 开花
pollen	['pɔlən] *n.* 花粉
petal	['petəl] *n.* 花瓣
calyx	['keiliks] *n.* （[*pl.*] calyxes, calyces）花萼
corolla	[kə'rɔlə] *n.* 花冠
fragrant	['freigrənt] *a.* 芳香的，有香味的
florescence	[flɔ:'resəns] *n.* 开花期
blossom	['blɔsəm] *n.* 开花 *v.*（植物）开花
blown	[bləun] *a.* 开了花的，（花）盛开的
wither	['wiðə] *v.* 枯萎，凋零
shrivel	['ʃrivəl] *v.*（使）蔫，枯萎（因热、冷或干所致）
wilt	[wilt] *v.* 使…凋谢，枯萎 *n.* 枯萎
defoliate	[di:'fəulieit] *v.*（使）落叶
blight	[blait] *n.* 植物枯萎病 *v.* 使…枯萎
decompose	[ˌdi:kəm'pəuz] *v.* 分解，（使）腐烂
rot	[rɔt] *v.*（使）腐烂 *n.* 腐烂
perish	['periʃ] *v.* 丧生，毁灭
putrefy	['pju:trifai] *v.* 使腐烂
toxin	['tɔksin] *n.* 毒素，毒质
stalk	[stɔːk] *n.* 茎，梗
stem	[stem] *n.* 茎，干
trunk	[trʌŋk] *n.* 树干
parasite	['pærəsait] *n.* 寄生物
transplant	[træns'plænt; træns'plɑːnt] *v.* 移栽，移种（植物等）
transpiration	[ˌtrænspi'reiʃən] *n.* 呼吸作用
photosynthesis	[ˌfəutəu'sinθsis] *n.* 光合作用
respiration	[ˌrespə'reiʃən] *n.* 呼吸
fertilizer	['fə:tilaizə] *n.* 肥料，化肥
lush	[lʌʃ] *a.* 繁茂的，茂盛的
thrive	[θraiv] *v.* 茁壮成长
ripe	[raip] *a.* 熟的，成熟的

| proliferous | [prəu'lifərəs] *a.* 繁殖的，多产的 |
| pullulate | ['pʌljuleit] *v.* 发芽；充满 |

Plant Colors 植物颜色

violet	['vaiəlit] *a.* 紫罗兰色的
lavender	['lævəndə] *a.* 淡紫色的
mauve	[məuv] *a.* 淡紫色的
purple	['pə:pl] *a.* 紫色的
magenta	[mə'dʒentə] *n./a.* 紫红色(的)
rosy	['rəuzi] *a.* 玫瑰色的
sanguine	['sæŋgwin] *a.* 血红色的
scarlet	['skɑ:lət] *a.* 猩红的，鲜红的 *n.* 猩红色
reddish	['rediʃ] *a.* 微红的
pink	[piŋk] *n./a.* 粉红色(的)，桃红色(的)
ivory	['aivəri] *n.* 象牙色，乳白色
milky	['milki] *a.* 乳白色的
jade	[dʒeid] *n.* 碧绿(色)，浅绿(色)
verdant	['və:dənt] *a.* 翠绿的，青葱的
maize	[meiz] *a.* 玉米色的，黄色的
yellowish	['jeləuiʃ] *a.* 微黄的；发黄的
golden	['gəuldən] *a.* 金(黄)色的
maroon	[mə'ru:n] *n./a.* 栗色(的)
chocolate	['tʃɔkələt] *n.* 巧克力色
sandy	['sændi] *a.* 沙色的
brown	[braun] *n./a.* 棕色(的)，褐色(的)
grizzle	['grizl] *a.* 灰色的
indigo	['indigəu] *n.* 靛青 *a.* 靛蓝色的
azure	['æʒə] *n.* 天蓝色 *a.* 蔚蓝的
pale	[peil] *a.* 浅色的

Plant Application 植物用途

bouquet	[buˈkei]	*n.* 花束；芳香
perfume	[ˈpəːfjuːm]	*n.* 香水
garland	[ˈgɑːiənd]	*n.* （作为胜利标志的）花环，奖品
wreath	[riːθ]	*n.* 花圈，花环
beautify	[ˈbjuːtifai]	*v.* 美化，装饰
textile	[ˈtekstail]	*n.* 纺织品 *a.* 纺织的
horticulture	[ˈhɔːtikʌltʃə]	*n.* 园艺，园艺学
carpenter	[ˈkɑːpəntə]	*n.* 木匠
charcoal	[ˈtʃɑːkəul]	*n.* 炭，木炭
nutriment	[ˈnjuːtrimənt]	*n.* 营养品；食物
honey	[ˈhʌni]	*n.* 蜜，蜂蜜
brew	[bruː]	*v.* 酿造（啤酒）；冲泡（茶、咖啡等）
popcorn	[ˈpɔpkɔːn]	*n.* 爆玉米花
yogurt	[ˈjɔgət]	*n.* 酸奶酪，酵母乳
beverage	[ˈbevəridʒ]	*n.* 饮料
wine	[wain]	*n.* （葡萄）酒

Astronomy and Geography 天文地理

Heavenly Bodies 天体种类

cosmos	[ˈkɔzmɔs]	*n.* 宇宙
milky way		银河
galaxy	[ˈgæləksi]	*n.* 星系；[the G-]银河系，银河
constellation	[ˌkɔnstəˈleiʃən]	*n.* 星座，星群

interstellar	[ˌintəˈstelə] a. 星际的
luminary	[ˈljuːminəri] n. 天体(如日、月等)
celestial	[siˈlestjəl] a. 天体的
solar	[ˈsəulə] a. 太阳的；(利用)太阳能的
nova	[ˈnəuvə] n. 新星
supernova	[ˌsjuːpəˈnəuvə] n. 超新星
stellar	[ˈstelə] a. 星的，星球的
cynosure	[ˈsinəˌzjuə] n. 小熊(星)座，北极星
shooting star	流星
comet	[ˈkɔmit] n. 彗星
nucleus	[ˈnjuːkliəs] n. 慧核
quasar	[ˈkweizɑː] n. 类星体
sidereal	[saiˈdiəriəl] a. 恒星的
starlet	[ˈstɑːlit] n. 小星星
planet	[ˈplænit] n. 行星
planetary	[ˈplænitəri] a. (似)行星的
Venus	[ˈviːnəs] n. 金星
Mars	[mɑːz] n. 火星
Saturn	[ˈsætən] n. 土星
Mercury	[ˈməːkjuri] n. 水星
Jupiter	[ˈdʒuːpitə] n. 土星
asteroid	[ˈæstərɔid] n. 小行星 a. 星状的
lunar	[ˈljuːnə] a. 月亮的

Astronomical Phenomena 天文现象

chromosphere	[ˈkrəuməˌsfiə] n. 色球
aureole	[ˈɔːriəul] n. 日冕
eclipse	[ikˈlips] n. (日、月)食
eyewitness	[ˈaiˈwitnis] n. 目击者
fantastic	[fænˈtæstik] a. 荒诞的，奇异的

sunset	['sʌnset]	n. 日落（时分）
sunglow	['sʌngləu]	n. 朝霞，晚霞；日光
impact	['impækt]	n. 碰撞（力）
polychrome	['pɔlikrəum]	a. 多色的
aurora	[ɔː'rɔːrə]	n. 极光（南北极夜晚所放彩光）
zenith	['ziːniθ; 'zeniθ]	n. 天顶，极点
solstice	['sɔlstis]	n. 至，至日，至点
nebula	['nebjulə]	n. 星云
meteorite	['miːtiərait]	n. 流星，陨石
meteor	['miːtiə]	n. 流星，陨星
sunspot	['sʌnspɔt]	n. （太阳）黑子，日斑
weightlessness	['weitlisnis]	n. 失重状态
revolution	[ˌrevəl'(j)uːʃən]	n. 旋转
rotation	[rəu'teiʃən]	n. 旋转，旋动
phase	[feiz]	n. （月）相，相位
crescent	['kresənt]	n. 新月形，月牙 a. 新月形的
coincidence	[kəu'insidəns]	n. 同时发生，同时存在
tide	[taid]	n. 潮，潮汐
astronomer	[ə'strɔnəmə]	n. 天文学家
drift	[drift]	v. 漂流，漂
float	[fləut]	v. （使）浮动，（使）飘动
horizon	[hə'raizən]	n. 地平线
axis	['æksis]	n. 轴，中心线
sphere	[sfiə]	n. 球（体）

Astronomical Technology 天文技术

astronaut	['æstrənɔːt]	n. 宇航员
cosmonaut	['kɔzmənɔːt]	n. 宇航员，航天员
spacecraft	['speiskrɑːft; 'speiskræft]	n. 航天器；宇宙飞船
shuttle	['ʃʌtl]	n. 航天飞机

hatch	[hætʃ] *n*. (飞机等的)舱门，船舱盖	
spacesuit	['speis'sju:t] *n*. 太空服，航天服	
rocket	['rɔkit] *n*. 火箭	
satellite	['sætəlait] *n*. 卫星，人造卫星	
controller	[kən'trəulə] *n*. 控制器	
instrument	['instrumənt] *n*. 仪器，工具	
module	['mɔdju:l; 'mɔdʒu:l] *n*. (航空器中的)舱	
cabinet	['kæbinit] *n*. 机箱	
prototype	['prəutəutaip] *n*. 原型，蓝本	
radar	['reidɑ:] *n*. 雷达	
screen	[skri:n] *n*. 屏幕	
screw	[skru:] *n*. 螺丝(钉) *v*. 拧，拧紧	
experimental	[ik,speri'mentəl] *a*. 实验(性)的	
maiden	['meidən] *a*. 首次的，初次的	
unmanned	[ˌʌn'mænd] *a*. 无人操纵的，自动的	
liftoff	['liftɔf] *n*. (航天器、火箭等)垂直升空，起飞	
launch	[lɔ:ntʃ] *n*./*v*. 发射	
eject	[i'dʒekt] *v*. (在紧急情况下将人从飞行器中)弹出	
kindle	['kindl] *v*. 点燃，使着火	
insulation	[ˌinsju'leiʃən; 'insəleiʃən] *n*. 绝缘	
sacrifice	['sækrifais] *v*. 牺牲；献出	
shock	[ʃɔk] *n*. 震动，冲击	
synchronous	['siŋkrənəs] *a*. 同步的	
deploy	[di'plɔi] *v*. 部署，调度	
accelerate	[ək'seləreit] *v*. (使)加速	
fuel	[fjuəl] *n*. 燃料 *v*. 给…加燃料	
observe	[əb'zə:v] *v*. 观察	
base	[beis] *n*. 总部	
planetarium	[ˌplæni'teəriəm] *n*. ([*pl*.] planetariums, planetaria) 天文馆；天象仪	
observatory	[əb'zə:vətəri] *n*. 天文台	

astrolabe	[ˈæstrəuleib]	n. 星盘
sundial	[ˈsʌndaiəl]	n. （通过太阳知道时间的）日规；日晷（仪）
almanac	[ˈɔːlmənæk]	n. 历书，天文历
astrology	[əˈstrələdʒi]	n. 占星术
horoscope	[ˈhɔrəskəup]	n. 占星术；算命天宫图
magnetosphere	[mægˈniːtə(u)sfiə]	n. （围绕地球或其他行星等天体的）磁层
orbit	[ˈɔːbit]	n. 轨道 v. 沿轨道运行
globe	[gləub]	n. 地球；球体
aerospace	[ˈeərəuspeis]	n. 宇宙空间
atmosphere	[ˈætməˌsfiə]	n. 大气层
light-year	[ˈlaitjəː]	n. 光年
mission	[ˈmiʃən]	n. 任务，使命
probe	[prəub]	v. 探索 n. 探测器
explode	[ikˈspləud]	v. （使某物）爆炸

Topographies and Landforms 地形地貌

terrain	[təˈrein; ˈterein]	n. 地势，地形
physiognomy	[ˌfiziˈɔgnəmi]	n. 地势，地貌
alpine	[ˈælpain]	a. 高山（性）的；阿尔卑斯山的
barren	[ˈbærən]	a. （土地等）贫瘠的
bluff	[blʌf]	n. 悬崖，峭壁
cliff	[klif]	n. 悬崖，峭壁
cape	[keip]	n. 海角，岬
crest	[krest]	n. 顶峰
bog	[bɔg]	n. 沼泽
marsh	[mɑːʃ]	n. 沼泽，湿地
moorland	[ˈmuələnd]	n./a. 〈主英〉高沼地（的）

canyon　　　　['kænjən] *n.* 峡谷

valley　　　　['væli] *n.* 山谷

cavern　　　　['kævən] *n.* 大洞穴

cove　　　　　[kəuv] *n.* （河）湾；小海湾

foothill　　　　['futhil] *n.* 山麓小丘，丘陵地带

highland　　　　['hailənd] *n.* 高原地区，山岳地带

plateau　　　　['plætəu；plæ'təu] *n.* 高原

tableland　　　　['teibllænd] *n.* 高原，台地

upland　　　　['ʌplənd] *n.* 高地，内陆地区

terrace　　　　['terəs] *n.* 梯田

meadow　　　　['medəu] *n.* 草地；低洼地

oasis　　　　　[əu'eisis] *n.* （[*pl.*] oases）（沙漠中的）绿洲

peninsula　　　　[pi'ninsjulə；pi'ninsələ] *n.* 半岛

plain　　　　　[plein] *n.* 平原，草原

prairie　　　　['preəri] *n.* （尤指北美的）大草原

reef　　　　　[ri:f] *n.* 礁，暗礁

iceberg　　　　['aisbə:g] *n.* 冰山

volcano　　　　[vɔl'keinəu] *n.* 火山

crater　　　　　['kreitə] *n.* （火山口的）碗状凹陷

slope　　　　　[sləup] *n.* 斜坡，斜面

tributary　　　　['tribjutəri] *n.* 支流

downstream　　　　['daun'stri:m] *ad.* 顺流而下，朝下游方向

delta　　　　　['deltə] *n.* 三角洲

Rocks and Minerals 岩石矿物

mineral　　　　['minərəl] *n.* 矿物，矿石

ore　　　　　[ɔ:] *n.* 矿，矿石

basalt　　　　['bæsɔ:lt] *n.* 玄武岩

bauxite　　　　['bɔ:ksait] *n.* 铝土岩

crystal　　　　['kristəl] *n.* 水晶，晶体

diamond	['daiəmənd] *n.* 钻石，金刚石	
dripstone	['dripstəun] *n.* 滴水石；钟乳石	
emerald	['emərəld] *n.* 祖母绿，翡翠	
flint	[flint] *n.* 火石，燧石	
gem	[dʒem] *n.* 宝石	
granite	['grænit] *n.* 花岗岩，花岗石	
jade	[dʒeid] *n.* 玉，翡翠	
lime	[laim] *n.* 石灰	
marble	['mɑ:bl] 大理石	
mineral deposit	矿床	
moonstone	['mu:nstəun] *n.* 月长石	
opal	['əupəl] *n.* 蛋白石；猫眼石	
quartz	[kwɔ:ts] *n.* 石英	
ruby	['ru:bi] *n.* 红宝石	
turquoise	['tə:kwɔiz] *n.* 绿松石	
spa	[spɑ:] *n.* 矿泉	
bedrock	[,bed'rɔk] *n.* 基岩	
gravel	['grævəl] *n.* 沙砾，砾石	
boulder	['bəuldə] *n.* 大石头	
cobble	['kɔbl] *n.* 圆石子，鹅卵石	
pebble	['pebl] *n.* 小鹅卵石	
coalmine	['kəulmain] *n.* 煤矿	
lode	[ləud] *n.* 矿脉	
quarry	['kwɔri] *n.* 采石场，石矿	
prospecting	['prɔspektiŋ;prəu'spektiŋ] *n.* 探矿	
dowse	[dauz] *v.* 探寻水源或矿藏	

Geographical Phenomena 地理现象

backwash	['bækwɔʃ] *n.* 逆流；浪涛	
cascade	[kæ'skeid] *n.* 小瀑布	

convection	[kən'vekʃən] *n.* 对流
debris flow	泥石流
erosion	[i'rəuʒən] *n.* 侵蚀，腐蚀
soil erosion	水土流失
landslide	['lændslaid] *n.* 山崩
rupture	['rʌptʃə] *n./v.* 破裂，裂开
sediment	['sediment] *n.* 沉淀物；沉积物
weathering	['weðəriŋ] *n.* 侵蚀，风化
circulation	[ˌsəːkju'leiʃən] *n.* (体液的)循环，(水、空气等的)流通
erupt	[i'rʌpt] *v.* (指火山)爆发
dormant	['dɔːmənt] *a.* 休眠的
collide	[kə'laid] *v.* 碰撞
deposit	[di'pɔzit] *v.* 使沉积 *n.* 沉淀物
scour	['skauə] *v.* 冲刷，冲刷成
alluvial	[ə'l(j)uːviəl] *a.* 冲积的，淤积的

Climate 气候

monsoon	[mɔn'suːn] *n.* 季风；雨季
subtropics	[sʌb'trɔpiks] *n.* 亚热带地方
subtropical	[sʌb'trɔpikəl] *a.* 亚热带的
littoral	['litərəl] *a.* 海岸的 *n.* 沿海地区
continental	[ˌkɔnti'nentəl] *a.* 大陆性的
coastal	['kəustəl] *a.* 沿(临)海的；沿岸的
oceanic	[ˌəuʃi'ænik] *a.* 海洋性的
Mediterranean	[ˌmeditə'reiniən] *n.* 地中海
moisture	['mɔistʃə] *n.* 潮湿
humid	['hjuːmid] *a.* 潮湿的
grassy	['grɑːsi;'græsi] *a.* 多草的，草茂盛的

drought	[draut] *n.* 干旱	
arid	['ærid] *a.* 干旱的	
semiarid	[ˌsemi'ærid] *a.* 半干旱的（尤指年降雨量约为 10～20 英寸的）	
seasonal	['siːzənəl] *a.* 季节性的；周期性的	
annual	['ænjuəl] *a.* 一年一次的	
variable	[ˌveəriəbi] *n.* 易变的	
global	['gləubəl] *a.* 全球性的	
regional	['riːdʒənəl] *a.* 地方（性）的，区域性的	
abnormality	[ˌæbnɔːˈmæləti] *n.* 异常，反常	
abominable	[əˈbɔminəbl] *a.* 讨厌的，可恶的	
disgusting	[disˈgʌstiŋ] *a.* 令人厌恶的	
wicked	['wikid] *a.* 有害的，引起祸害的	
vile	[vail] *a.* 恶劣的	
execrable	['eksikrəbl] *a.* 恶劣的，糟透的	
delightful	[diˈlaitful] *a.* 使人快乐的，令人愉快的	
pleasant	['plezənt] *a.* 舒适的，令人愉快的	
temperate	['tempərət] *a.* 温和的	
polar	['pəulə] *a.* 极地的，近极地的	

Weather 天气

forecast	['fɔːkɑːst] *n.*/*v.* 预报	
weather forecast	天气预报	
predict	[priˈdikt] *v.* 预言，预测	
blizzard	['blizəd] *n.* 暴风雪	
drizzle	['drizl] *n.* 毛毛雨，蒙蒙雨 *v.* 下毛毛雨	
downpour	['daunpɔː] *n.* 暴雨	
sleet	[sliːt] *n.* 冰雨，雨夹雪 *v.* 下雨雪，下冰雹	
raindrop	['reindrɔp] *n.* 雨滴，雨点	
intermittent	[ˌintəˈmitənt] *a.* 断断续续的，间歇的	

freakish	[ˈfriːkiʃ] *a.* 反复无常的
barometric	[ˌbærəuˈmetrik] *a.* 气压(表)的
scale	[skeil] *n.* 规模；刻度
subzero	[sʌbˈziərəu] *a.* 零度以下的
frost	[frɔst] *n.* 霜冻，霜 *v.* 结霜
icicle	[ˈaisikl] *n.* 冰柱，冰锥
flake	[fleik] *n.* 雪片 *v.* 雪片般落下
chilly	[ˈtʃili] *a.* 寒冷的
icy	[ˈaisi] *a.* 结冰的
frigid	[ˈfridʒid] *a.* 寒冷的
dew	[djuː; duː] *n.* 露水
hail	[heil] *n.* 雹 *v.* 下冰雹
lightning	[ˈlaitniŋ] *n.* 闪电
fog	[fɔg] *n.* 雾
thunder	[ˈθʌndə] *n.* 雷，雷声 *v.* 打雷
moderate	[ˈmɔdərət] *a.* 适度的
violent	[ˈvaiələnt] *a.* 厉害的，极度的
squall	[skwɔːl] *n.* 短暂、突然且猛烈的风暴
trade	[treid] *n.* 信风
breeze	[briːz] *n.* 微风，轻风
gale	[geil] *n.* 大风，风暴
cyclone	[ˈsaikləun] *n.* 飓风；龙卷风
hurricane	[ˈhʌrikən] *n.* 飓风
typhoon	[taiˈfuːn] *n.* 台风
tornado	[tɔːˈneidəu] *n.* 龙卷风
headwind	[ˈhedwind] *n.* 顶头风，逆风
gusty	[ˈgʌsti] *a.* 阵风的
flood	[flʌd] *v.* 淹没 *n.* 洪水
tsunami	[tsuˈnɑːmi] *n.* 海啸
smoky	[ˈsməuki] *a.* 多烟的
muggy	[ˈmʌgi] *a.* (指天气)闷热而潮湿的

sultry	['sʌltri] *a.* 闷热的
scorching	['skɔːtʃiŋ] *a.* 酷热的
smother	['smʌðə] *v.* 使窒息，闷死

Geographic Terminology 地理学术语

equator	[i'kweitə] *n.* 赤道
meridian	[mə'ridiən] *n.* 子午线 *a.* 子午线的
latitude	['lætitjuːd] *n.* 纬度
longitude	['lɔndʒitjuːd; 'lɔndʒitjud] *n.* 经度，经线
perigee	['peridʒiː] *n.* 近地点
torrid	['tɔrid] *a.* 酷热的，热带的
tropical	['trɔpikəl] *a.* 热带的
macroclimate	['mækrəuˌklaimit] *n.* 大气候
continental shelf	大陆架
oceanic trench	海沟
glacial	['gleisjəl] *a.* 冰期的，冰川期的
megarelief	[ˌmegə'riliːf] *n.* 大地形
mollisol	['mɔlisɔl] *n.* 软土
permafrost	['pəːməfrɔst] *n.* 永冻土
migration	[mai'greiʃən] *n.* 迁移，移动
markstone	['maːkstəun] *n.* 标石
vegetation	[ˌvedʒi'teiʃən] *n.* 植物，草木
humidity	[hjuː'midəti] *n.* 湿度
multimeter	['mʌltimiːtə] *n.* 万用表
multisensor	[ˌmʌlti'sensə] *n.* 多传感器
nephograph	['nefəgraːf] *n.* 云图摄影机
nonius	['nəuniəs] *n.* 游标
pantograph	['pæntəugraːf] *n.* 缩放仪
pedometer	[pi'dɔmitə] *n.* 计步器，里程计

| penetrometer | [ˌpeniˈtrɔmitə] n. 硬度测量计 |
| perforator | [ˈpəːfəreitə] n. 穿孔机 |

Living Environment 生存环境

biosphere	[ˈbaiəsfiə] n. 生命层，生物圈
ecosystem	[ˈiːkəuˌsistəm] n. 生态系统
environment	[inˈvaiərənmənt] n. 周围状况，环境
fauna	[ˈfɔːnə] n. (某地区或某时期的)所有动物
fenland	[ˈfenlænd] n. 沼泽地
flora	[ˈflɔːrə] n. (某地区或时代的)一切植物，植物区系
mountainous	[ˈmauntinəs] a. 多山的
preserve	[priˈzəːv] n. 野生动物保护区
reciprocal	[riˈsiprəkəl] a. 相互的，互惠的
reserve	[riˈzəːv] n. 自然保护区
settlement	[ˈsetlmənt] n. 居留地
tropic	[ˈtrɔpik] n. 热带
wetland	[ˈwetlænd] n. [常用复] 潮湿的土壤，沼泽地
zone	[zəun] n. 地区，区域

Pollution 污染

infrared	[ˌinfrəˈred] n. 红外线 a. 红外线的
ultraviolet	[ˌʌltrəˈvaiələt] a. 紫外(线)的
radiation	[ˌreidiˈeiʃən] n. 放射线；辐射的热、能等
ozone	[ˈəuzəun] n. 臭氧
ozone layer	臭氧层
noxious	[ˈnɔkʃəs] a. 有害的，有毒的
toxic	[ˈtɔksik] a. 有毒的

waste	[weist] *n.* 废弃物
solid waste	固体垃圾
sewage disposal	污水处理
purification	[ˌpjuərifiˈkeiʃən] *n.* 净化
decibel	[ˈdesibel] *n.* 分贝
dump	[dʌmp] *v.* 倾卸，倾倒
ecologist	[iːˈkɔlədʒist] *n.* 生态学家，生态学者
rain forest	雨林
food chain	食物链
pollution-free	*a.* 无污染的
pollutant	[pəˈluːtənt] *n.* 污染物质
acid	[ˈæsid] *n.* 酸，酸性物质
acid rain	酸雨
carcinogen	[kɑːˈsinədʒən] *n.* 致癌物
contamination	[kənˌtæmiˈneiʃən] *n.* 污染，玷污
pollute	[pəˈluːt] *v.* 弄脏，污染
pollution	[pəˈluːʃən] *n.* 污染
discharge	[disˈtʃɑːdʒ] *n./v.* 排出
disposable	[disˈpəuzəbl] *a.* 一次性使用的
drainage	[ˈdreinidʒ] *n.* 排水；排出物
effluent	[ˈefluənt] *n.* 废水
leakage	[ˈliːkidʒ] *n.* 渗漏，漏出
sewage	[ˈsjuːidʒ] *n.* （下水道里的）污物
emission	[iˈmiʃən] *n.* （光、热等的）散发，发射
greenhouse effect	温室效应
radioactive	[ˌreidiəuˈæktiv] *a.* 放射性的
misshapen	[ˌmisˈʃeipən] *a.* 畸形的
exhaust	[igˈzɔːst] *n.* （机器排出的）废气
fume	[fjuːm] *n.* 烟
spit	[spit] *v.* 吐痰
junk	[dʒʌŋk] *n.* 垃圾

litter	['litə] *n.* 垃圾
trash	[træʃ] *n.* 垃圾，废物
lumber	['lʌmbə] *v.* 砍伐
overexploitation	['əuvər,eksplɔi'teiʃən] *n.* (对资源等的)过度开采
exhaustion	[ig'zɔːstʃən] *n.* 用尽，枯竭
abate	[ə'beit] *v.* (数量)减少，降低
shortage	['ʃɔːtidʒ] *n.* 不足，缺少
desertification	[,dezətifi'keiʃən] *n.* 沙(漠)化，土壤贫瘠化
destruction	[di'strʌkʃən] *n.* 毁坏，消灭
deterioration	[di,tiəriə'reiʃən] *n.* 恶化
endangered	[in'deindʒəd] *a.* 有危险的；濒临灭绝的
disaster	[di'zɑːstə] *n.* 灾难，灾祸
hazardous	['hæzədəs] *a.* 危险的
red tide	赤潮
sandstorm	['sændstɔːm] *n.* 沙暴

Environmental Protection Measures 环保措施

administration	[əd,mini'streiʃən] *n.* 管理
convention	[kən'venʃən] *n.* 公约，协议
declaration	[,deklə'reiʃən] *n.* 宣言，声明
awareness	[ə'weənis] *n.* 意识
obligation	[,ɔbli'geiʃən] *n.* 责任，义务
penalty	['penəlti] *n.* 处罚，罚款
propagandize	[,prɔpə'gændaiz] *v.* 宣传
utilization	[,juːtilai'zeiʃən] *n.* 利用
afforestation	[æ,fɔri'steiʃən] *n.* 造林
windbreak	['windbreik] *n.* 防风林
greening	['griːniŋ] *n.* 绿化
landscaping	['lænd,skeipiŋ] *n.* 景观美化

green industry		绿色产业
protection	[prəu'tekʃən]	n. 保护，防护
conservation	[ˌkɔnsə'veiʃən]	n. 保存，保持
decontaminate	[ˌdi:kən'tæmineit]	v. 排除污染，净化
purifier	['pjuərifaiə]	n. 清洁器
disposal	[di'spəuzəl]	n. 丢掉，清除
filtration	[fil'treiʃən]	n. 过滤
separator	['sepəreitə]	n. 分离器
dike	[daik]	n. 土堤，堤坝
landfill	['lændfil]	n. 垃圾填筑地，废渣埋填法
biodegradable	[ˌbaiəudi'greidəbl]	a. 可由生物降解的
degradable	[di'greidəbl]	a. 可降解的
environment-friendly		a. 有利于环境的
economization	[iˌkɔnəmai'zeiʃən]	n. 节约
recovery	[ri'kʌvəri]	n. 恢复
sustainable	[sə'steinəbl]	a. 可持续的
recycle	[ˌri:'saikl]	v. 回收利用(废物等)
recyclable	[ˌri:'saikləbl]	a. 可回收利用的
renewable	[ri'nju:əbl]	a. 可延长有效期的；可更新的

Scientific Research 科研

Archeology 考古研究

ruin	['ru:in]	n. 遗迹，废墟
remains	[ri'meinz]	n. 遗迹，遗骸
relic	['relik]	n. 遗物，文物
antique	[æn'ti:k]	a. 古时的，古老的 n. 古物

antiquity	[æn'tikwəti] n. 古代，古物	
archeologist	[ˌɑːki'ɔlədʒist] n. 考古学家	
excavation	[ˌekskə'veiʃən] n. 挖掘，发掘	
excavate	['ekskəveit] v. 挖掘，掘出	
unearth	[ˌʌn'əːθ] v. 发掘或挖出某物	
artifact	['ɑːtifækt] n. 人工制品	
archaeology	[ˌɑːki'ɔlədʒi] n. 考古学	
acclimate	[ə'klaimit; 'æklə,meit] v. 使适应新环境	
accustom	[ə'kʌstəm] v. 使习惯于	
adapt	[ə'dæpt] v. 使适合	
adjust	[ə'dʒʌst] v. 改变…以适应	
ancient	['einʃənt] a. 古代的，古老的	
biological	[ˌbaiəu'lɔdʒikəl] a. 生物的，生物学的	
degenerate	[di'dʒenəreit] v. 退化	
evidence	['evidəns] n. 根据，证据	
evolution	[ˌiːvə'luːʃən] n. 进化，进化论	
evolve	[i'vɔlv] v. (使)进化	
extinct	[ik'stiŋkt] a. 灭绝的	
fossil	['fɔsəl] n. 化石	
gene	[dʒiːn] n. 基因	
genetic	[dʒi'netik] a. 遗传的	
gradual	['grædʒuəl] a. 逐渐的，逐步的	
inheritance	[in'heritəns] n. 遗传	
maladaptive	[ˌmælə'dæptiv] a. 不适应的	
optimization	[ˌɔptimai'zeiʃən] n. 最优化	
origin	['ɔridʒin; 'ɔːridʒin] n. 起源	
procedure	[prə'siːdʒə] n. 步骤	
species	['spiːʃiːz] n. 物种	
supersede	[ˌsjuːpə'siːd] v. 淘汰	
survive	[sə'vaiv] v. 幸存	
variation	[ˌveəri'eiʃən] n. 变异，变种	

Technological Production 科技产品

digital	['didʒitəl]	a. 数字的
device	[di'vais]	n. 设备
monitor	['mɔnitə]	n. 监控器，(计算机)显示器
sensor	['sensə]	n. 传感器，敏感元件(或装置)
scanner	['skænə]	n. 扫描仪
laptop	['læptɔp]	n. 便携式电脑
LCD		液晶显示器
processor	['prəusesə; 'prɔsesə]	n. 处理器
hardware	['hɑːdweə]	n. 硬件
cable	['keibl]	n. 电缆
interface	['intəfeis]	n. 接口
software	['sɔftweə]	n. 软件
operating system		操作系统
network	['netwəːk]	n. 网络
homepage	['həumpeidʒ]	n. 主页
multi-media	[ˌmʌlti'miːdiə]	n. 多媒体
download	['daunləud]	n./v. 下载
password	['pɑːswəːd; 'pæswəːd]	n. 密码
accessory	[ək'sesəri]	n. 附件
portable	['pɔːtəbl]	a. 便于携带的，手提式的

Application and Development 应用和发展

innovation	[ˌinəu'veiʃən]	n. 创新，改革
computerize	[kəm'pjuːtəraiz]	v. (使)计算机化
internet	['intənet]	n. [the～]国际互联网，因特网
log on		登录
log off		注销，退出(在网络上终止连接主机的操作)

hyperlink	['haipə,link] *n.* ［计］超链接	
online	['ɔn'lain] *n.* 联机，在线	
memory	['meməri] *n.* 存储(器)	
decipher	[di'saifə] *v.* 破译，解释	
commercial	[kə'məːʃəl] *a.* 商务的	
profitable	['prɔfitəbl] *a.* 有利可图的	
automatic	[,ɔːtə'mætik] *a.* 自动的	
intricate	['intrikət] *a.* 复杂的，难懂的	
substitute	['sʌbstitjuːt; 'sʌbstituːt] *n.* 代用品，代替品	
technology	[tek'nɔlədʒi] *n.* 技术，工艺	
robot	['rəubɔt] *n.* 机器人；自动机械	
impact	['impækt] *v.* 冲击	
overthrow	[,əuvə'θrəu] *n./v.* 推翻；使终止	

Invention and Creation 发明创造

create	[kriː'eit] *v.* 创造	
creation	[kriː'eiʃən] *n.* 创造	
invent	[in'vent] *v.* 发明，创造	
invention	[in'venʃən] *n.* 发明，创造	
devise	[di'vaiz] *v.* 发明，设计	
contrive	[kən'traiv] *v.* 设计，发明	
originate	[ə'ridʒəneit] *v.* 发明，创办	
originality	[ə,ridʒə'næləti] *n.* 独创性	
patent	['peitənt] *a.* 专利的 *n.* 专利权(证书)	
multifunction	[,mʌlti'fʌŋkʃən] *n.* 多功能	
apply	[ə'plai] *v.* 使用，运用	
necessity	[ni'sesəti] *n.* 必要性	
advanced	[əd'vɑːnst; əd'vænst] *a.* 先进的	
profit	['prɔfit] *n.* 利润，收益	
valuable	['væljuəbl] *a.* 贵重的；有价值的	

Enterprise 企业

Trades 行业分类

agriculture	['ægrikʌltʃə]	*n.* 农业
fishery	['fiʃəri]	*n.* 渔业，水产业
butchery	['butʃəri]	*n.* 屠宰业
manufacture	[,mænju'fæktʃə]	*n.* 制造业
masonry	['meisənri]	*n.* 石匠业
joinery	['dʒɔinəri]	*n.* 细木匠业
lumbering	['lʌmbəriŋ]	*n.* 木材业
glazing	['gleiziŋ]	*n.* 玻璃装配业
mining	['mainiŋ]	*n.* 矿业
shipbuilding	['ʃip,bildiŋ]	*n.* 造船业
aviation	[,eivi'eiʃən]	*n.* 航空工业
utilities	[ju:'tilətis]	*n.* 公用事业
journalism	['dʒə:nəlizəm]	*n.* 新闻业
insurance	[in'ʃuərəns]	*n.* 保险业
tourism	['tuərizəm]	*n.* 旅游业
retailing	['ri:teiliŋ]	*n.* 零售业
advertising	['ædvətaiziŋ]	*n.* 广告业
moonlighting	['mu:n,laitiŋ]	*n.* 从事第二职业
intermediary	[,intə'mi:diəri]	*n.* 中介
underwriter	['ʌndə,raitə]	*n.* 保险商
hairdressing	['heə,dresiŋ]	*n.* 美容美发
textile	['tekstail]	*n.* 纺织品
hosiery	['həuziəri]	*n.* 针织品

Modern Agriculture 现代农业

agricultural	[ˌægriˈkʌltʃərəl]	*a*. 农业的
silt	[silt]	*n*. （由流水带到河口、港口的）淤泥，淤沙
clod	[klɔd]	*n*. 土块
agrarian	[əˈgreəriən]	*a*. 土地的，农业的
pilot	[ˈpailət]	*a*. 试验性的
rural	[ˈruərəl]	*a*. 乡村的，农村的
idyllic	[aiˈdilik]	*a*. 田园风光的，田园诗般的
irrigation	[ˌiriˈgeiʃən]	*n*. 灌溉，冲洗
farm animal	家畜	
farm car	农用拖车	
farm crane	农用装载机	
farm product	农产品	
farm vehicle	农用运输车	
farm working	农活儿	
farming	[ˈfɑːmiŋ]	*n*. 农事，农业
farming season	农忙期	
autarkic	[ɔːˈtɑːkik]	*a*. 自给自足的，经济独立的
tractor	[ˈtræktə]	*n*. 拖拉机
combine	[kəmˈbain]	*n*. 联合收割机
cowboy	[ˈkaubɔi]	*n*. 牧童
ranch	[ræntʃ; rɑːntʃ]	*n*. 大牧场，饲养场 *v*. 经营牧场
cross	[krɔs; krɔːs]	*v*. （使）杂交
pasture	[ˈpɑːstʃə; ˈpæstʃə]	*n*. 牧草；牧场 *v*. 放牧
contract	[ˈkɔntrækt] *n*. 合同，契约 [kənˈtrækt] *v*. 签合同	
mechanize	[ˈmekənaiz]	*v*. 机械化
smallholder	[ˈsmɔːlˌhəuldə]	*n*. 小农，小佃农
pastoral	[ˈpɑːstərəl; ˈpæstərəl]	*a*. 田园生活的；宁静的
graze	[greiz]	*n*./*v*. 放牧

nomadic	[nəu'mædik] *a*. 游牧的

Enterprise Classification 企业分类

venture	['ventʃə] *n*. 风险投资,风险项目
joint venture	合资企业
enterprise	['entəpraiz] *n*. 企业,事业
SOE	(state owned enterprise) 国有企业
FOE	(foreign owned enterprise) 外资企业
Sino-foreign joint ventures	中外合资企业
private enterprise	私营企业
individually-run enterprise	民营企业
cartel	[kɑ:'tel] *n*. 企业联合,卡特尔
combine	[kəm'bain] *n*. 联合企业 *v*. 联合,结合
conglomerate	[kən'glɔmərət] *n*. 大公司,企业集团
cooperative	[kəu'ɔpərətiv] *a*. 合作的,协作的 *n*. 合作社,合作企业
corporation	[ˌkɔ:pə'reiʃən] *n*. 团,公司,企业
lose-making	*a*. 亏损的
profit-making	*a*. 赢利的
public institution	事业单位

Competition 职业竞争

opponent	[ə'pəunənt] *n*. 对手 *a*. 对抗的

rival	['raivəl] *n.* 竞争对手 *a.* 竞争的 *v.* 竞争
respectable	[ri'spektəbl] *a.* 值得尊敬的；正派的
admirable	['ædmərəbl] *a.* 令人钦佩的；绝妙的
upright	['ʌprait] *a.* 诚实的，正直的
appreciate	[ə'priːʃieit] *v.* 赏识；感激
sportsmanship	['spɔːtsmənʃip] *n.* 公正大度的品质或精神
impartial	[im'pɑːʃəl] *a.* 不偏不倚的，公正的
unjust	[ˌʌn'dʒʌst] *a.* 不公平的
inimical	[i'nimikəl] *a.* 敌意的
vilify	['vilifai] *v.* 诽谤，辱骂
befoul	[bi'faul] *v.* 污蔑，中伤
telltale	['telteil] *n.* 告密的人，告发者
skullduggery	[skʌl'dʌgəri] *n.* 舞弊
malign	[mə'lain] *v.* 诽谤，中伤(某人)
underestimate	[ˌʌndər'estimeit] *n./v.* 低估
undercut	['ʌndəkʌt] *v.* 削价，与…抢生意
outbid	[ˌaut'bid] *v.* 出高于…的价钱
promotion	[prə'məuʃən] *n.* 广告宣传，推销活动
appraise	[ə'preiz] *v.* 评价，评定
debt	[det] *n.* 债
bankrupt	['bæŋkrʌpt] *a.* 破产的 *v.* 破产

Import and Export 进出口贸易

importation	[ˌimpɔː'teiʃən] *n.* 进口，输入品
exportation	[ˌekspɔː'teiʃən] *n.* 出口，输出品
commerce	['kɔməːs] *n.* 贸易
transaction	[træn'zækʃən] *n.* 交易
rebate	['riːbeit] *n.* 折扣 *v.* 打折扣
purchase	['pəːtʃəs] *n./v.* 买，购买

bulk	[bʌlk] *n.* 大批
bulk sale	批发
distribution	[ˌdistriˈbjuːʃən] *n.* 销售，分配
hire-purchase	[ˈhaiəˈpəːtʃəs] *n.* 分期付款购买
installment	[inˈstɔːlmənt] *n.* 部分
installment plan	分期付款购买
dispute	[disˈpjuːt] *n./v.* 争论，争吵
consultation	[ˌkɔnsəlˈteiʃən] *n.* 咨询；磋商
mediation	[ˌmiːdiˈeiʃən] *n.* 仲裁，调节
tariff	[ˈtærif] *n.* 关税 *v.* 课以关税
delivery	[diˈlivəri] *n.* 交货，递送
transit	[ˈtrænsit] *n.* 搬运，运输
warehouse	[ˈweəhaus] *n.* 仓库，货栈 *v.* 存入仓库
endorse	[inˈdɔːs] *v.* 在票据背面签名，签署
receipt	[riˈsiːt] *n.* 收据，收条
clearance	[ˈkliərəns] *n.* 票据交换，清算
liquidation	[ˌlikwiˈdeiʃən] *n.* 清算
dumping	[ˈdʌmpiŋ] *n.* 倾销
anti-dumping	[ˌæntiˈdʌmpiŋ] *n.* 反倾销
barrier	[ˈbæriə] *n.* 壁垒
trade barrier	贸易壁垒
domestic	[dəˈmestik] *a.* 国内的
external	[eksˈtəːnl] *a.* 外国的
overseas	[ˈəuvəˈsiːz] *a.* 外国的 *ad.* 在国外

Products and Services 产品及服务

commodity	[kəˈmɔditi] *n.* 商品
merchandise	[ˈməːtʃəndaiz] *n.* [总称] 商品，货物
appliance	[əˈplaiəns] *n.* 用具

utensil	[juːˈtensəl] *n*. 用具，器皿
machinery	[məˈʃiːnəri] *n*. 机器
component	[kəmˈpəunənt] *n*. 零部件
assemble	[əˈsembl] *v*. 装配
condiment	[ˈkɔndimənt] *n*. 调味品，作料
confectionery	[kənˈfekʃənəri] *n*. 糖果点心类
cosmetic	[kɔzˈmetik] *n*. 化妆品
dairy	[ˈdeəri] *n*. 乳品店；奶制品
feedstuff	[ˈfiːdstʌf] *n*. 饲料
mobile	[ˈməubail] *n*. 移动电话
telecommunication	[ˈtelikəˌmjuːniˈkeiʃən] *n*. 电讯
electronic	[ˌilekˈtrɔnik] *a*. 电子的
energy-saving	*a*. 节能的
glassware	[ˈglɑːsweə；ˈglæsweə] *n*. 玻璃器具，玻璃制品
porcelain	[ˈpɔːsəlin] *n*. 瓷，瓷器
headwear	[ˈhedweə] *n*. (＝headgear)头饰
household	[ˈhaushəuld] *a*. 家用的
logistic	[ləuˈdʒistik] *a*. 后勤的
stationery	[ˈsteiʃənəri] *n*. 文具

Advertising and Publicizing 广告宣传

advertisement	[ˌædvəˈtaizmənt；ədˈvəːtismənt] *n*. 广告
brand	[brænd] *n*. 商标，牌子
communication	[kəˌmjuːniˈkeiʃən] *n*. 传播
target	[ˈtɑːgit] *n*. 目标，对象
consumer	[kənˈsjuːmə] *n*. 消费者
customer	[ˈkʌstəmə] *n*. 消费者
persuasion	[pəˈsweiʒən] *n*. 说服，说服力
cognition	[kɔgˈneiʃən] *n*. 认知，认知力

motivation	[ˌməuti'veiʃən]	n. 刺激
marketing	['mɑːkitiŋ]	n. 行销，买卖
brainwash	['breinwɔʃ]	n./v. 洗脑
promote	[prə'məut]	v. 宣传，推销
model	['mɔdəl]	n. 模特；模型 v. 模仿
strategy	['strætidʒi]	n. 策略，战略
popularity	[ˌpɔpju'lærəti]	n. 普及，流行
magnify	['mægnifai]	v. 放大，夸大
exaggerate	[ig'zædʒəreit]	v. 夸张，夸大
impact	['impækt]	n./v. 影响
irreplaceable	[ˌiri'pleisəbl]	a. 不可替代的，不可调换的
irresponsible	[ˌiris'pɔnsəbl]	a. 不负责的，不可靠的
nonprofit	[nɔn'prɔfit]	a. 非赢利的
leaflet	['liːflit]	n. 传单
tract	[trækt]	n. 小册子
junk mail		垃圾邮件
billboard	['bilbɔːd]	n. 户外广告板，广告牌
poster	['pəustə]	n. 招贴，海报

Commercial Policy 贸易政策

convention	[kən'venʃən]	n. 协定；大会
alliance	[ə'laiəns]	n. 联合，联盟
policy	['pɔləsi]	n. 政策，方针
implement	['implimənt]	v. 贯彻，执行
bilateral	[ˌbai'lætərəl]	a. 双边的，两面的
mutual	['mjuːtʃuəl]	a. 相互的，共有的
mutually	['mjuːtʃuəli]	ad. 相互地，互助地
recognition	[ˌrekəg'niʃən]	a. 公认，承认
abide	[ə'baid]	v. 坚持，遵守

negotiate	[ni'gəuʃieit]	v. 谈判；买卖
repeal	[ri'pi:l]	n./v. 废除，撤销
countervail	[ˌkauntə'veil]	v. 补偿，抵消
violate	['vaiəleit]	v. 违反，妨碍
undermine	[ˌʌndə'main]	v. 破坏
elimination	[iˌlimi'neiʃən]	n. 排除，消除
liberalization	[ˌlibərəlai'zeiʃən]	n. 自由化
beneficial	[ˌbeni'fiʃəl]	a. 有益的；有使用权的
intransigence	[in'trænsidʒəns]	n. 不让步，不妥协
economic	[ˌi:kə'nɔmik]	a. 经济的，经济上的
operational	[ˌɔpə'reiʃənəl]	a. 可使用的；操作的
investment	[in'vestmənt]	n. 投资，可获利的东西
guarantee	[ˌgærən'ti:ˌˌgɑ:rən'ti:]	n. 抵押品；保证书 v. 保证，担保
property	['prɔpəti]	n. 所有权，所有物

Commercial Organizations 贸易机构

WTO	(World Trade Organization) 世贸组织
IMF	(International Monetary Fund) 国际货币基金会
CTG	(Council for Trade in Goods) 货物贸易理事会
EFTA	(European Free Trade Association) 欧洲自由贸易协会
AFTA	(ASEAN Free Trade Area) 东盟自由贸易区
JCCT	(Sino-US Joint Commission on Commerce and Trade) 中美商贸联委会
NAFTA	(North American Free Trade Area) 北美自由贸易区
UNCTAD	(United Nations Conference on Trade and Development) 联合国贸易与发展会议
GATT	(General Agreement on Tariffs and Trade) 关贸总协定

Price and Insurance 价格与保险

duty	[ˈdjuːti; ˈduːti] *n.* 税	
customs	[ˈkʌstəmz] *n.* 关税	
charge	[tʃɑːdʒ] *n.* 费用	
freight	[freit] *n.* 运费	
due	[djuː] *n.* [常用复] 应付款	
commission	[kəˈmiʃən] *n.* 佣金	
surcharge	[səˈtʃɑːdʒ] *n.* 额外费用；追加罚款 *v.* 追加罚款	
import surcharge	进口附加税	
allowance	[əˈlauəns] *n.* 津贴，补助	
damage	[ˈdæmidʒ] *n.* [常用复] 赔偿金	
variable	[ˈveəriəbl] *a.* 可变的	
import variable duties	进口差价税	
FOB	(free on board) 离岸价	
net	[net] *n.* 净利润 *v.* 净赚	
capital	[ˈkæpitəl] *n.* 资金，资产	
fund	[fʌnd] *n.* 资金，基金 *v.* 投资	
retail	[ˈriːteil] *n.* 零售 *a.* 零售的	
retail price	零售价	
wholesale	[ˈhəulseil] *n.* 批发 *a.* 批发的	
wholesale price	批发价	
fluctuate	[ˈflʌktjueit] *v.* 波动，变动	
compensation	[ˌkɔmpenˈseiʃən] *n.* 补偿，赔偿	
pilferage	[ˈpilfəridʒ] *n.* 行窃，偷盗	
valuation	[ˌvæljuˈeiʃən] *n.* 估价，评估	

Organization Structure 组织架构

head office	总公司

parent company	总公司，母公司
directorate	[di'rektərət] n. 理事会，董事会
chairman	['tʃeəmən] n. 主席；董事长
headquarter	[‚hed'kwɔːtə] v. 设总公司于
personnel	[‚pəːsə'nel] n. 全体人员；人事部门
branch office	分公司
business office	营业部
personnel department	人事部
human resources department	人力资源部
general affairs department	总务部
general accounting department	财务部
accounting	[ə'kauntiŋ] n. 会计；会计学
auditing	['ɔːditiŋ] n. 查账，审计
sales	[seilz] a. 销售的 n. 销售额
sales department	销售部
sales promotion department	促销部
international department	国际部
public relations department	公共关系
planning department	企划部
brainpower	['brein‚pauə] n. 智囊，智囊团
research and development department(R&D)	研发部
secretarial	[‚sekrə'teəriəl] a. 秘书(的工作)的
secretarial pool	秘书室
teamwork	['tiːmwəːk] n. 有组织的合作；协力合作
united	[juː'naitid] a. (为共同目标)团结的；结盟的

— 53 —

Position 工作职位

administrator	[əd'ministreitə]	n. 管理人
president	['prezidənt]	n. 总统；（大学）校长；董事长
principal	['prinsəpəl]	n. 负责人；校长
minister	['ministə]	n. 部长，大臣
ambassador	[æm'bæsədə]	n. 大使
official	[ə'fiʃəl]	n. 官员，行政人员
director	[di'rektə]	n. 主管
director general		局长，处长
executive	[ig'zekjutiv]	n. 经理
supervisor	['sju:pəvaizə]	n. 监督者；主管
accountant	[ə'kauntənt]	n. 会计师
broker	['brəukə]	n. 经纪人
cashier	[kæ'ʃiə]	n. 收银员，出纳员
jobber	['dʒɔbə]	n. 股票经纪人
analyst	['ænəlist]	n. 分析家；化验员
coordinator	[kəu'ɔːdineitə]	n. 协调者
decorator	['dekəreitə]	n. 装饰者；制景人员
architect	['ɑːkitekt]	n. 建筑师，设计师
engineer	[,endʒi'niə]	n. 工程师，机械师
technician	[tek'niʃən]	n. 技术员，技师
professor	[prə'fesə]	n. 教授
assistant	[ə'sistənt]	n. 助教
lecturer	['lektʃərə]	n. （大学、学院中的）讲师
tutor	['tju:tə]	n. 家庭教师，导师
librarian	[lai'breəriən]	n. 图书馆馆长或馆员
consultant	[kən'sʌltənt]	n. 顾问
intern	[in'tə:n]	n. 实习生
proofreader	['pru:f,ri:də]	n. 校对员

agent	['eidʒənt] n. 代理人，代理商
receptionist	[ri'sepʃənist] n. 招待员，接待员
recruiter	[ri'kru:tə] n. 征兵人员；招聘人员
security	[si'kjuərəti] n. 警卫，保安
staff	[stɑːf; stæf] n. 全体职工

Responsibility 工作职责

arrange	[ə'reindʒ] v. 安排；筹划
cooperate	[kəu'ɔpəreit] v. 与他人合作，配合
demonstration	[,demən'streiʃən] n. 示范
disposition	[,dispə'ziʃən] n. 处理；部署
handle	['hændl] v. 处理，应付
documentation	[,dɔkjumen'teiʃən] n. 证件
registration	[,redʒi'streiʃən] n. 登记；注册
statistic	[stə'tistik] n. 统计资料
fulltime	['ful'taim] n. 专职
permanent	['pə:mənənt] a. 固定的
part-time	['pɑːt'taim] a. 兼职的
temporary	['tempərəri] a. 暂时的
installation	[,instə'leiʃən] n. 就职
interpret	[in'tə:prit] v. 口译，翻译
modification	[,mɔdifi'keiʃən] n. 修改，改正
negotiation	[ni,gəuʃi'eiʃən] n. 商议，谈判
promotion	[prə'məuʃən] n. 广告宣传；升职

Labor Unions 工会组织

| organize | ['ɔ:gənaiz] v. 组织 |
| union | ['ju:njən] n. 协会，联盟 |

guild	[gild] *n.* 行会，行业协会
society	[sə'saiəti] *n.* 社，社团
association	[ə,səusi'eiʃən] *n.* 协会，联合
consortium	[kən'sɔ:tjəm] *n.* 社团，协会
unionize	['ju:njənaiz] *v.* 统一；成立工会
guildhall	['gild'hɔ:l] *n.* 会馆
advocate	['ædvəkeit] *v.* 提倡 ['ædvəkət] *n.* 提倡者
convener	[kən'vi:nə] *n.* 会议召集人
conflict	['kɔnflikt]/[kən'flikt] *n./v.* 冲突，抵触
defuse	[,di:'fju:z] *v.* 使缓和
instigate	['instigeit] *v.* 鼓动
safeguard	['seifgɑ:d] *v.* 维护，捍卫
nonunion	[nɔn'ju:njən] *a.* 不属于工会的，不承认工会的
voluntary	['vɔləntəri] *a.* 非官办的，自愿的
non-governmental	['nɔn,gʌvən'mentəl] *a.* 非政府的

Office Supplies 办公用品

computer	[kəm'pju:tə] *n.* 电脑
mouse	[maus] *n.* 鼠标
keyboard	['ki:bɔ:d] *n.* 键盘
printer	['printə] *n.* 打印机
electrograph	[i'lektrəgrɑ:f] *n.* 传真机
cabinet	['kæbinit] *n.* 橱柜
drawer	[drɔ:ə] *n.* 抽屉
notebook	['nəutbuk] *n.* 笔记本
ball-point	['bɔ:lpɔint] *n.* 圆珠笔
vase	[vɑ:z; veis] *n.* 瓶，花瓶
pencil vase	笔筒
clip	[klip] *n.* 回形针 *v.* 夹住
tack	[tæk] *n.* 大头针 *v.* 以大头针钉住

file	[fail] *n*. 文件，文档 *v*. 将…归档
envelope	['envələup] *n*. 信封，封套
lamp	[læmp] *n*. 灯 *v*. 照亮

Job Hunting and Recruitment 求职招聘

want ad	招聘广告，征求广告
recruit	[ri'kru:t] *v*. 征募
request	[ri'kwest] *n*./*v*. 要求，请求
applicant	['æplikənt] *n*. 申请人
application	[ˌæpli'keiʃən] *n*. 申请，申请表
apply	[ə'plai] *v*. 请求，申请
recommendation	[ˌrekəmen'deiʃən] *n*. 推荐，推荐信
résumé	['rezju:mei] *n*. 简历
job-hopping	['dʒɔbˌhɔpiŋ] *n*. 跳槽
job-hunt	['dʒɔbhʌnt] *v*. 找工作
investigate	[in'vestigeit] *v*. 调查
identify	[ai'dentifai] *v*. 认出，识别
assessment	[ə'sesmənt] *n*. 确定，评定
candidate	['kændideit] *n*. 候选人
inform	[in'fɔ:m] *v*. 通知
interview	['intəvju:] *n*./*v*. 面试
hesitate	['heziteit] *v*. 犹豫，踌躇
relax	[ri'læks] *v*. 放松
ease	[i:z] *v*. 减轻；安心
presentation	[ˌprezən'teiʃən] *n*. 介绍
describe	[di'skraib] *v*. 描写，描述
confident	['kɔnfidənt] *a*. 有信心的，自信的
contact	['kɔntækt] *n*./*v*. 联系
participate	[pɑ:'tisipeit] *v*. 参与，参加

| feedback | ['fi:dbæk] *n*. 反馈，反馈信息 |
| panel | ['pænəl] *n*. 专门小组 |

Job Requirements 工作要求

accountable	[ə'kauntəbl] *a*. 应负责的
aggressive	[ə'gresiv] *a*. 有进取心的
adaptable	[ə'dæptəbl] *a*. 有适应能力的
capable	['keipəbl] *a*. 有能力的，能干的
diploma	[di'pləumə] *n*. 资格证书；毕业证书
bachelor	['bætʃələ] *n*. 学士，学士学位
collaboration	[kə,læbə'reiʃən] *n*. 合作
coordination	[kəu,ɔ:di'neiʃən] *n*. 协作
team work	协同工作
sedulity	[si'dju:ləti] *n*. 勤奋，勤勉
diligence	['dilidʒəns] *n*. 勤勉，勤奋
faithful	['feiθful] *a*. 可信赖的，认真的
initiative	[i'niʃiətiv] *n*. 主动性，首创精神
persistent	[pə'sistənt] *a*. 坚持不懈的
practical	['præktikəl] *a*. 切合实际的，实用的
experienced	[ik'spiəriənst] *a*. 富有经验的
familiarity	[fə,mili'ærəti] *n*. 熟悉，通晓
professional	[prə(u)'feʃənəl] *a*. 职业的，专业的
proficiency	[prə'fiʃənsi] *n*. 熟练，精通
proficient	[prə'fiʃənt] *a*. 熟练的，精通的
resourceful	[ri'sɔ:sful] *a*. 机智的
tactful	['tæktful] *a*. 机智的；老练的
knowledgeable	['nɔlidʒəbl] *a*. 有见识的；在行的
logical	['lɔdʒikəl] *a*. 有逻辑头脑的
flexibility	[,fleksə'biləti] *n*. 适应性，机动性

Employment 就业

employment	[im'plɔimənt]	n. 雇用；职业
counselor	['kaunsələ]	n. 法律顾问，顾问
inquiry	[in'kwaiəri]	n. 调查
career	[kə'riə]	n. 职业
content	[kən'tent]	a. 满足的，满意的 v. 使满足
job market		就业市场
well-paid	['wel'peid]	a. 高薪的
white-collar	['wait'kɔlə]	a. 白领阶层的
blue-collar	['blu:'kɔlə]	a. 蓝领阶层的
overtime	['əuvətaim]	a./ad. 加班的(地)
qualified	['kwɔlifaid]	a. 有资格的；合格的
cautious	['kɔːʃəs]	a. 十分小心的，谨慎的
enthusiasm	[in'θju:ziæzəm; in'θu:ziæzəm]	n. 积极性；热心
attitude	['ætitju:d; ætitu:d]	n. 态度，意见
motivation	[,məuti'veiʃən]	n. 动力
compete	[kəm'pi:t]	v. 竞争
team spirit		团队精神
impression	[im'preʃən]	n. 印象
letter of reference		介绍信
appoint	[ə'pɔint]	v. 任命
nominate	['nɔmineit]	v. 任命，推荐
promote	[prə(u)'məut]	v. 提升，晋升
annoy	[ə'nɔi]	v. 使烦恼；打搅
isolate	['aisəleit]	v. 孤立；隔离
bossy	['bɔsi]	a. 专横的
dismiss	[dis'mis]	v. 解职，开除
shelve	[ʃelv]	v. 解雇
lay off		解雇

layoff	['leɪɔf] *n.* 解雇；下岗工人
pension	['penʃən] *n.* 养老金
bonus	['bəunəs] *n.* 奖金，红利
tax	[tæks] *n.* 税 *v.* 纳税
enrollment	[in'rəulmənt] *v.* 登记，注册
register	['redʒistə] *v.* 注册，登记
leave	[li:v] *n.* 请假，假期
attendance	[ə'tendəns] *n.* 出席
check on work attendance	记考勤
schedule	['skedʒu:əl; 'ʃedju:əl] *n.* 时间表 *v.* 确定时间表
agenda	[ə'dʒendə] *n.* 议程

Career Development 职业前景

entrepreneur	[ˌɔntrəprə'nə:] *n.* 企业家
prospect	['prɔspekt] *n.* 前景，前途
expand	[ik'spænd] *v.* 扩张，发展
improvement	[im'pru:vmənt] *n.* 改进，进步
promising	['prɔmisiŋ] *a.* 有希望的；有前途的
lifelong	['laiflɔŋ] *a.* 终身的
raise	[reiz] *n.* （工资、薪金的）提升

Culture 文化

Art Genres 艺术流派

| classicism | ['klæsisizəm] *n.* 古典主义，古典风格 |
| romanticism | [rəu'mæntisizəm] *n.* 浪漫主义 |

realism	['riəlizəm] *n*. 现实主义	
symbolism	['simbəlizəm] *n*. 象征主义	
impressionism	[im'preʃənizəm] *n*. 印象主义	
expressionism	[ik'spreʃənizəm] *n*. 表现主义	
naturalism	['nætʃərəlizəm] *n*. 自然主义	
existentialism	[ˌegzis'tenʃəlizəm] *n*. 存在主义	
fauvism	['fəuvizəm] *n*. 野兽派	
abstract art	抽象派，抽象主义	
cubism	['kju:bizəm] *n*. 立体派，立体主义	
Byzantine	[bi'zæntain] *n*. 拜占庭式	
futurism	['fju:tʃərizəm] *n*. 未来主义	
Romanesque	[ˌrəumə'nesk] *n*. 罗马式	
Gothic	['gɔθik] *n*. 哥特式	
Baroque	[bə'rəuk] *n*. 巴洛克式	

Painting and Sculpture 绘画与雕塑

exhibition	[ˌeksi'biʃən] *n*. 展览，展览会	
gallery	['gæləri] *n*. 画廊，美术馆	
salon	['sɔlɔ:n] *n*. 沙龙	
inspiration	[ˌinspə'reiʃən] *n*. 灵感，启发	
artist	['ɑ:tist] *n*. 大师，艺术家	
sculptor	['skʌlptə] *n*. 雕刻家	
pigment	['pigmənt] *n*. 颜料	
crayon	['kreiən] *n*. 蜡笔	
brush	[brʌʃ] *n*. 画笔	
chalk	[tʃɔ:k] *n*. 粉笔	
frame	[freim] *n*. 画框，框架	
canvas	['kænvəs] *n*. 画布，帆布	
sketch	[sketʃ] *n*. 草稿	
portrait	['pɔ:trit] *n*. 画像	

watercolor	['wɔtə,kʌlə]	n. 水彩画
landscape	['lændskeip]	n. 风景画，山水画
seascape	['siːskeip]	n. 海景画，海景
engraving	[in'greiviŋ]	n. 版画，雕版
nude	[njuːd]	n. 裸体画，裸体 a. 裸体的
caricature	['kærikətjuə]	n. 漫画
tracing	['treisiŋ]	n. 临摹
plaster	['plɑːstə; 'plæstə]	n. 石膏，灰泥
clay	[klei]	n. 黏土，泥土
profile	['prəufail]	n. 轮廓，外形
engrave	[in'greiv]	v. 雕刻
carve	[kɑːv]	v. 雕刻
statue	['stætʃuː; 'stætjuː]	n. 雕像，塑像
bronze	[brɔnz]	n. 铜像，青铜
vivid	['vivid]	a. 生动的，逼真的
lifelike	['laiflaik]	a. 逼真的，栩栩如生的

Literature and Drama 文学与戏剧

masterpiece	['mɑːstəpiːs]	n. 杰作
essay	['esei]	n. 随笔
anthology	[æn'θɔlədʒi]	n. 选集
prose	[prəuz]	n. 散文
novel	['nɔvəl]	n. 小说
biography	[bai'ɔgrəfi]	n. 自传
allegory	['æligəri]	n. 寓言
myth	[miθ]	n. 神话，虚构的故事
fiction	['fikʃən]	n. 虚构，小说
science fiction	科幻小说	
criticism	['kritisizəm]	n. 评论
satire	['sætaiə]	n. 讽刺文学

reportage	[ˌrepɔːˈtɑːʒ] *n.*	报告文学
attractive	[əˈtræktiv] *a.*	吸引人的，有魅力的
thought-provoking	[ˈθɔːtprəˌvəukiŋ] *a.*	发人深省的，引人思考的
copyright	[ˈkɔpirait] *n.*	版权，著作权
poet	[ˈpəuit] *n.*	诗人
poetry	[ˈpəuitri] *n.*	诗歌
poem	[ˈpəuim] *n.*	诗
ode	[əud] *n.*	颂歌，赋
sonnet	[ˈsɔnit] *n.*	十四行诗
verse	[vəːs] *n.*	（诗）节，诗句
rhyme	[raim] *n.*	韵脚，押韵
playwright	[ˈpleirait] *n.*	编剧，剧作家
theatre	[ˈθiətə] *n.*	戏剧；剧院
drama	[ˈdrɑːmə] *n.*	话剧，戏剧艺术
comedy	[ˈkɔmidi] *n.*	喜剧，喜剧性的事情
farce	[fɑːs] *n.*	滑稽剧，闹剧
mummery	[ˈmʌməri] *n.*	哑剧
perform	[pəˈfɔːm] *v.*	表演，演出
plot	[plɔt] *n.*	情节，结构
episode	[ˈepisəud] *n.*	一段情节；插曲
denouement	[deinuːˈmɔŋ] *n.*	结局

Language Origin and Usage 语言的来源及运用

aboriginal	[ˌæbəˈridʒənəl] *a.*	原来的
exotic	[igˈzɔtik] *a.*	外来的
Latin	[ˈlætin] *n.* 拉丁文 *a.*	拉丁文的
Greek	[griːk] *n.* 希腊语 *a.*	希腊语的
Rome	[rəum] *n.*	罗马
French	[ˈfrentʃ] *n.* 法语 *a.*	法语的

orient	[ˈɔːriənt] *n.* 东方 *a.* 东方的	
communicate	[kəˈmjuːnikeit] *v.* 沟通，交流	
lingual	[ˈliŋgwəl] *a.* 语言的	
bilingual	[baiˈliŋgwəl] *a.* (说)两种语言的	
linguist	[ˈliŋgwist] *n.* 语言学家	
linguistic	[liŋˈgwistik] *a.* 语言学的	
verbal	[ˈvəːbəl] *a.* 口头的	
oral	[ˈɔːrəl] *a.* 口头的	
pronunciation	[prəuˌnʌnsiˈeiʃən] *n.* 发音，读法	
accent	[ˈæksənt] *n.* 重音，口音	
stress	[stres] *n.* 重音，强调 *v.* 重读	
fluent	[ˈfluːənt] *a.* 流利的，流畅的	
coherent	[kəuˈhiərənt] *a.* 一致的，连贯的	
articulate	[ɑːˈtikjuleit] *v.* 清晰地说 [ɑːˈtikjulət] *a.* 发音清晰的	
vocabulary	[vəˈkæbjuləri] *n.* 词汇，词汇量	
expression	[ikˈspreʃən] *n.* 措辞，词语	
phrase	[freiz] *n.* 短语，词组 *v.* 叙述	
clause	[klɔːz] *n.* 从句	
adage	[ˈædidʒ] *n.* 格言，谚语	
byword	[ˈbaiwəːd] *n.* 格言，谚语；笑柄	
idiom	[ˈidiəm] *n.* 成语，习惯用语	
proverb	[ˈprɔvəːb] *n.* 谚语	
motto	[ˈmɔtəu] *n.* 座右铭，格言	
slang	[slæŋ] *n.* 俚语，行话	
jargon	[ˈdʒɑːgən] *n.* 行话	
irony	[ˈaiərəni] *n.* 反话，讽刺	

Music and Dance 音乐与舞蹈

musician	[mjuːˈziʃən] *n.* 音乐家	

songster	['sɔŋstə] *n*. 歌唱家	
pianist	['piənist] *n*. 钢琴家	
soloist	['səuləuist] *n*. 独唱者	
soprano	[sə'prɑːnəu] *n*. 女高音	
tenor	['tenə] *n*. 男高音	
bass	[beis] *n*. 男低音，贝司	
conductor	[kən'dʌktə] *n*. 指挥	
rap	[ræp] *n*. 说唱音乐	
rock	[rɔk] *n*. 摇滚乐，摇滚舞；摇摆	
jazz	[dʒæz] *n*. 爵士乐	
symphony	['simfəni] *n*. 交响乐	
blues	[bluːz] *n*. 蓝调音乐（忧郁布鲁斯音乐）	
R & B	(Rhythm & Blues)节奏布鲁斯	
bassoon	[bə'suːn] *n*. 低音管	
flute	[fluːt] *n*. 长笛	
violin	[ˌvaiə'lin] *n*. 小提琴，小提琴手	
piano	[pi'ænəu] *n*. 钢琴	
pantomime	['pæntəmaim] *n*. 舞剧	
opera	['ɔpərə] *n*. 歌剧	
ballet	['bælei] *n*. 芭蕾，芭蕾舞剧	
anthem	['ænθəm] *n*. 圣歌，赞美诗	
solo	['səuləu] *n*. 独奏，独唱 *a*. 单独的	
lyrics	['liriks] *n*. 歌词；抒情诗 *a*. 抒情的	
melody	['melədi] *n*. 悦耳的音调；旋律	
rhythm	['riðəm] *n*. 节奏，韵律	
time	[taim] *n*. 节拍	
composition	[ˌkɔmpə'ziʃən] *n*. 创作，作曲	
cassette	[kæ'set] *n*. 盒式磁带	
microphone	['maikrəfəun] *n*. 麦克风，扩音器	
step	[step] *n*. 舞步	

ballroom	['bɔ:lrum] n. 舞厅，跳舞场
arena	[ə'ri:nə] n. 舞台；竞技场
pop	[pɔp] a. 流行的，通俗的

Movie 电影艺术

filmdom	['filmdəm] n. 电影界
first-run cinema	首轮影院
continuous performance cinema	循环场电影院
projector	[prə'dʒektə] n. 放映机
showing	['ʃəuiŋ] n. 放映
screening	['skri:niŋ] n. 放映
premiere	[pri'miə] n./v. 首次公演
festival	['festəvəl] n. 节，节日，喜庆日
film festival	电影节
certificate	[sə'tifikeit] n. 证(明)书；执照
censor's certificate	审查级别
distributor	[di'stribjutə] n. 发行人
director	[di'rektə] n. 导演
producer	[prə(u)'dju:sə] n. (电影)制片人，制作人；监制
adaptation	[ˌædæp'teiʃən] n. 改编
adapter	[ə'dæptə] n. 编剧者，改编者
scenarist	['si:nərist; si'na:rist] n. 剧作家
stagehand	['steidʒhænd] n. 舞台管理
actor	['æktə] n. 男演员
leading actor	男主角
actress	['æktris] n. 女演员
leading actress	女主角
supporting role	配角

costar	['kəustɑ:] n./v. (影视中)(使)共同主演，合演
cinematographer	[ˌsinəmə'tɔgrəfə] n. 电影摄影技师，放映技师
utility man	饰演小角色的演员，跑龙套
stand-in	n. 替身，代替演员
stunt	[stʌnt] n. 惊险动作，特技(表演)
stunt man	特技替身演员
swordsman	['sɔ:dzmən] n. 剑客
cast	[kɑ:st；kæst] n. 演员表，全体演员
screenplay	['skri:nplei] n. 电影剧本
script	[skript] n. 剧本，脚本
exterior	[ik'stiəriə] n. 外景
lighting	['laitiŋ] n. 灯光
shooting	['ʃu:tiŋ] n. 摄制
shooting schedule	摄制计划
special effects	特技
slow motion	慢镜头
montage	[mɔn'tɑ:ʒ] n. 蒙太奇
sound effects	音响效果
dub	[dʌb] v. 为(电影等)配音；译制(影片)
studio	['stju:diəu；'stu:diəu] n. 摄影室，摄影棚；(电影)制片厂
property	['prɔpəti] [常用复] n. 道具
spotlight	['spɔtlait] n. 聚光灯
serial	['siəriəl] n. 连续剧；系列片
trailer	['treilə] n. 预告片
silent cinema	无声电影
sound motion picture	有声电影
newsreel	['nju:zri:l] n. 新闻影片
documentary	[ˌdɔkju'mentəri] n. 纪录片 a. 文件的，文献的
literary film	文艺片

musical	['mju:zikəl] n. 音乐喜剧，音乐剧
tragedy	['trædʒidi] n. 悲剧（艺术）
swordsmen film	武侠片
detective film	侦探片
ethical	['eθikəl] a. 道德的，伦理的
ethical film	伦理片
affectional	[ə'fekʃənəl] a. 情感的，爱情的
affectional film	爱情片

Broadcasting 广播

broadcast	['brɔ:dkɑ:st；'brɔ:dkæst] n./v. 广播，播放
wave	[weiv] n. 波，波浪
transmitter	[trænz'mitə] n. 发射机，发射台
receiver	[ri'si:və] n. 接收器
signal	['signəl] n. 信号 v. 发信号
preside	[pri'zaid] v. 主持
anchor	['æŋkə] n. 新闻节目主持人 v. 主持（新闻广播节目）
anchorperson	['æŋkə,pə:sn] n. 新闻节目主持人
newscast	['nju:zkɑ:st；'nju:zkæst] n. 新闻广播
newscaster	['nju:z,kɑ:stə；'nju:z,kæstə] n. 新闻广播员，新闻评论员
audience	['ɔ:diəns] n. 听众，观众
fair-sounding	['feə'saundiŋ] a. 动听的
talkative	['tɔ:kətiv] a. 话多的，健谈的
DJ	(disc jockey)流行音乐播音员，流行音乐节目主持人
BBC	英国广播公司
VOA	美国之音
program	['prəugræm] n. 节目 v. 安排节目

rank	[ræŋk] *n*. 等级 *v*. 将…分等级
ranks	[ræŋks] *n*. 排行，排行榜
hotline	['hɔtlain] *n*. 热线
consult	[kən'sʌlt] *v*. 请教，咨询
announce	[ə'nauns] *v*. 宣布，通告

News 新闻传播

press	[pres] *n*. 报刊；新闻界
news agency	通讯社
wire service	通讯社
news conference	记者招待会
carry	['kæri] *v*. 刊登，刊载
censor	['sensə] *v*. 审查；新闻审查
release	[ri'li:s] *v*. 发表，发布
journalist	['dʒə:nəlist] *n*. 新闻记者
accredit	[ə'kredit] *v*. 信任，授权
accredited journalist	特派记者
correspondent	[,kɔri'spɔndənt] *n*. 驻外记者；常驻外埠记者
stringer	['striŋə] *n*. 特约记者；通讯员
contributing editor	特约编辑
copy editor	文字编辑
contributor	[kən'tribjutə] *n*. 投稿人
columnist	['kɔləmnist] *n*. 专栏作家
free-lancer	['fri:'la:nsə] *n*. 自由撰稿人
journal	['dʒə:nəl] *n*. 定期刊物，杂志，日报
weekly	['wi:kli] *n*. 周报
periodical	[,piəri'ɔdikəl] *n*. 期刊
quarterly	['kwɔ:təli] *n*. 季刊
newssheet	['nju:zʃi:t] *n*. 单张报纸

extra	['ekstrə] *n.* (报纸)号外
supplement	['sʌpliment] *n.* 号外；副刊，增刊
chart	[tʃɑːt] *n.* (每周流行音乐等)排行榜；畅销目录
column	['kɔləm] *n.* 专栏；栏目
contribution	[ˌkɔntriˈbjuːʃən] *n.* (投给报刊的)稿件，投稿
press release	新闻稿
title	['taitl] *n.* 标题，题目
caption	['kæpʃən] *n.* 标题；(图片)说明文字
cartoon	[kɑːˈtuːn] *n.* 卡通画，漫画
photograph	['fəutəɡrɑːf; 'fəutəɡræf] *n.* 照片
headline	['hedlain] *n.* 大字标题；[常用复]新闻提要
banner	['bænə] *n.* 通栏大字标题
update	[ʌpˈdeit] *n.* 更新；最新报道 *v.* 更新；校正
newsletter	['njuːzˌletə] *n.* 时事通讯
breaking news	突发新闻
fudge	[fʌdʒ] *n.* 报纸中特载的新闻或最后的新闻
bulletin	['bulitin] *n.* 简明新闻；公告
highlight	['hailait] *n.* 最重要的事件 *v.* 强调，突出
affair	[əˈfeə] *n.* 桃色新闻；绯闻
anecdote	['ænikdəut] *n.* 短故事；轶事
back alley news	小道消息
rumor	['ruːmə] *n.* 传闻，小道消息
slander	['slɑːndə] *n./v.* 诋毁，中伤
grapevine	['greipvain] *n.* 小道消息
expose	[ikˈspəuz] *n.* 揭丑新闻；曝光
abstract	['æbstrækt] *n.* 摘要，梗概 [æbˈstrækt] *v.* 做…的摘要
brief	[briːf] *n.* 简讯，概要
boil down	压缩(篇幅)，摘要
digest	['daidʒest] *n.* 文摘
editorial	[ˌediˈtɔːriəl] *n.* 社论

Traditions and Customs 习俗

convention	[kən'venʃən]	n. 习俗，惯例
custom	['kʌstəm]	n. 习惯，风俗
habitude	['hæbitjuːd]	n. 习俗
civilization	[ˌsivilai'zeiʃən;ˌsivili'zeiʃən]	n. 文明，教化
legacy	['legəsi]	n. 遗产
aboriginal	[ˌæbə'ridʒənəl]	n. 土著人 a. 土著的
ancestor	['ænsestə]	n. 祖宗，祖先
background	['bækgraund]	n. 出身背景
antiquated	['æntikweitid]	a. 陈旧的
timeworn	['taimwɔːn]	a. 陈旧的，老朽的
dated	['deitid]	a. 有年头的
unique	[juː'niːk]	a. 惟一的；独特的
folk	[fəuk]	a. 民间的
extinction	[ik'stiŋkʃən]	n. 灭绝
preserve	[pri'zəːv]	v. 维持
diversity	[dai'vəːsəti]	n. 多样性；差异

Folkways 民风

folkway	['fəukwei]	n. 社会习俗
civilian	[si'viljən]	a. 市民的；民间的 n. 平民
honest	['ɔnist]	a. 诚实的，正直的
virtuous	['vəːtʃuəs]	a. 有道德的；贞节的
unsophisticated	[ˌʌnsə'fistikeitid]	a. 不懂世故的，单纯的
sophisticated	[sə'fistikeitid]	a. 老于世故的
hypocritical	[ˌhipə'kritikəl]	a. 虚伪的
plain	[plein]	a. 朴素的；简单的
sincere	[sin'siə]	a. 诚挚的，真诚的

warmhearted	[ˈwɔːmˈhɑːtid]	a. 热心肠的
zealous	[ˈzeləs]	a. 热心的
intense	[inˈtens]	a. 热情的
hospitable	[ˈhɔspitəbl]	a. 好客的，殷勤的
humane	[hjuːˈmein]	a. 仁慈的，慈悲的

Transcultural Communication 跨文化交流

communication	[kəˌmjuːniˈkeiʃən]	n. 交流，交际
culture	[ˈkʌltʃə]	n. 文化，文明
misunderstanding	[ˌmisʌndəˈstændiŋ]	n. 误会，误解
barrier	[ˈbæriə]	n. 障碍，隔阂
promote	[prəˈməut]	v. 促进，增进
enhance	[inˈhɑːns; inˈhæns]	v. 提高，增强
exchange	[iksˈtʃeindʒ]	n./v. 交换，互换
respect	[riˈspekt]	n./v. 尊敬；尊重

Publishing 出版

press	[pres]	n. 出版社；印刷机
compile	[kəmˈpail]	v. 编译，编辑
edit	[ˈedit]	v. 编辑 n. 编辑工作
proofread	[ˈpruːfriːd]	v. 校对，校正
publish	[ˈpʌbliʃ]	v. 出版；发表
stack	[stæk]	n. [常用复] 书架，书库；堆；叠 v. 堆叠
volume	[ˈvɔljuːm]	n. 卷，册
dictionary	[ˈdikʃənəri]	n. 字典
subscribe	[səbˈskraib]	v. 订阅
issue	[ˈiʃjuː]	n. 出版；期 v. 出版，发行
hardcover	[ˈhɑːdˈkʌvə]	n. 精装书 a. 精装的
paperback	[ˈpeipəbæk]	n. 平装本

e-book	['i:buk] *n*. 电子图书	
edition	[i'diʃən] *n*. 版本	
handbook	['hændbuk] *n*. 手册	
pirated	['paiərətid] *a*. 翻印的，盗版的	
catalogue	['kætəlɔg] *n*. 目录	
table of contents	目录，目次	
content	['kɔntent] *n*. 内容，目录	
flyleaf	['flaili:f] *n*. 扉页	
preface	['prefis] *n*. 序文，前言 *v*. 做序言	
index	['indeks] *n*. 索引 *v*. 编索引	
introduction	[ˌintrə'dʌkʃən] *n*. 导言，绪论	
chapter	['tʃæptə] *n*. 章节	
author	['ɔ:θə] *n*. 作者	
signature	['signətʃə] *n*. 签名，署名	

Living 生活

Clothing 服饰

costume	['kɔstju:m] *n*. (特定场合穿的)成套服装；服饰	
dress	[dres] *n*. 服装，衣服	
suit	[sju:t; su:t] *n*. 一套衣服	
tuxedo	[tʌk'si:dəu] *n*. 无尾礼服	
jacket	['dʒækit] *n*. 短上衣，夹克衫	
sweater	['swetə] *n*. 厚运动衫，毛线衫	
sportswear	['spɔ:tsweə] *n*. 运动装	
vest	[vest] *n*. 汗衫，背心 *v*. 穿衣服	
shirt	[ʃə:t] *n*. 衬衫，衬衣	
tie	[tai] *n*. 领带，领结	

pant	[pænt] *n*. [常用复] 裤子，短裤
sock	[sɔk] *n*. [常用复] 短袜 *v*. 给···穿短袜
sneaker	['sniːkə] *n*. 运动鞋
blouse	[blauz] *n*. 女式衬衫
skirt	[skəːt] *n*. 裙子
jumper	['dʒʌmpə] *n*. 女式套头外衣；海员上衣
jean	[dʒiːn] *n*. 裤子，牛仔裤
underwear	['ʌndəweə] *n*. 内衣
bikini	[bi'kiːni] *n*. 比基尼
gown	[gaun] *n*. 长袍，睡衣
robe	[rəub] *n*. 长袍，罩衣
lace	[leis] *n*. 花边，缎带 *v*. 饰以花边
cap	[kæp] *n*. 帽子，军帽
hat	[hæt] *n*. 帽子
scarf	[skɑːf] *n*. 围巾 *v*. 围围巾
glove	[glʌv] *n*. 手套
shabby	['ʃæbi] *a*. 褴褛的
gorgeous	['gɔːdʒəs] *a*. 华丽的，灿烂的
luxurious	[lʌg'zjuəriəs] *a*. 奢华的
formfitting	['fɔːmˌfitiŋ] *a*. 合身的
skintight	['skin'tait] *a*. 紧身的
corpulent	['kɔːpjulənt] *a*. 肥大的
layette	[lei'et] *n*. 婴儿的全套用品
mantle	['mæntl] *n*. 披风，斗篷
cloak	['kləuk] *n*. 斗篷，披风
hood	['hud] *n*. 风帽，兜帽
shawl	[ʃɔːl] *n*. （妇女用）披肩
brief	['briːf] *n*. [常用复] 贴身短内裤
waistcoat	['weistkəut] *n*. 背心
slipper	['slipə] *n*. 拖鞋；便鞋
sandal	['sændəl] *n*. 凉鞋

trainer	['treinə] n. 软运动鞋
gumshoe	['gʌmʃuː] n. 橡胶鞋
high heels	高跟鞋
loafer	['ləufə] n. 平底便鞋；懒人鞋
wellies	['weliz] n. 长统雨靴，长统胶靴
boot	[buːt] n. 靴子，长统靴
dot	[dɔt] n. 小圆点；圆点花
stripe	[straip] n. 条纹
embroidery	[im'brɔidəri] n. 刺绣，刺绣品
linen	['linin] n. 亚麻织品，亚麻布
knitting	['nitiŋ] n. 编织（法）；编织物，针织品
knitwear	['nitweə] n. 针织品
tweed	[twiːd] n. 粗花呢
corduroy	['kɔːdərɔi] n. 灯芯绒
satin	['sætin] n. 缎子，缎 a. 缎子做的；缎子般的
flannel	['flænəl] n. 法兰绒（一种布）a. 法兰绒的

Habitation 居住

province	['prɔvins] n. 省
town	[taun] n. 镇，市镇；市区，市中心
county	['kaunti] n. 〈英〉郡，〈美〉县
countryside	['kʌntrisaid] n. 乡下，农村
capital	['kæpitəl] n. 首都，首府
metropolis	[mi'trɔpəlis] n. 首府，都会；大城市
shopping centre	商业区
downtown	['daun'taun] ad. 往(在)市区 a. 市区的
uptown	['ʌp'taun] a./ad. 位于或向着市镇外围住宅区(的)
district	['distrikt] n. 地区，区域；管区，行政区
residential	[ˌrezi'denʃəl] a. 居住的，住宅的

residential area	居民区，住宅区
urban	['ə:bən] *a*. 城市的
suburb	['sʌbə:b] *n*. 市郊，郊区
outskirt	['autskə:t] *n*. [常用复] 郊区，郊外
slum	[slʌm] *n*. [常用复] 贫民窟，贫民区
village	['vilidʒ] *n*. 乡村，村庄
hamlet	['hæmlit] *n*. 村子；〈英〉（无教堂的）小村庄
locality	[ləu'kæləti] *n*. 地点，位置
shelter	['ʃeltə] *n*. 庇护所
house	[haus] *n*. 房屋，住宅
building	['bildiŋ] *n*. 建筑物，房屋；建筑
skyscraper	['skai,skreipə] *n*. 摩天大楼
flat	[flæt] *n*. 一套房间；公寓套房
shed	[ʃed] *n*. 棚屋，小屋
cabin	['kæbin] *n*. 小木屋
hut	[hʌt] *n*. 简陋的房子，棚屋
refuge	['refju:dʒ] *n*. 庇护所，藏身处
townhouse	['taunhaus] *n*. 城市住宅
cell	[sel] *n*. 单人小室
basement	['beismənt] *n*. 地下室
apartment	[ə'pɑ:tmənt] *n*. 一套公寓
villa	['vilə] *n*. 别墅
tent	[tent] *n*. 帐篷
castle	['kɑ:sl; 'kæsl] *n*. 城堡

House Decoration 室内装修

decorate	['dekəreit] *v*. 装饰，装修
decoration	[,dekə'reiʃən] *n*. 装饰，装饰品
ornament	['ɔ:nəmənt] *n*. 装饰物 *v*. 装饰，装修

layout	['leiaut]	n. 规划，设计
outline	['autlain]	n. 轮廓，外形 v. 描画轮廓
furniture	['fə:nitʃə]	n. 家具；设备
heater	['hi:tə]	n. 加热器，发热器
ceiling	['si:liŋ]	n. 天花板
skylight	['skailait]	n. 天窗
spacious	['speiʃəs]	a. 广阔的，宽敞的
capacious	[kə'peiʃəs]	a. 面积大的，宽敞的
simple	['simpl]	a. 简单的，简朴的
crude	[kru:d]	a. 天然的；粗糙的
traditional	[trə'diʃənəl]	a. 传统的
classical	['klæsikəl]	a. 古典的
modern	['mɔdən]	a. 现代的，摩登的
fashionable	['fæʃənəbl]	a. 流行的，时髦的
stylish	['stailiʃ]	a. 时髦的，流行的
comfortable	['kʌmfətəbl]	a. 舒适的
toilet	['tɔilit]	n. 厕所，盥洗室
lavatory	['lævətəri;'lævə,tɔri]	n. 盥洗室，厕所
washroom	['wɔʃrum]	n. 盥洗室；厕所(尤指公共建筑物中的)
balcony	['bælkəni]	n. 阳台
transom	['trænsəm]	n. (门窗上端的)横楣，横档；气窗，扇形窗
windowsill	['windəusil]	n. 窗沿，窗台

Housewares 家居用品

armchair	[ɑ:m'tʃeə]	n. (单座的)沙发；扶手椅
easy chair		安乐椅
stool	[stu:l]	n. 凳子
footstool	['futstu:l]	n. 脚凳

bench	[bentʃ] *n.* 长椅子
tea table	茶几
bookcase	['bukkeis] *n.* 书柜(架)`
wardrobe	['wɔːdrəub] *n.* 衣橱
built-in wardrobe	壁橱
bookshelf	['bukʃelf] *n.* 书架
closet	['klɔzit] *n.* 橱，壁橱
chest of drawers	五斗橱
sofa	['səufə] *n.* 沙发
screen	[skriːn] *n.* 屏风，帘，纱窗
rug	[rʌg] *n.* (小)地毯；围毯
carpet	['kɑːpit] *n.* 地毯 *v.* 以地毯覆盖
mattress	['mætris] *n.* 床垫，垫褥
quilt	[kwilt] *n.* 被子
blanket	['blæŋkit] *n.* 毯子；厚的覆盖物
tapestry	['tæpistri] *n.* 织锦，挂毯
sheet	[ʃiːt] *n.* 被单
bedspread	['bedspred] *n.* 床单，床罩
dressing table	梳妆台
bath towel	浴巾
towel rack	毛巾架
sponge	[spʌndʒ] *n.* 海绵 *v.* 用湿海绵(或布)擦，揩
curtain	['kəːtən] *n.* 窗帘，门帘
shutter	['ʃʌtə] *n.* 百叶窗
kettle	['ketl] *n.* 水壶，罐
cooker	['kukə] *n.* 炊具；厨灶
pressure cooker	压力锅
ladle	['leidl] *n.* 长柄勺
oven	['ʌvən] *n.* 烤箱，烤炉；灶
microwave	['maikrəuweiv] *n.* 微波(炉)

toaster	['təustə] n. 烤面包机
dishwasher	['diʃ,wɔʃə] n. 洗碗机
air-condition	['eəkən,diʃən] v. 给…装上空调；用空调调节（空气）
air-conditioning	['eəkən,diʃəniŋ] n. 空调设备，空调系统
electric	[i'lektrik] a. 电动的，电的
electric cooker	电饭锅
electric fan	电扇
electric iron	电熨斗
chandelier	[,ʃændə'liə] n. 枝形吊灯（烛台）
pendant	['pendənt] n. 垂饰，下垂物
pendant lamp	吊灯
fluorescent	[,fluə'resənt] a. 荧光的，发光的
fluorescent lamp	日光灯
reading lamp	台灯
desk lamp	桌灯，台灯
bedside lamp	床头灯
floor lamp	落地灯
lampshade	['læmpʃeid] n. 灯罩
bulb	[bʌlb] n. 灯泡
bulb holder	灯头，灯座
switch	[switʃ] n. 开关，电闸
socket	['sɔkit] n. 插座；插口管，插口
plug	[plʌg] n. 插头，插座
refrigerator/fridge	[ri'fridʒəreitə] n. 冰箱，冷藏库
television/TV	['teli,viʒən] n. 电视（机）
washer	['wɔʃə] n. 洗衣机
washing machine	洗衣机
flashlight	['flæʃlait] n. 手电筒
vacuum	['vækjuəm] n. 真空吸尘器 v. 用吸尘器清扫
vacuum cleaner	真空吸尘器

Nutrition 营养

nutrition	[nju:'triʃən] *n.* 营养，营养学
variety	[və'raiəti] *n.* 品种；多样性
nourishment	['nʌriʃmənt; 'nə:riʃmənt] *n.* 营养品
vitamin	['vaitəmin; 'vitəmin] *n.* 维他命，维生素
protein	['prəuti:n] *n.* 蛋白质 *a.* 蛋白质的
fiber	['faibə] *n.* 纤维
dextrose	['dekstrəus] *n.* 葡萄糖
amino acid	氨基酸
grain	['grein] *n.* 谷物，粮食
cereal	['siəriəl] *n.* 谷类食品，谷物
vegetable	['vedʒitəbl] *n.* 蔬菜
vegetarian	[ˌvedʒi'teəriən] *n.* 素食者，食草动物 *a.* 素食的
choosy	['tʃu:zi] *a.* 挑剔的，慎重选择的
tasteless	['teistlis] *a.* 没味道的
nutrient	['nju:triənt] *a.* 有营养的
balanced	['bælənst] *a.* 平衡的，平稳的
intake	['inteik] *n.* 引入的量，摄入量
digest	[dai'dʒest] *v.* 消化
metabolism	[mi'tæbəlizəm] *n.* 新陈代谢
indigestion	[ˌindi'dʒestʃən] *n.* 消化不良
nourish	['nʌriʃ; 'nə:riʃ] *v.* 滋养，使强壮
absorb	[əb'sɔ:b] *v.* 吸收

Food and Drink 食品与饮料

beef	[bi:f] *n.* 牛肉
veal	[vi:l] *n.* 小牛肉

pork	[pɔːk] n. 猪肉
mutton	[ˈmʌtən] n. 羊肉
lamb	[læm] n. 羔羊
duck	[dʌk] n. 鸭子；鸭肉
seafood	[ˈsiːfuːd] n. 海鲜，海味
shrimp	[ʃrimp] n. 虾
crab	[kræb] n. 螃蟹
bacon	[ˈbeikən] n. 咸肉，熏肉
ham	[hæm] n. 火腿
sausage	[ˈsɔsidʒ; ˈsɔːsidʒ] n. 香肠，腊肠
frankfurter	[ˈfræŋk,fəːtə] n. 法兰克福香肠
steak	[steik] n. 肉片，肉排
rib	[rib] n. 肋骨
cream	[kriːm] n. 奶油，乳酪
butter	[ˈbʌtə] n. 黄油，牛油 v. 涂黄油
cheese	[tʃiːz] n. 干酪
snack	[snæk] n. 小吃，快餐
junk food	垃圾食品，无营养的食品
biscuit	[ˈbiskit] n. 饼干，小点心
hamburger	[ˈhæmbəːgə] n. 汉堡包，牛肉饼
toast	[təust] n. 烤面包片，吐司面包片 v. 烤面包
cookie	[ˈkuki] n. 甜面包，小甜饼
sandwich	[ˈsænwidʒ] n. 三明治
pizza	[ˈpiːtsə] n. 比萨饼
spaghetti	[spəˈgeti] n. 意大利面
dessert	[diˈzəːt] n. 餐后甜点
pudding	[ˈpudiŋ] n. 布丁
broth	[brɔθ] n. 肉汤
salad	[ˈsæləd] n. 沙拉
pepper	[ˈpepə] n. 胡椒粉
vinegar	[ˈvinigə] n. 醋

spice	[spais]	n. 香料，调味品
seasoning	['siːzəniŋ]	n. 调味品，调料
stew	[stjuː]	v. 炖，闷 n. 炖肉，炖菜
appetite	['æpitait]	n. 食欲，胃口
juice	[dʒuːs]	n. 果汁
lemonade	[ˌleməˈneid]	n. 柠檬汁
soda	['səudə]	n. 苏打水，碳酸水
cocktail	['kɔkteil]	n. 鸡尾酒
sherry	['ʃeri]	n. 雪利酒，葡萄酒
champagne	[ˌʃæmˈpein]	n. 香槟酒

Restaurant 餐馆

restaurant	['restərɔnt]	n. 饭店
cafeteria	[ˌkæfiˈtiəriə]	n. 自助餐厅
dining-room		n. 餐厅
flavor	['fleivə]	n. 风味
delicious	[diˈliʃəs]	a. 美味的
spicy	['spaisi]	a. 辛辣的
horrible	['hɔrəbl]	a. 可怕的，恐怖的
terrible	['terəbl]	a. 糟糕的，极差的
book	[buk]	v. 预定，登记
reserve	[riˈzəːv]	v. 预定
chef	[ʃef]	n. 厨师
waitress	['weitris]	n. 女服务生
waiter	['weitə]	n. 服务生
knife	[naif]	n. 餐刀，刀
fork	[fɔːk]	n. 叉子
menu	['menjuː]	n. 菜单
bill	[bil]	n. 账单 v. 开账单

| tip | [tip] *n.* 小费 *v.* 给小费 |
| economical | [ˌekəˈnɔmikəl] *a.* 节约的，经济的 |

Shopping 购物

supermarket	[ˈsjuːpəˌmɑːkit] *n.* 超市
department	[diˈpɑːtmənt] *n.* 部
department store	百货商店
mall	[mɔːl] *n.* 购物商场，商业街
flea market	跳蚤市场
clerk	[ˈkləːk; klɑːk] *n.* 店员，职员
sales promotion	促销
discount	[ˈdiskaunt] *n.* 折扣
reduction	[riˈdʌkʃən] *n.* 减少
secondhand	[ˈsekəndˈhænd] *a.* 二手的，旧的
bargain	[ˈbɑːgin] *n.* 便宜货 *v.* 议价
stock	[stɔk] *n.* 库存 *v.* 存储，进货

Body-Building 健身

gymnasium	[dʒimˈneiziəm] *n.* 健身馆，体育馆
coach	[kəutʃ] *n.* 教练 *v.* 训练
equipment	[iˈkwipmənt] *n.* 器械，器材
instruction	[inˈstrʌkʃən] *n.* 指示，指导
aerobics	[eəˈrəubiks] *n.* 有氧健身法，增氧健身法
aerobic	[eəˈrəubik] *a.* 增氧健身法的
oxygen	[ˈɔksidʒən] *n.* 氧气
endurance	[inˈdjuərəns] *n.* 忍耐力，持久力
muscle	[ˈmʌsl] *n.* 肌肉
tired	[ˈtaiəd] *a.* 疲劳的，疲倦的

massage	['mæsɑːʒ;mə'sɑːʒ] *n./v.* 按摩	
pant	[pænt] *n./v.* 气喘	
gasp	[gɑːsp;gæsp] *v.* 气喘，喘息	
physical	['fizikəl] *a.* 身体的 *n.* 体格检查	
stature	['stætʃə] *n.* 身材，身高	
bonny	['bɔni] *a.* 漂亮的；健美的	
towel	['tauəl] *n.* 毛巾 *v.* 用毛巾擦	
sweat	[swet] *n.* 汗水 *v.* 出汗	
membership	['membəʃip] *n.* 会员资格	
fee	[fiː] *n.* 费用	
shadowboxing	['ʃædəu,bɔksiŋ] *n.* 太极拳	
kickboxing	['kik,bɔksiŋ] *n.* 跆拳道	
Yoga	['jəugə] *n.* 瑜伽	
jog	[dʒɔg] *n./v.* 漫步，慢跑	
hike	[haik] *n./v.* 远足	

Vehicle 交通

vessel	['vesəl] *n.* 船只（总称）
dugout	['dʌgaut] *n.* 独木舟
rowboat	['rəubəut] *n.* 划艇
canoe	[kə'nuː] *n.* 独木舟 *v.* 乘独木舟，划独木舟
ferry	['feri] *n.* 渡船 *v.* 运送
ferryboat	['feribəut] *n.* 渡船，渡轮
raft	[rɑːft;ræft] *n.* 木排，木筏
skiff	[skif] *n.* 轻舟，小船
steamer	['stiːmə] *n.* 汽船，轮船
yacht	[jɔt] *n.* 快艇，（竞赛用的)帆船，游艇 *v.* 驾游艇
motorboat	['məutəbəut] *n.* 摩托艇
lifeboat	['laifbəut] *n.* 救生艇
cabin	['kæbin] *n.* 机舱，船舱

stateroom	['steitrum] *n.* (轮船的)特等客舱	
tourist class	普通舱，经济舱	
first class	头等舱	
first-class cabin	头等舱	
steerage	['stiəridʒ] *n.* 最低票价的舱位，下等客舱	
freighter	['freitə] *n.* 货船	
cargo boat	货船	
tanker	['tæŋkə] *n.* 油轮	
patrol boat	巡逻艇	
frigate	['frigit] *n.* (小型)护卫舰	
gunboat	['gʌnbəut] *n.* 炮舰	
bus	[bʌs] *n.* 公共汽车	
minibus	['minibʌs] *n.* 小型公共汽车	
coach	[kəutʃ] *n.* 长途公共汽车；四轮大马车	
taxi	['tæksi] *n.* 出租汽车 *v.* 乘出租车	
taxi rank	计程汽车停车行列	
taxi stand	计程汽车车站	
taxicab	['tæksikæb] *n.* 出租车	
trailer	['treilə] *n.* 拖车，挂车	
compact car	小型汽车	
lorry	['lɔri；'lɔ:ri] *n.* 载货汽车，卡车	
wagon	['wægən] *n.* 四轮马车，大篷车	
moped	['məuped] *n.* 机动脚踏两用车	
motorbike	['məutəbaik] *n.* 摩托车	
motorcycle	['məutə,saikl] *n.* 摩托车	
ambulance	['æmbjuləns] *n.* 救护车	
jeep	['dʒi:p] *n.* 吉普车	
limousine	['liməzi:n] *n.* 大客车；豪华轿车	
roadster	['rəudstə] *n.* 敞篷车，跑车	
trolley/trolly	['trɔli] *n.* 手推车，小车；(=trolley bus)电车	
tramcar	['træmkɑ:] *n.* 有轨电车	
streetcar	['stri:tkɑ:] *n.* 路面电车	

underground	[ˈʌndəgraund] n. 地铁	
tube	[tjuːb;tuːb] n. 地铁	
subway	[ˈsʌbwei] n. 地铁	
conductor	[kənˈdʌktə] n. 售票员	
railway	[ˈreilwei] n. 铁路	
railroad	[ˈreilrəud] n. 铁路 v. 由铁道运输	
express train	特别快车	
fast train	快车	
through train	直达快车	
stopping train	慢车	
excursion train	游览列车	
commuter	[kəˈmjuːtə] n. 经常往返者；通勤者	
commuter train	往返于市区与郊区之间的火车	
suburban train	市郊火车	
carriage	[ˈkæridʒ] n. 客车车厢	
sleeper	[ˈsliːpə] n. (火车等的)卧铺	
berth	[bəːθ] n. (船、车、飞机等的)座(铺)位；卧铺	
bunk	[bʌŋk] n. 铺位，卧铺	
booking office	售票处	
ticket office	售票处	
ticket collector	检票员，验票员	
platform	[ˈplætfɔːm] n. 站台，月台	
platform ticket	站台票	
left-luggage office	行李暂存处	
terminal	[ˈtəːminəl] n. 终点站	
terminus	[ˈtəːminəs] n. (火车，汽车)终点站	
car attendant	(火车车厢)列车员	
train attendant	列车员	
rack	[ræk] n. 挂架，搁架	
transfer	[trænsˈfəː] n./v. 换乘，转车	
civil aviation	民用航空	
aircraft	[ˈeəkrɑːft] n. 飞机；航空器	

airplane	['eəplein] *n*. 飞机	
airliner	['eə,lainə] *n*. (大型民航)班机；航线客机	
jet	[dʒet] *n*. 喷气式飞机，喷气发动机 *v*. 乘喷气式飞机	
airline	['eəlain] *n*. [常用复] 航空公司；航线	
boarding check/card/pass	登机牌	
airport	['eəpɔːt] *n*. 机场；航空港	
air terminal	航空集散站	
tarmac	['tɑːmæk] *n*. 停机坪	
air hostess	空中小姐	
stewardess	['stjuədis] *n*. (轮船、飞机或火车上的)女服务员	
steward	['stjuəd] *n*. (飞机、轮船等的)乘务员，服务员	
aircraft crew	机组，机务人员	
pilot	['pailət] *n*. 飞行员；领航员 *v*. 驾驶，为…引航	
takeoff	['teikɔf] *n*. 起飞	

Voyage 旅行

tourist	['tuərist] *n*. 游客，旅行者
journey	['dʒəːni] *n*. 旅行，旅程 *v*. 旅行
route	[ruːt] *n*. 路线，路程
itinerary	[ai'tinərəri] *n*. 路线
do-it-yourself	[,duːitjɔː'self] *n*. 自己做 *a*. 自己动手的
independent	[,indi'pendənt] *a*. 独立自主的
guide	[gaid] *n*. 向导，导游 *v*. 指导，带领
travel agent	旅行代办人
agency	['eidʒənsi] *n*. 代理处
travel agency	旅行社
guidebook	['gaidbuk] *n*. 旅行指南

transportation	[ˌtrænspəˈteiʃən] n. 运输，运送
vehicle	[ˈviːikl] n. 交通工具，车辆
voyage	[ˈvɔiidʒ] n./v. 航行，航海
destination	[ˌdestiˈneiʃən] n. 目的地
sightsee	[ˈsaitsiː] v. 观光
sight	[sait] n. 情景，景象，奇观；[常用复] 风景，名胜
scene	[siːn] n. 景象，景观
scenery	[ˈsiːnəri] n. 风景，景色
motel	[məuˈtel] n. 汽车旅馆
reservation	[ˌrezəˈveiʃən] n. 保留，预定
passport	[ˈpɑːspɔːt; ˈpæspɔːt] n. 护照
expire	[ikˈspaiə] v. 期满，终止
luggage	[ˈlʌgidʒ] n. 行李，皮箱
memento	[miˈmentəu] n. 纪念品
souvenir	[ˌsuːvəˈniə] n. 纪念品

Family Relations 家庭关系

family tree	家谱
generation	[ˌdʒenəˈreiʃən] n. 一代人
lineage	[ˈliniidʒ] n. 宗系，世系；血统
stock	[stɔk] n. 世系，血统
origin	[ˈɔridʒin; ˈɔːridʒin] n. [常用复] 出身，血统
kin	[kin] n. [集合词] 家属；亲戚；血缘关系
ancestry	[ˈænsestri] n. 家系，血统
extraction	[ikˈstrækʃən] n. 血统，家世，出身
descent	[diˈsent] n. 血统，世系
noble birth	贵族出身
humble birth	平民出身
next of kin	近亲
forebear	[ˈfɔːbeə] n. 祖宗，祖先

forefather	[ˈfɔːˌfɑːðə] *n.* 祖先，祖宗
affinity	[əˈfinəti] *n.* 嫡亲关系，嫡戚关系
offspring	[ˈɔfspriŋ] *n.* 子孙，后代
descendant	[diˈsendənt] *n.* 后代，后裔
progeny	[ˈprɔdʒəni] *n.* 后代，子女
relative	[ˈrelətiv] *n.* 亲属，亲戚
relation	[riˈleiʃən] *n.* 关系；亲属
premarital	[priːˈmæritəl] *a.* 婚前的
cousin	[ˈkʌzən] *n.* 堂（或表）兄弟；堂（或表）姊妹
sibling	[ˈsibliŋ] *n.* 兄弟或姊妹
rely	[riˈlai] *v.* 依赖；信赖
newlywed	[ˈnjuːliwed] *n.* 新婚的人
bride	[braid] *n.* 新娘
bridegroom	[ˈbraidgrum] *n.* 新郎
bridesmaid	[ˈbraidzmeid] *n.* 女傧相
beatific	[ˌbiːəˈtifik] *a.* 祝福的
harmony	[ˈhɑːməni] *n.* 和谐，融洽
rapport	[ræˈpɔː] *n.* 和睦
reverent	[ˈrevərənt] *a.* 尊敬的，虔诚的
gracious	[ˈgreiʃəs] *a.* 和蔼的，宽厚的
venerate	[ˈvenəreit] *v.* 崇敬，敬仰
spoil	[spɔil] *v.* 宠坏，溺爱
cosset	[ˈkɔsit] *v.* 宠爱，溺爱 *n.* 宠儿
henpecked	[ˈhenpekt] *a.* 顺从妻子的，惧内的
gentle	[ˈdʒentl] *a.* 温柔的，慈祥的
gap	[gæp] *n.* 隔阂
illegitimate	[ˌiliˈdʒitimət] *a.* 私生的
strict	[strikt] *a.* 严格的，严厉的
scold	[skəuld] *v.* 责骂，训斥
brutal	[ˈbruːtəl] *a.* 无情的，冷酷的
tough	[tʌf] *a.* 强硬的

separate	['sepəreit] *v.* 分居
divorce	[di'vɔːs] *n.* /*v.* 离婚
abandon	[ə'bændən] *v.* 遗弃
adopt	[ə'dɔpt] *v.* 收养
stepfather	['step,fɑːðə] *n.* 继父
stepmother	['step,mʌðə] *n.* 继母
stepson	['stepsʌn] *n.* 继子
orphan	['ɔːfən] *n.* 孤儿
rejoin	[riˈdʒɔin] *v.* 团圆

Friendship and Love 友情与爱情

pal	[pæl] *n.* 伙伴，好友 *v.* 结成朋友
colleague	['kɔliːg] *n.* 同事
roommate	['ruːmmeit] *n.* 室友
fraternal	[frə'təːnəl] *a.* 兄弟的；友善的
neighborly	['neibəli] *a.* 邻居似的，友好的
reliable	[ri'laiəbl] *a.* 可靠的
loyalty	['lɔiəlti] *n.* 忠诚，忠心
easygoing	['iːzi,gəuiŋ] *a.* 随和的
deceptive	[di'septiv] *a.* 虚伪的
sociable	['səuʃəbl] *a.* 友善的；好交际的
gauche	[gəuʃ] *a.* 不擅交际的，不圆滑的
unfriendly	[,ʌn'frendli] *a.* 不友善的
eccentric	[ik'sentrik] *a.* 古怪的 *n.* 古怪的人
betray	[bi'trei] *v.* 背叛，出卖
cheat	[tʃiːt] *n.* /*v.* 欺骗，骗取
dump	[dʌmp] *v.* 抛弃
quarrel	['kwɔrəl] *n.* /*v.* 争吵
indifferent	[in'difərənt] *a.* 冷漠的
passive	['pæsiv] *a.* 被动的；冷淡的

impassive	[im'pæsiv]	a. 无动于衷的，无感情的
nonchalant	['nɔnʃələnt]	a. 冷漠的
troublemaker	['trʌbl,meikə]	n. 惹麻烦的人；捣乱者
odious	['əudiəs]	a. 可憎的，讨厌的
censorious	[sen'sɔ:riəs]	a. 爱挑剔的，吹毛求疵的
tolerate	['tɔləreit]	v. 容许；忍受
bighearted	['big'hɑ:tid]	a. 善良的；宽大的
ingenuous	[in'dʒenjuəs]	a. 淳朴的，单纯的
amiable	['eimjəbl]	a. 和蔼的，亲切的
beneficent	[bi'nefisənt]	a. 行善的；慷慨的
charm	[tʃɑ:m]	n. 魅力 v. 吸引
lovesick	['lʌvsik]	a. 害相思病的
amorous	['æmərəs]	a. 多情的
passionate	['pæʃənət]	a. 充满激情的，强烈的
beloved	[bi'lʌvid]	a. 所钟爱的，心爱的
pious	['paiəs]	a. 虔诚的
pursue	[pə'sju:; pə'su:]	v. 追求
engage	[in'geidʒ]	v. 订婚
marry	['mæri]	v. 结婚
wedding	['wediŋ]	n. 婚礼
church	[tʃə:tʃ]	n. 教堂
partner	['pɑ:tnə]	n. 配偶
null	[nʌl]	a. 无效的

Diseases 常见疾病

autism	['ɔ:tizəm]	n. 自闭症
barrenness	['bærənnis]	n. 不孕症
complication	[,kɔmpli'keiʃən]	n. 并发症
anemia	[ə'ni:miə]	n. 贫血，贫血症
amnesia	[æm'ni:zjə]	n. 健忘症

allergy	[ˈælədʒi]	n. 敏感症
sleepwalking	[ˈsliːpˌwɔːkiŋ]	n. 夜游症
phobia	[ˈfəubjə]	n. 恐惧症
tuberculosis	[tjuːˌbəːkjuˈləusis]	n. 肺结核
rabies	[ˈreibiːz]	n. 狂犬病
pinkeye	[ˈpiŋkai]	n. 红眼病
sunstroke	[ˈsʌnstrəuk]	n. 中暑
asthma	[ˈæsmə]	n. 哮喘
tumor	[ˈtjuːmə]	n. 瘤
virus	[ˈvaiərəs]	n. 病毒
alcoholism	[ˈælkəhɔlizəm]	n. 酒精中毒
pathology	[pəˈθɔlədʒi]	n. 病理学
psychiatric	[ˌsaikiˈætrik]	a. 精神病学的
venereal	[vəˈniəriəl]	a. 性病的
inflamed	[inˈfleimd]	a. 发炎的，红肿的
tumid	[ˈtjuːmid]	a. 肿胀的，肿大的
turgid	[ˈtəːdʒid]	a. 肿胀的
wan	[wɔn]	a. 苍白的；病态的
paralytic	[ˌpærəˈlitik]	a. 瘫痪的 n. 瘫痪病人
chronic	[ˈkrɔnik]	a. 慢性的
acute	[əˈkjuːt]	a. 急性的
communicable	[kəˈmjuːnikəbl]	a. 可传染的
contagious	[kənˈteidʒəs]	a. 传染性的，有传染力的
remittent	[riˈmitənt]	a. 间歇性的，忽好忽坏的
infect	[inˈfekt]	v. 传染，感染

Medicine 药品

heal	[hiːl]	v. 治愈，医治
therapy	[ˈθerəpi]	n. 治疗

convalesce	[ˌkɔnvəˈles] v. 渐渐康复，渐愈
recuperate	[riˈkjuːpəreit] v. 复原，康复
hospitalization	[ˌhɔspitəlaiˈzeiʃən] n. 住院治疗
medicate	[ˈmedikeit] v. 用药物治疗
psychoanalyze	[ˌsaikəuˈænəlaiz] v. 用心理分析法治疗
antidote	[ˈæntidəut] n. 解毒剂；矫正法
relapse	[riˈlæps] n. 复发 v. 旧病复发
exacerbate	[ekˈsæsəbeit] v. 恶化
aggravate	[ˈægrəveit] v. 使恶化，加重
surgery	[ˈsəːdʒəri] n. 外科，外科学
specialist	[ˈspeʃəlist] n. 专门医师，专家
surgeon	[ˈsəːdʒən] n. 外科医生
physician	[fiˈziʃən] n. 医师；内科医生
dentist	[ˈdentist] n. 牙医
oculist	[ˈɔkjulist] n. 眼科医生
pediatric	[ˌpiːdiˈætrik] a. 小儿科的
chemist	[ˈkemist] n. 药剂师
dispenser	[disˈpensə] n. 药剂师，配药员
matron	[ˈmeitrən] n. 护士长
remediable	[riˈmiːdiəbl] a. 可医治的，可矫正的
incurable	[inˈkjuərəbl] a. 不能治愈的
curative	[ˈkjuərətiv] a. 医疗的 n. 药品
analgesic	[ˌænælˈdʒiːsik] a. 止痛的 n. 止痛剂
antibacterial	[ˌæntibækˈtiəriəl] a. 抗菌的 n. 抗菌药
balm	[bɑːm] n. 止痛药膏，镇痛剂
cure-all	[ˈkjuərɔːl] n. 万灵药，百宝丹
sanatorium	[ˌsænəˈtɔːriəm] n. 疗养院，修养地
scalpel	[ˈskælpəl] n. 手术刀，解剖刀
sickbay	[ˈsikbei] n. 船上的医务室
ward	[wɔːd] n. 病房
sickbed	[ˈsikbed] n. 病床

medication	[ˌmediˈkeiʃən] *n*. 药物疗法；药剂
remedy	[ˈremidi] *n*. 药物，治疗法
pill	[pil] *n*. 药丸，药片
tablet	[ˈtæblit] *n*. 药片
capsule	[ˈkæpsjuːl] *n*. 胶囊
powder	[ˈpaudə] *n*. 粉，粉末
dose	[dəus] *n*. 一剂；剂量
dosage	[ˈdəusidʒ] *n*. 剂量，服用量
aspirin	[ˈæspərin] *n*. 阿司匹林，阿司匹林药片
tranquillizer	[ˈtræŋkwilaizə] *n*. 镇静剂
laxative	[ˈlæksətiv] *n*. 轻泻药
pain-killer	[ˈpeinˌkilə] *n*. 止痛片
antibiotic	[ˌæntibaiˈɔtik] *n*. 抗生素
drug	[drʌg] *n*. 药；麻药
lotion	[ˈləuʃən] *n*. 洗液，洗剂
tonic	[ˈtɔnik] *n*. 滋补品 *a*. 滋补的
prescription	[priˈskripʃən] *n*. 处方，药方
pharmacy	[ˈfɑːməsi] *n*. 药剂学，制药业
symptom	[ˈsimptəm] *n*. 症状
generic drug	非品牌配方药物
pharmaceutical	[ˌfɑːməˈsjuːtikəl] *a*. 制药的，药学的
herb	[həːb] *n*. 药草，草本植物
injection	[inˈdʒekʃən] *n*. 注射；注射剂
cure	[kjuə] *v*. 治愈
treatment	[ˈtriːtmənt] *n*. 治疗，疗法
course	[kɔːs] *n*. 疗程
alleviate	[əˈliːvieit] *v*. 减轻，缓解
soothe	[suːð] *v*. 缓和(痛苦等)，减轻
medical	[ˈmedikəl] *n*. 医生
pharmacist	[ˈfɑːməsist] *n*. 药剂师，配药者
side effect	副作用

potent	['pəutənt]	a. (药等)效力大的
effective	[i'fektiv]	a. 有效的，生效的

Bad Habits 不良习惯

inhale	[in'heil]	v. 吸入，吸气
marijuana	[,mæriju'ɑːnə]	n. 大麻
poppy	['pɔpi]	n. 罂粟
addiction	[ə'dikʃən]	n. 上瘾，沉溺
junkie	['dʒʌŋki]	n. 有毒瘾者
stub	[stʌb]	n. 烟蒂
tobacco	[tə'bækəu]	n. 烟草
cigarette	[,sigə'ret]	n. 香烟，纸烟
ashtray	['æʃtrei]	n. 烟灰缸
drunkard	['drʌŋkəd]	n. 酒鬼，醉汉
inebriate	[i'niːbriət]	v. 灌醉
libation	[lai'beiʃən]	n. 饮酒
bibulous	['bibjuləs]	a. 嗜酒的，饮酒的
alcohol	['ælkəhɔl]	n. 酒精，酒
liquor	['likə]	n. 酒精饮料 v. 喝酒
tipple	['tipl]	n. 烈酒 v. 不断地喝，饮烈酒
toast	[təust]	v. 敬酒
refrain	[ri'frein]	v. 节制
abstinence	['æbstinəns]	n. 戒酒；节制
teetotal	[tiː'təutəl]	a. 绝对戒酒的
temperance	['tempərəns]	n. 戒酒，节欲
gamble	['gæmbl]	v. 赌博
gluttony	['glʌtəni]	n. 暴食
oversleep	[,əuvə'sliːp]	v. 睡过头
vigil	['vidʒil]	n. 守夜，熬夜
indulge	[in'dʌldʒ]	v. 纵容

| abuse | [əˈbjuːz] v. 滥用；虐待 |
| wallow | [ˈwɔləu] v. 沉迷 n. 堕落 |

Social Issues 社会问题

Social Configuration 社会形态

slave	[sleiv] n. 奴隶
slavery	[ˈsleivəri] n. 奴隶制
kingdom	[ˈkiŋdəm] n. 王国
capitalist	[ˈkæpitəlist] n. 资本家
feudalism	[ˈfjuːdəlizəm] n. 封建制度
feudalist	[ˈfjuːdəlist] n. 封建论者
capitalism	[ˈkæpitəlizəm] n. 资本主义
communism	[ˈkɔmjunizəm] n. 共产主义
communist	[ˈkɔmjunist] n. 共产主义者

Race 种族

race	[reis] n. 种族
racial	[ˈreiʃəl] a. 种族的，人种的
ethnic	[ˈeθnik] a. 种族的，民族的
racism	[ˈreisizəm] n. 种族歧视，种族主义
segregation	[ˌsegriˈgeiʃən] n. 种族隔离
racialism	[ˈreiʃəlizəm] n. 种族主义；种族歧视
genocidal	[ˌdʒenəuˈsaidəl] a. 种族灭绝的
minority	[maiˈnɔrəti] n. 少数民族
ethnicity	[eθˈnisəti] n. 少数民族

look down upon		歧视
discriminate	[dis'krimineit]	v. 歧视
discrimination	[dis,krimi'neiʃən]	n. (种族等的)歧视
prejudice	['predʒudis]	n. 偏见，成见
riot	['raiət]	n. 暴乱，骚乱
segregate	['segrigeit]	v. 隔离
isolation	[,aisə'leiʃən]	n. 孤立；隔绝
equal	['i:kwəl]	a. 平等的
dark-skinned		a. 黑皮肤的
ghetto	['getəu]	n. 犹太人区
immigrant	['imigrənt]	n. 移民，侨民

Crime 犯罪

crime	[kraim]	n. 罪行，犯罪
commit	[kə'mit]	v. 犯罪
delinquency	[di'liŋkwənsi]	n. 过失；行为不良
sin	[sin]	n. 过失，罪过
offence	[ə'fens]	n. 犯规，犯法
kidnap	['kidnæp]	v. 绑架，勒赎
abduct	[æb'dʌkt]	v. 绑架，诱拐
robbery	['rɔbəri]	n. 抢劫；盗窃
blackmail	['blækmeil]	n./v. 敲诈，勒索
extortion	[ik'stɔ:ʃən]	n. 勒索，敲诈
hijack	['haidʒæk]	v. 劫持(尤指劫机)
murder	['mə:də]	v. 谋杀
assassinate	[ə'sæsineit]	v. 暗杀
violence	['vaiələns]	n. 暴力行为
rape	[reip]	v. 强奸
arson	['ɑ:sən]	n. 纵火，放火
counterfeiting	['kauntəfitiŋ]	n. 伪造

pirate	['paiərət] v. 非法窃印（或复制），盗印	
computer fraud	计算机犯罪	
smuggle	['smʌgl] v. 走私；偷运	
smuggling	['smʌgliŋ] n. 走私活动	
traffic	['træfik] v. （非法）交易	
drug trafficking	贩毒	
swindle	['swindl] n./v. 诈骗	
guilty	['gilti] a. 有罪的，犯罪的	
criminal	['kriminəl] a. 犯罪的，罪恶的 n. 罪犯，犯人	
gangster	['gæŋstə] n. 匪徒，强盗	
blackguard	['blægɑːd] n. 流氓	
ringleader	['riŋˌliːdə] n. 魁首；元凶	
polarization	[ˌpəuləraiˈzeiʃən; ˌpəuləriˈzeiʃən] n. 极化，分裂	
soar	[sɔː] v. 猛增，剧增	
frustration	[frʌˈstreiʃən] n. 不满	
desperation	[ˌdespəˈreiʃən] n. 绝望	
unemployment	[ˌʌnimˈplɔimənt] n. 失业	

Judicature 司法

prosecution	[ˌprɔsiˈkjuːʃən] n. 起诉	
accuse	[əˈkjuːz] v. 指责，指控	
adjudicate	[əˈdʒuːdikeit] v. 充当裁判；判决	
convict	[kənˈvikt] v. 定罪，证明…有罪	
deprive	[diˈpraiv] v. 剥夺	
verdict	['vəːdikt] v. 调查	
evidence	['evidəns] n. 根据，证据	
criminal record	犯罪记录	
intention	[inˈtenʃən] n. 意图，目的	
motivation	[ˌməutiˈveiʃən] n. 动机	
gang	[gæŋ] v. 合伙（对付他人）	

court	[kɔːt] *n*. 法庭，法院	
judge	[dʒʌdʒ] *n*. 法官	
jury	['dʒuəri] *n*. 陪审团，评判委员会	
trial	['traiəl] *n*. 审判，审讯	
justice	['dʒʌstis] *n*. 司法，审判	
judicial	[dʒuːˈdiʃəl] *a*. 审判的，司法的	
courtroom	['kɔːtrum] *n*. 审判室，法庭	
venue	['venjuː] *n*. （审判或犯罪）地点	
witness	['witnis] *n*. 目击者，见证人	
victim	['viktim] *n*. 受害者	
lawyer	['lɔːjə] *n*. 律师	
attorney	[əˈtəːni] *n*. 〈美〉律师	
defend	[diˈfend] *v*. 为…辩护	
sanction	['sæŋkʃən] *v*. 批准，认可	
arrest	[əˈrest] *n*./*v*. 拘留	
illegal	[iˈliːgəl] *a*. 不合法的，违法的	
legitimate	[liˈdʒitimət] *a*. 合法的；正当的	

Feminism 女权

feminism	['feminizəm] *n*. 女权主义	
feminist	['feminist] *n*. 女权主义者	
equality	[iːˈkwɔləti] *n*. 平等，相等	
opportunity	[ˌɔpəˈtjuːnəti] *n*. 机会，时机	
campaign	[kæmˈpein] *n*. （政治性）活动	
revolution	[ˌrevəˈluːʃən] *n*. 革命，革命活动	
sponsor	['spɔnsə] *n*. 发起者，赞助人	
involve	[inˈvɔlv] *v*. 使参与	
approve	[əˈpruːv] *v*. 赞成	
decry	[diˈkrai] *v*. 责难	
criticize	['kritisaiz] *v*. 批评，责备	

Athletic Sports 体育运动

Ball Games 球类运动

tennis	['tenis] *n.* 网球
basketball	['bɑːskitbɔːl] *n.* 篮球
volleyball	['vɔlibɔːl] *n.* 排球
badminton	['bædmintən] *n.* 羽毛球
baseball	['beisbɔːl] *n.* 棒球
soccer	['sɔkə] *n.* 英式足球
hockey	['hɔki] *n.* 曲棍球
golf	[gɔlf] *n.* 高尔夫球
bat	[bæt] *n.* 球棒 *v.* 用球棒击
rugby	['rʌgbi] *n.* 橄榄球
handball	['hændbɔːl] *n.* 手球；手球运动
cricket	['krikit] *n.* 板球运动
ice hockey	冰球
football	['futbɔːl] *n.* 足球；橄榄球
billiards	['biljədz] *n.* 台球
bowls	['bəulz] *n.* 保龄球运动
forecourt	['fɔːkɔːt] *n.* (在网球、羽毛球等球场中)前场
forehand	['fɔːhænd] *n./a.* (网球等的)正手打(的)
ballplayer	['bɔːlˌpleiə] *n.* 棒球手
ballpark	['bɔːlpɑːk] *n.* 棒球场
infield	['infiːld] *n.* (棒球、垒球球场)内场
outfield	['autfiːld] *n.* (棒球、垒球球场)外场
backboard	['bækbɔːd] *n.* (篮球架上的)篮板
court	[kɔːt] *n.* 球场

goal	[gəul] n. 球门；得分	
goalpost	['gəulpəust] n. 门柱	
judge	[dʒʌdʒ] n. 裁判员	
goalkeeper	['gəul,ki:pə] n. 守门员	
fullback	['fulbæk] n. （足球）后卫	
backfield	['bækfi:ld] n. （足球）后卫	
forward	['fɔːwəd] n. 前锋	
center	['sentə] n. 中锋	

Track and Field 田径运动

athlete	['æθli:t] n. 运动员，田径运动员
relay	['riːlei] n. 接替 v. 分程传递
relay race	接力赛
hurdling	['həːdliŋ] n. 跨栏赛跑
marathon	['mærəθən] n. 马拉松
sprint	[sprint] v. 快跑，疾跑
dash	[dæʃ] n./v. 飞奔，冲刺
pole-vault	['pəulvɔːlt] v. 撑杆跳
gavelock	['gævəlɔk] n. 标枪
race	[reis] n. （速度的）比赛，赛跑
middle-distance race	中长跑
cross-country race	越野跑
hurdle	['həːdl] n. 跳栏，栏 v. 进行跨栏赛；越过障碍架
the 400-meter hurdle	400 米栏
hurdler	['həːdlə] n. 跳栏比赛选手，跨栏运动员
decathlon	[di'kæθlɔn] n. 十项全能运动
high jump	跳高
long jump	跳远
broad jump	跳远
triple jump	三级跳

hop	[hɔp] v. (人) 单足跳跃，单足跳行
hop, step and jump	三级跳
vault	[vɔːlt] n. 撑杆跳 v. 撑杆跳过
throwing	['θrəuiŋ] n. 投掷运动
shot	[ʃɔt] n. 铅球
putting the shot	推铅球
shot put	推铅球
discus	['diskəs] n. 铁饼
throwing the discus	掷铁饼
hammer	['hæmə] n. 锤，链锤
throwing the hammer	掷链锤
javelin	['dʒævlin] n. 标枪
throwing the javelin	掷标枪
walk	[wɔːk] n. 竞走
foot race	竞走

Others 其他

champion	['tʃæmpiən] n. 冠军
skiing	['skiːiŋ] n. 滑雪
skating	['skeitiŋ] n. 溜冰，滑冰
boxing	['bɔksiŋ] n. 拳击
jogging	['dʒɔgiŋ] n. 慢跑
diving	['daiviŋ] n. 潜水；跳水
springboard	['spriŋbɔːd] n. 跳板
gymnast	['dʒimnæst] n. 体操运动员
gymnastics	[dʒim'næstiks] n. 体操，体育
horizontal	[,hɔri'zɔntəl] a. 水平的，平坦的
horizontal bar	单杠
parallel bars	双杠
ring	[riŋ] [常用复] n. 吊环

trapeze	[trə'piːz] *n*. 吊秋千	
side horse	鞍马	
pommel	['pʌml] *n*. (马鞍)前鞍	
pommelled horse	鞍马	
weight lifting	举重	
wrestling	['reslin] *n*. 摔跤，格斗	
Greece-Roman wrestling	古典式摔跤	
judo	['dʒuːdəu] *n*. 柔道	
fencing	['fensin] *n*. 剑术，击剑	
winter sports	冬季运动	
downhill race	速降滑雪赛，滑降	
slalom	['slɑːləm] *n*. 障碍滑雪赛	
ski jump	跳高滑雪	
ice skating	滑冰	
figure skating	花样滑冰	
roller skating	滑旱冰	

第二部分 同义词汇归纳记忆

安静的 (quiet, tranquil, peaceful, placid, pacific, still, sedate, restful)

soothe [suːð] v. 抚慰、缓和、减轻.

quiet	['kwaiət] *a.* 安静的，静止的 (making very little or no noise)
	【例】I prefer *quiet* soothing music.
tranquil	['træŋkwil] *a.* 宁静的 (calm or with no sound)
	【例】He grew up in a *tranquil* village.
peaceful	['piːsful] *a.* 安静的，宁静的 (calm and free from disturbance)
	【例】The children look so *peaceful* when they are sleeping.
placid	['plæsid] *a.* 安静的，平静的 (calm and without a lot of action or movement)
	【例】You can see fishes under the *placid* water of the lake.
pacific	[pə'sifik] *a.* 平静的，平和的 (peaceful in character or intent)
	【例】The hotel is set in *pacific* surroundings.

still	[stil] *a.* 静止的，寂静的 (not moving)
	【例】Just sit *still* and I will finish the work in a minute.
sedate	[si'deit] *a.* 安静的 (quiet or slow, and not likely to shock people or attract attention)
	【例】The couple walked at a *sedate* pace.
restful	['restful] *a.* 宁静的 (relaxing and with no noise)
	【例】There is a *restful* quality about that apartment.

安慰 (comfort, console, reassure, solace)

comfort	['kʌmfət] *v.* 安慰 (to make someone feel less sad, worried, or disappointed)
	【例】I tried to *comfort* Joanna after she failed the examination.
console	[kən'səul] *v.* 安慰，抚慰 (to try to make someone feel better when they are unhappy or disappointed)
	【例】After his home was destroyed by the flood, Alan *consoled* himself with the thought that it might have been worse.
	【用】console sb. for/on sth. 在…（问题上）安慰…
reassure	[,ri:ə'ʃuə] *v.* 使…安心，安慰 (to make someone feel less worried about something)
	【例】Rebecca just *reassured* me that everything was fine.
	【用】reassure sb. about sth. 使…在…（问题上）安心
solace	['sɔləs] *v.* 安慰 (to make someone feel better when they are sad or upset)
	【例】Jessica *solaced* herself by playing the flute.

昂贵的 (expensive, costly, valuable, invaluable, precious, priceless)

expensive	[ik'spensiv] *a.* 昂贵的 (costing a lot of money)
	【例】It can be very *expensive* to train new personnel.
costly	['kɔstli] *a.* 昂贵的，代价高的 (costing a lot of money)
	【例】Changing your company's management style can be a *costly* business.
valuable	['væljuəbl] *a.* 贵重的 (having considerable monetary or material value for use or exchange)

【例】Where did you get the **valuable** collection of paintings?

【用】sth. prove valuable 证明…的价值无可估量

invaluable ［in'væljuəbl］*a.* 无价的，极宝贵的（valuable beyond estimation）

【例】Those **invaluable** ancient scrolls were all destroyed by the fire.

precious ['preʃəs] *a.* 珍贵的，贵重的（worth a lot of money）

【例】Here is a historic house with rare and **precious** contents.

priceless ['praislis] *a.* 无价的，珍贵的（very valuable and impossible to replace）

【例】The supreme craftsmanship of this sculpture makes it **priceless**.

包围（beset, besiege, surround, siege, encircle, blockade, close off）

beset ［bi'set］*v.* 包围（to hem in）

【例】The mountains **beset** the lake round.

besiege ［bi'si:dʒ］*v.* 包围，围攻（to surround a place with an army and prevent the people there from getting food and supplies）

【例】Our troops had **besieged** the enemy's headquarters.

【用】besiege sb. with sth. 以…(问题、请求等)使…应接不暇

surround ［sə'raund］*v.* 包围（to be all around or on all sides of someone or something）

【例】When the car stopped in the town square it was **surrounded** by soldiers and militiamen.

【用】surround sth. with sth. 用…包围…

siege ［si:dʒ］*v.* 包围，围攻（to surround with hostile forces）

【例】Our reinforcement was trying to send supplies to the city which had been **sieged** by the enemy.

encircle	[in'səːkl] *v.* 环绕，围绕（to completely surround something） 【例】The jail was *encircled* by a forty-foot-high concrete wall.
blockade	[blɔ'keid] *v.* 封锁（to prevent people or goods from moving from one place to another） 【例】Police *blockaded* the commercial building which had been exploded.
close off	关闭，封锁（block off the passage through） 【例】Terrorists *closed off* the government building.

保护（safeguard, protect, shield, secure, defend, guard）

safeguard	['seifgaːd] *v.* 保护，捍卫（to protect something or someone from being harmed or having problems） 【例】We hope that world leaders can agree on a plan to *safeguard* the environment. 【用】safeguard against sb. /sth. 为预防…而采取保护措施
protect	[prə'tekt] *v.* 保护，保卫（to keep someone or something safe from harm, injury, damage, or loss） 【例】Are you prepared to *protect* yourself in case of attack? 【用】protect sb. /sth. against/from sth. 保护…免受…的侵害
shield	[ʃiːld] *v.* 保卫，保护（to protect something, usually from being hit, touched, or seen） 【例】Tina *shielded* her eyes against the sun's glare. 【用】shield sb. /sth. (from/against sb. /sth.) 保护…免受伤害
secure	[si'kjuə] *v.* 使安全，保卫（to make an area or building safe） 【例】We have done our best to *secure* the embassy against terrorist attacks. 【用】secure sth. against/from sth. 保护…免受…的威胁
defend	[di'fend] *v.* 保卫，保护（to protect someone or something from attack） 【例】Thousands of young men came forward, willing to *defend* their country. 【用】defend sb. /sth. (from/against sb. /sth.) 保护…免受伤害
guard	[gaːd] *v.* 守卫，保卫（to protect someone or something from something dangerous or unpleasant）

【例】There were two soldiers *guarding* the main gate.
【用】guard against sth. 预防…

抱怨 (yammer, complain, gripe, grumble, moan, whine)

yammer [ˈjæmə] *v.* 抱怨 (to utter persistent complaints)
【例】Don't *yammer* any more，OK? We have work to do.
【用】yammer on/about sth. /sb. 抱怨…

complain [kəmˈpleɪn] *v.* 抱怨，诉苦 (to express grief, pain, or discontent)
【例】Mary is always *complaining* about something. Why can't she be pleasant?
【用】complain about/of sb. /sth 抱怨…，申诉…

gripe [graɪp] *v.* 抱怨 (to complain with grumbling)
【例】The boss didn't want his employees to have anything to *gripe* about.
【用】gripe about sb. /sth. 抱怨…

grumble [ˈgrʌmbl] *v.* 抱怨，发牢骚 (to mutter in discontent)
【例】Tom has everything he needs and has nothing to *grumble* about.
【用】grumble at/to sb. 向…抱怨；grumble about/over/at sth. 抱怨…

moan [məʊn] *v.* 抱怨，发牢骚 (to complain about sth. in a way that other people find annoying)
【例】Stop *moaning*，it doesn't help solve your trouble.
【用】moan about sth. 抱怨…

whine [waɪn] *v.* 抱怨，牢骚 (to complain with or as if with a plaintive, high-pitched, protracted sound)
【例】Don't be a baby and *whine* about trifles.
【用】whine about sth. 因…发牢骚

爆发，喷出 (erupt, burst forth, spout, gush, eject, belch)

erupt [iˈrʌpt] *v.* 爆发，喷出 (to start suddenly with a lot of violence or noise)

【例】The volcano *erupted* after years of dormancy.

【用】erupt in/into 爆发

| burst forth | **爆发，喷出**（be unleashed） |

【例】Flames *burst forth* from the ceiling.

| spout | ［spaut］*v.* **喷出，涌出**（to gush forth in a rapid stream or in spurts） |

【例】The square has a fountain that *spouts* water 40 feet into the air.

【用】spout out of /from sth. 从…喷出，涌出；spout sth. out/up 喷出…

| gush | ［gʌʃ］*v.* **（突然大量地）流出，泻出**（to flow forth suddenly in great volume） |

【例】Water *gushed* from the hydrant and the fire was soon put out.

【用】gush out from sth. 从…（突然大量地）流出

| eject | ［i'dʒekt］*v.* **喷出；弹出**（to throw out especially by physical force，authority，or influence） |

【例】Lava was *ejected* from the volcano.

【用】eject sth. from 从…喷出

| belch | ［beltʃ］*v.* **（火山）喷出**（to erupt or explode） |

【例】The volcano *belched* smoke and ashes.

【用】belch out/into 喷出

（使）爆裂（burst, pop, fly apart, blow up, bust, split）

| burst | ［bə:st］*v.* **（使）爆裂，爆发**（to break open，apart，or into pieces usually from impact or from pressure within） |

【例】The bottle *burst* under the big pressure.

【用】burst forth 突发，爆发

| pop | ［pɔp］*v.* **砰的一声爆开**（to burst open with a short，sharp explosive sound） |

【例】The bottle cork *popped* when Jim pulled it out.

【用】pop out 跳出来，冒出来

| fly apart | **飞散，粉碎** |

【例】The cup *flew apart* when it was heated.

| blow up | **爆炸**（to explode） |

【例】The ammunition dump *blew up* when it was hit by a mortar.

bust	[bʌst] *v.* 打破，打碎（to break or damage something very badly） 【例】A couple of drunken guests *busted* all the balloons. 【用】bust up〈口〉破坏，使…破裂
split	[split] *v.* 撕裂（to make a long thin cut or break in something） 【例】He *split* his pants when he bent over. 【用】split with sb. 和…闹翻，断绝关系

悲痛（lament, mourn, grieve, weep, wail, shed tears, sorrow, bewail, deplore）

lament	[ləˈment] *v.* 悲痛（to show publicly that you feel sad or disappointed about something） 【例】We all *lament* his passing. 【用】lament for/over sb. /sth. 为…感到悲痛，哀悼
mourn	[mɔːn] *v.* 哀悼；悲痛（to feel extremely sad because someone has died, and express this in public） 【例】Anna *mourned* for her dead husband. 【用】mourn for/over sb. /sth. 因丧失…而悲痛，表示哀悼
grieve	[griːv] *v.* 感到悲痛（to feel extremely sad because someone has died） 【例】Mary *grieved* over her father's sudden death. 【用】grieve for sb. 为（死去的、失去的）…而悲伤；grieve over/about sb. /sth. 因失去…而悲伤
weep	[wiːp] *v.* 悲叹，哀悼（to cry because you feel unhappy or have some other strong emotion） 【例】Daisy began to *weep* in desperation after her husband left her.
wail	[weil] *v.* 悲叹，哀号（to shout or cry with a long high sound to show that you are in pain or very sad） 【例】The boy is *wailing*, curling low to avoid the bear's paws. 【用】wail about/over sth. 为…大哭，诉苦
shed tears	流泪，哭泣（to cry or feel very sad） 【例】They *shed tears* on one another's neck when they parted.
sorrow	[ˈsɔrəu] *v.* 感到悲痛（to feel or show great sadness） 【例】Della's friends *sorrowed* for her in her loss of the child. 【用】sorrow at/for/over sth. 为…感到、表示悲哀或懊悔

bewail	[bi'weil] *v.* 哀悼，悲泣（to cry over; lament） 【例】Jean **bewailed** and lamented her own sufferings.
deplore	[di'plɔː] *v.* 悲悼，表示悲痛（to feel or express grief for） 【例】They **deplored** the incident, but accepted our apologies.

本地的 (native, aboriginal, indigenous, domestic, native-born, local)

native	['neitiv] *a.* 当地(人)的（living in a particular country, area, or city since birth） 【例】My wife's a **native** New Yorker, but I'm from Atlanta.
aboriginal	[ˌæbə'ridʒənəl] *a.* 土著的（relating to the people or animals that have lived in a place or country since the earliest times） 【例】This last bit of **aboriginal** life should be preserved.
indigenous	[in'didʒinəs] *a.* 本地的（having originated in and being produced, growing, living, or occurring naturally in a particular region or environment） 【例】Pandas are **indigenous** to China.
domestic	[dəu'mestik] *a.* 本国的（of, relating to, or originating within a country and especially one's own country） 【例】The **domestic** economy showed no improvement.
native-born	*a.* 土生土长的（belonging to a place by birth） 【例】Some **native-born** Americans objected to new immigrants entering their country.
local	['ləukəl] *a.* 当地的（in or related to the area you live in, or to the particular area you are talking about） 【例】The **local** newspaper regards itself as the voice of the community.

崩溃，倒塌 (collapse, crumple, crumble, topple, founder, buckle, slump, fold up)

collapse	[kə'læps] *v.* 崩溃，倒塌（to fall or shrink together abruptly and completely; to break down completely） 【例】The roof **collapsed** under the weight of the snow. 【用】collapse under the strain/pressure 在压力下崩溃

crumple ['krʌmpl] *v.* 崩溃，垮台 (to break down completely)

【例】This kind of regime finally *crumpled*.

【用】crumple up 打垮，使崩溃

crumble ['krʌmbl] *v.* 弄碎，崩溃 (to give away; collapse)

【例】His parents were born in an age that *crumbled* under pressure.

【用】crumble sth. into/to sth. 将…弄碎成

topple ['tɒpl] *v.* 倾覆，推倒 (to stop being steady and fall, or make someone or something do this)

【例】Strong winds *toppled* trees and electricity lines.

【用】topple down 推翻，颠覆，倒塌

founder ['faʊndə] *v.* 崩溃，倒塌 (to begin to fail; break down)

【例】The company *foundered* during the last recession.

buckle ['bʌkl] *v.* 崩溃 (to break down)

【例】Gavin finally *buckled* under the excessive demands of the job.

slump [slʌmp] *v.* 突然倒下，猛然落下 (to suddenly fall or sit because people are very tired or unconscious)

【例】Angela *slumped* into a chair.

【用】slump over sth. 伏倒在…上

fold up 坍塌，垮掉 (collapse; come to an end)

【例】The old shelf *folded up* under the heavy weight.

必要的 (necessary, needful, indispensable, essential)

necessary ['nesəseri] *a.* 必要的，必需的 (essential or needed in order to do something, provide something, or make something happen)

【例】What type of clothing is *necessary* for survival at these altitudes?

【用】be necessary for sth. /to do sth. 对…是必不可少的

needful ['niːdful] *a.* 必要的，需要的 (necessary or essential)

【例】You have promised to do what is *needful*.

indispensable [ˌindis'pensəbl] *a.* 必不可少的，必需的 (difficult or impossible to exist or do something without)

【例】International cooperation is *indispensable* to resolving the problem of the drug trade.

essential　[i'senʃəl] *a.* 基本的，必需的（completely necessary or most basic and necessary）
【例】In large organizations，good internal communication is ***essential***.
【用】be essential to/for sth. 对…是不可或缺的；it is essential to do sth. 做…是很必要的

避免（avoid, dodge, elude, evade, shun, keep away from）

avoid　[ə'vɔid] *v.* 避免，避开（to try not to go near someone or something or to prevent something from happening）
【例】They could not ***avoid*** being drawn into the argument.
【用】avoid doing sth. 避免做…

dodge　[dɔdʒ] *v.* 闪开，躲避（to avoid someone or something by moving quickly，especially so that something does not hit you）
【例】Shoppers had to ***dodge*** flying glass when the bomb exploded.
【用】dodge doing sth. 避免做…

elude　[i'lju:d] *v.* 躲避，逃避（to manage to escape or hide from someone or something）
【例】The criminal ***eluded*** the authorities for six years.

evade　[i'veid] *v.* 躲开，避开（to avoid being caught，especially after you have done something illegal）
【例】The armed robbers ***evaded*** capture，escaping in a stolen vehicle.

shun　[ʃʌn] *v.* 避开，避免（to deliberately avoid a person，place，or activity）
【例】Josie ***shunned*** his friends by living alone in the woods.
【用】shun doing sth. 避开做…

keep away from　避开（to avoid someone or something）
【例】You can't ***keep*** the kids ***away from*** the computer.

边缘（edge, brim, rim, margin, verge, border）

edge　[edʒ] *n.* 边，边缘（the line where an object or area begins or ends）

【例】Victoria was sitting on the *edge* of the cliff.

【用】on the edge of 在…的边缘

brim [brim] *n.* 边缘 (the top edge of a cup or bowl)

【例】Jody lifted her cup and looked at us over the *brim*.

【用】be filled/full to the brim 满到边缘

rim [rim] *n.* 边缘 (the edge of an open container or circular object)

【例】Ivy's glasses had gold *rims*.

【用】on the rim of 在…的边缘

margin ['mɑ:dʒin] *n.* 边，边缘 (the edge of a place or thing)

【例】The Andes run along the western *margin* of South America.

【用】margin of…的边缘

verge [və:dʒ] *n.* 边缘 (a border along the side of a road, often covered with grass)

【例】Heavy trucks damaged the grass *verge*.

【用】on the verge of 在…即将发生之际

border ['bɔ:də] *n.* 边缘，边界 (an outer part or edge)

【例】Rushes grew on the *borders* of the lake.

【用】on the border of 在…的边缘

编辑，校订 (edit, revise, correct, refine, rewrite, polish, proofread, redact)

edit ['edit] *v.* 编辑，校订 (to make a book or document ready to be published by correcting the mistakes and making other changes)

【例】The original text has been heavily *edited*.

【用】edit out 编辑

revise [ri'vaiz] *v.* 修订，修改 (to change, improve, or make additions to something such as a book, law, or piece of writing)

【例】Three editors *revised* the article for publication.

【用】a revised edition/version 修订版

correct [kə'rekt] *v.* 改正，纠正 (to make or set right, to alter or adjust so as to bring to some standard or required condition)

【例】I want to *correct* the false impression that people have of me.

【用】correct oneself 自我更正

refine	［ri'fain］v. 精炼；使变得完善（to make some changes to something to improve it） 【例】We've **refined** the system since it was first launched.
rewrite	［ˌriː'rait］v. 重写，改写（to make changes to a piece of writing in order to make it better） 【例】It's much easier to **rewrite** your work on the computer. 【用】rewrite history 改写历史
polish	［'pɔliʃ］v. 修改，润色（to improve something by correcting，making small changes or adding new material） 【例】If you **polish** the article，we will print it in the newspaper. 【用】polish up 润色
proofread	［'pruːfriːd］v. 校对，校正（to read something written or printed and mark any mistakes so that they can be corrected） 【例】Frank spent three days **proofreading** his novel.
redact	［ri'dækt］v. 编辑，修订（to select or adapt for publication or release） 【例】Your article needs **redacting** before it is published.

表明或证明…正当（或有理）（warrant, legitimize, substantiate, rationalize, exonerate）

warrant	［'wɔrənt］v. 证明（某事物）正当（to make an action seem reasonable or necessary） 【例】They are now of sufficient standing to **warrant** their entering the married state. 【用】I warrant 我保证
legitimize	［li'dʒitimaiz］v.（使）合法（to make something legal） 【例】The mayor wants to **legitimize** the current order.
substantiate	［səb'stænʃieit］v. 证实（to provide evidence that proves something） 【例】The hypothesis was **substantiated** soon afterward by Dr. Smith's discovery.
rationalize	［'ræʃənəlaiz］v. 试图使（自己的行动、情感等）有合理的依据（to try to find a reasonable explanation for behavior that is not reasonable or appropriate）

【例】Mary looked at Tom, trying to **rationalize** the conversation they had already had.

exonerate	[ig'zɔnəreit] *v.* 确定无罪 (to officially state or prove that someone is not to blame for something)

【例】Duane was to be **exonerated** free with those evidences.

【用】exonerate sb. from sth. 宣布…无罪

不合适的 (improper, unbecoming, inappropriate, indecorous, offensive, unseemly, unsuitable)

improper	[im'prɔpə] *a.* 不适当的，不合适的 (not accordance with accepted rules or standards, especially of morality or honesty)

【例】Laughing and joking are considered **improper** behavior at a funeral.

unbecoming	[ˌʌnbi'kʌmiŋ] *a.* 不合适的；不得体的 (not according with the standards appropriate to one's position or condition of life)

【例】I felt very sorry for my **unbecoming** speech.

【用】be unbecoming to/for sb. 不得体

inappropriate	[ˌinə'prəupriət] *a.* 不适合的，不相称的 (not suitable or proper in the circumstances)

【例】Maggie's speech is **inappropriate** to the occasion.

【用】be inappropriate to/for sb. /sth. 对…不恰当

indecorous	[in'dekərəs] *a.* 不合礼节的 (not in keeping with good taste and propriety; improper)

【例】It is **indecorous** to laugh aloud during a wedding ceremony.

offensive	[ə'fensiv] *a.* 冒犯的，无礼的 (not polite)

【例】The ad is **offensive** to women.

unseemly	[ˌʌn'si:mli] *a.* 不适当的，不宜的 (not suitable for time or place)

【例】It used to be thought **unseemly** for women to go to church without a hat.

unsuitable	[ˌʌn'sju:təbl] *a.* 不合适的，不相称的 (not appropriate for a particular situation, purpose, or person)

【例】Amy's shoes were **unsuitable** for walking long distance.

【用】be unsuitable for/to sb. /sth. 不适合或不适宜…

不可避免的 (unavoidable, inevitable, inescapable)

unavoidable　[ˌʌnə'vɔidəbl] *a*. 不可避免的 (impossible to stop from happening)

【例】Traffic jams are ***unavoidable*** on a holiday weekend.

inevitable　[in'evitəbl] *a*. 不可避免的，必然(发生)的 (impossible to avoid or prevent)

【例】War between those two countries now seems almost ***inevitable***.

【用】It is inevitable that... …是不可避免的。

inescapable　[ˌini'skeipəbl] *a*. 不可逃避的，不可避免的 (impossible to avoid or ignore)

【例】The ***inescapable*** fact is that the situation is changing.

不可信的，可疑的 (unbelievable, doubtful, incredible, questionable, unconvincing, suspicious)

unbelievable　[ˌʌnbi'liːvəbl] *a*. 不可信的；难以置信的 (too unlikely to be true or believed)

【例】The congestion at the theater last night was ***unbelievable***.

doubtful　['dautful] *a*. 可疑的 (not certain or likely to happen or to be true)

【例】I think the manuscript is of ***doubtful*** authenticity.

【用】It is doubtful (that) /whether/if... … 令人怀疑。be doubtful about sth. 对…表示怀疑

incredible　[in'kredəbl] *a*. 不能相信的，不可信的 (surprising or difficult to believe)

【例】This novel is about an almost ***incredible*** story of triumph and tragedy.

【用】It is incredible that... …是不能令人信服的。

questionable　['kwestʃənəbl] *a*. 可疑的，不可靠的 (possibly not true, accurate, or complete)

【例】The teacher feels that the results of the test are ***questionable***.

unconvincing　[ˌʌnkən'vinsiŋ] *a*. 不令人信服的 (not capable of persuading you that something is true or right)

— 117 —

【例】He gave an *unconvincing* explanation of the cause of the accident.

suspicious	［sə'spiʃəs］ *a.* 可疑的，怀疑的（having or showing a cautious distrust of someone or something） 【例】Did you observe anything *suspicious* in that case? 【用】be suspicious of sth. 对…表示怀疑

不清楚的（unclear，vague，indefinite，obscure，indistinct）

unclear	［ˌʌn'kliə］ *a.* 不清楚的（not obvious, definite, or easy to understand） 【例】The police said the motive for the attack was still *unclear*. 【用】be unclear about sth. 对…不清楚
vague	［veig］ *a.* 含糊的，不明确的（not clearly or fully explained） 【例】Witnesses gave only a *vague* description of the murderer. 【用】be vague about sth. 对…不了解
indefinite	［in'definət］ *a.* 不清楚的，不明确的（not clear） 【例】I gave Jim an *indefinite* answer.
obscure	［əb'skjuə］ *a.* 模糊的（not clearly expressed or not easy to understand） 【例】The rules for the competition are more or less *obscure*.
indistinct	［ˌindis'tiŋkt］ *a.* 不清楚的（not clear or sharply defined） 【例】The point of what Kirk had said was *indistinct*.

不同的，有差异的（unlike，dissimilar，distinct，diverse，various，disparate）

unlike	［ˌʌn'laik］ *a.* 不同的，不相似的（not similar to, different） 【例】These two boys are so *unlike* that nobody would believe they are brothers.
dissimilar	［di'similə］ *a.* 不同的，相异的（different from someone or something else） 【例】Vicky's latest album is *dissimilar* to her previous one. 【用】dissimilar to 与…不同

distinct	[dis'tiŋkt] *a.* 有区别的，不同的（different in nature or quality） 【例】They were classified into two ***distinct*** groups. 【用】distinct from 与…不同
diverse	[dai'vəːs] *a.* 不同的，多样的（made up of distinct characteristics, qualities, or elements） 【例】The magazine aims to cover a ***diverse*** range of issues.
various	['veəriəs] *a.* 各种各样的，不同的（different and more than a few） 【例】There are ***various*** hats and pants in the store. 【用】many and various 多种多样，五花八门
disparate	['dispərət] *a.* 迥然不同的（fundamentally different in kind; entirely dissimilar） 【例】The three experiments gave ***disparate*** results.

不注意的（oblivious, unconscious, forgetful, unaware, mindless）

oblivious	[ə'bliviəs] *a.* 不注意的（not noticing something or not knowing about it） 【例】The student seemed completely ***oblivious*** to the noise around her. 【用】be oblivious of/to sth. 未注意到…，未觉察到…
unconscious	[ˌʌn'kɔnʃəs] *a.* 未察觉的（not aware） 【例】Monica was ***unconscious*** of my presence.
forgetful	[fə'getful] *a.* 不经心的，不留心的（marked by neglectful or heedless failure to remember） 【例】Roger was accused of being ***forgetful*** of his duties. 【用】be forgetful of sb. /sth. 对…不留心，对…疏忽
unaware	[ˌʌnə'weə] *a.* 未意识到的（not realizing that something exists or is happening） 【例】Mary carried on reading, seemingly ***unaware*** of my presence. 【用】be unaware of sth. 未意识到…
mindless	['maindlis] *a.* 不注意的；粗心大意的（showing little attention or care） 【例】They proceeded, ***mindless*** of the dangers.

嘲笑 (jeer, taunt, scoff, ridicule, sneer, laugh at, tease, deride)

jeer ［dʒiə］ v. 嘲笑 (to shout or laugh at someone in an unkind way that shows you have no respect for them)

【例】The students *jeered* the speaker off the stage.

【用】jeer at sb. /sth. 嘲笑，嘲弄…

taunt ［tɔːnt］ v. 嘲笑 (jeer at sb.)

【例】The little girl felt that she was *taunted* by her classmates.

【用】taunt sb. with sth. 以…嘲笑…

scoff ［skɔf］ v. 嘲笑 (to laugh or say things to show that you think someone or something is stupid)

【例】At first I *scoffed* at the notion.

【用】scoff at sb. /sth. 嘲笑…

ridicule ［'ridikjuːl］ v. 嘲笑 (to try to make someone or something seem silly by making fun of them in an unkind way)

【例】His sisters and brothers refused to help him，and instead *ridiculed* him when he was in troubles.

sneer ［sniə］ v. 嘲笑，嗤笑 (to speak in an unpleasant way that shows you do not respect someone or something)

【例】If you go to a club and you don't look right，you will be *sneered* at.

【用】sneer at sb. /sth. 嘲笑…

laugh at 嘲笑 (to treat lightly; scoff at)

【例】You are said to *laugh at* the students when they make mistakes.

tease ［tiːz］ v. 戏弄 (to say something to someone in order to have fun by embarrassing or annoying them)

【例】You promise you won't ever *tease* me about my birth mark.

deride [diˈraid] *v.* 嘲笑（to criticize someone or something by suggesting that they are stupid, unimportant, or useless）

【例】They *derided* my efforts as childish.

【用】deride sb. /sth. as sth. 嘲笑或嘲弄…

承认 (admit, confess, fess/ fess up, acknowledge, own, avow)

admit [ədˈmit] *v.* 承认，供认（to agree that something is true）

【例】"I spent all the money", she *admitted* at last.

【用】admit to sth. /doing sth. 承认做了…

confess [kənˈfes] *v.* 承认，供认（to admit that you have committed a crime）

【例】The murderer *confessed* his crime to the judge.

【用】confess to sth. /doing sth. 承认做了…（错误、罪行等）；confess sth. to sb. 向…坦白

fess/fess up [fes] *v.* 〈口〉供认，坦白（to admit that something is true or that you have done something wrong）

【例】Come on, *fess up*.

acknowledge [əkˈnɔlidʒ] *v.* 承认…属实（to accept or admit that something exists, is true, or is real）

【例】The losing football team *acknowledged* their defeat.

【用】acknowledge sth. /sb. as sth. 承认…为…

own [əun] *v.* 坦白地承认（to admit that something is true）

【例】Her boyfriend was reluctant to *own* to being dismissed.

【用】own up to sth. （就…）承认有错

avow [əˈvau] *v.* 承认；公开宣称（to publicly claim or promise something）

【例】His father *avowed* that he had voted Labour in every election.

澄清，阐明 (clarify, clear up, explain, define, illuminate, interpret)

clarify [ˈklærifai] *v.* 澄清，阐明（to explain something more clearly so that it is easier to understand）

【例】The bank spokesman was unable to *clarify* the situation.

【用】clarify one's stand 阐明…的立场

clear up 清除疑虑（to make free from confusion or ambiguity；make clear）

【例】There should be someone to whom you can turn for any advice or to *clear up* any problems.

explain ［ik'splein］ *v.* 讲解，说明（to tell someone something in a way that helps them understand it better）

【例】The lawyer *explained* the new law to us. ·

【用】explain oneself 说明自己的意图

define ［di'fain］ *v.* 下定义，限定（to describe clearly and exactly what something is）

【例】In this paragraph，the writer *defined* the term.

【用】define sth. as sth. 给…下定义

illuminate ［i'lju:mineit］ *v.* 阐明，说明（to make something clear and easy to understand）

【例】Our teacher was trying to *illuminate* a point by reference to current life.

interpret ［in'tə:prit］ *v.* 解释，说明（to explain the meaning of something）

【例】We'll need some help to *interpret* all this data.

【用】interpret sth. as sth. 理解…为…

持续，维持 (last, endure, survive, persist, persevere, keep on, outlast, hold out)

last ［lɑ:st］ *v.* 持续，维持（to continue existing until a particular time）

【例】Our Christmas holiday *lasts* 20 days.

【用】last out 足够维持

endure ［in'djuə］ *v.* 维持，持续（to last for a long time）

【例】The Forbidden City has *endured* for centuries.

survive ［sə'vaiv］ *v.* 继续存在（to continue to exist，especially in a difficult or dangerous situation）

【例】The crops *survived* the drought.

【用】survive on sth. 靠…继续生存

persist	[pə'sist] *v.* 持续（to continue to do or say something in a determined way; to continue in existence） 【例】The hostilities between the two families have ***persisted*** for years. 【用】persist in/with sth. 不畏困难继续做…
persevere	[,pə:si'viə] *v.* 坚持做某事（to continue trying to achieve something difficult） 【例】Despite failures, he ***persevered*** in his research. 【用】persevere at/in/with sth. 坚持做…
keep on	继续做某事（to continue doing something） 【例】Although the weather is bad, we'll ***keep on*** heading for that mountain.
outlast	[,aut'lɑ:st; ,aut'læst] *v.* 比…耐久（to last longer or continue to be successful for longer than someone or something else） 【例】Most people agree that the economic reform may continue and ***outlast*** the political reform.
hold out	继续，坚持（to continue; to persist） 【例】Can you ***hold out*** just a little longer?

重新得到（recover, regain, retrieve）

recover	[ri'kʌvə] *v.* 重新获得，重新得到（to get back something that you lost or that someone stole from you） 【例】Though the thieves were caught, many of the items were never ***recovered***.
regain	[ri'gein] *v.* 收回，重新夺得（to get back something you lost, especially an ability or a mental state） 【例】After losing the second set, Tim ***regained*** his confidence and won the third set.
retrieve	[ri'tri:v] *v.* 重新得到（to get something back, especially something that is not easy to find） 【例】Government had made great rescue efforts to ***retrieve*** the bodies of the victims.

充足的 (enough, sufficient, ample, generous, adequate, extensive)

enough
[i'nʌf] *a.* 充足的，足够的 (as much or as many as required)
【例】A pound of butter is barely *enough* for a month.
【用】be enough for sth. 对…来说足够了；be enough to do sth. 足够做…

sufficient
[sə'fiʃənt] *a.* 充分的，充足的 (as much as is needed)
【例】We don't have *sufficient* time for the report.
【用】be sufficient for sth. 对…来说是充足的；be sufficient to do sth. 足够做…

ample
['æmpl] *a.* 富足的，充足的 (enough, and often more than you need)
【例】There is *ample* evidence to judge him.

generous
['dʒenərəs] *a.* 大量的，丰富的 (larger or more plentiful than is usual or necessary)
【例】The Indian dish is with *generous* pepper.

adequate
['ædikwət] *a.* 足够的，充分的 (good enough or large enough for a particular purpose)
【例】The state needs to maintain an *adequate* supply of qualified doctors.
【用】adequate for 对…来说是足够的；be adequate to do sth. 足够做…

extensive
[ik'stensiv] *a.* 大量的 (very large in amount or degree)
【例】The professor had an *extensive* knowledge of history.

丑陋的 (ugly, unattractive, hideous, homely, unsightly, plain)

ugly
['ʌgli] *a.* 难看的，丑陋的 (displeasing to the eye)
【例】What an *ugly* scene!

unattractive
[ˌʌnə'træktiv] *a.* 没有吸引力的，不美的 (with an ugly appearance or unpleasant or not enjoyable)
【例】I'm living in a very *unattractive* building.

hideous
['hidiəs] *a.* 极其丑陋的，难看的 (very ugly or frightening in appearance)
【例】The corpse had a *hideous* expression on its face.

homely	['həumli] *a.* 〈美〉不漂亮的（not good looking） 【例】The woman will be angry if you say that she has a **homely** kid.

unsightly [ˌʌn'saitli] *a.* 不好看的，不悦目的（unpleasant to look at; ugly）

【例】The car accident left an **unsightly** scar on his face.

plain [plein] *a.* 不漂亮的，不好看的（lacking beauty or distinction）

【例】She has a **plain** face, but she is beautiful inside.

传递（deliver, dispatch, send over, transmit, forward）

deliver [di'livə] *v.* 传送，递送（to take something, especially goods or letters, to a place）

【例】The package was **delivered** this afternoon.

【用】deliver sth. to sth. /sb. 将…运送到/给…

dispatch [di'spætʃ] *v.* 派遣，分派（to send someone or something somewhere）

【例】The new machines are **dispatched** from a warehouse.

【用】dispatch sb. /sth. to 把…派遣到

send over 发送（to send out something）

【例】Didn't you notice the signal I **sent over**?

transmit [trænz'mit] *v.* 传送，传递（to send out an electronic signal such as a radio or television signal）

【例】A telegram will be the most efficient way to **transmit** the message.

【用】transmit sth. from A to B 将…由 A 传送到 B

forward ['fɔːwəd] *v.* 转递，转送（to send a letter, package, e-mail, etc. to another address）

【例】The customer's enquiry has been **forwarded** to the head office.

【用】forward sth. to sb. 将…传送给…

传统的（traditional, conventional, customary, prescriptive）

traditional [trə'diʃənəl] *a.* 传统的，惯例的（an inherited, established, or customary pattern of thought, action, or behavior）

【例】Many women have abandoned their *traditional* role as wife and mother.

conventional [kən'venʃənəl] *a*. 惯例的，传统的（of the usual or accepted type, instead of being new and different）

【例】George wanted a *conventional* marriage with a wife and kids.

customary ['kʌstəməri] *a*. 惯例的（based on or established by custom; commonly practiced, used, or observed）

【例】It is *customary* to offer the repairman a cup of coffee in our country.

prescriptive [pri'skriptiv] *a*. 惯例的，约定俗成的（acquired by, founded on, or determined by long-standing custom）

【例】These are *prescriptive* policies of our country.

刺 (pierce, puncture, penetrate, perforate, stick, bore, stab, prick)

pierce [piəs] *v*. 刺穿，刺破（to cut or pass through with or as if with a sharp instrument）

【例】Jack *pierced* the rubber ball with a knife.

【用】pierce through sth. 刺入…；穿过或进入…

puncture ['pʌŋktʃə] *v*. 在…穿孔，刺穿（to make a small hole in the surface of something）

【例】The tyre is guaranteed never to *puncture* or go flat.

penetrate ['penitreit] *v*. 刺穿，渗入（to get inside an object or body by getting through something）

【例】The shrapnel had *penetrated* his head and chest.

perforate ['pə:fəreit] *v*. 打洞（to pierce, punch, or bore a hole or holes in）

【例】I refused to wear headphones because they can *perforate* your eardrums.

stick [stik] *v*. 刺，戳（to pierce, puncture, or penetrate with a pointed instrument）

【例】The knife *stuck* in the ground at Bill's feet.

【用】stick sth. in/into/through sth. 将…插入或刺穿…；stick in/into/through sth.（指尖物）插入或刺穿…

bore [bɔ:] *v*. 钻（孔），挖（洞）（to make a deep hole in something hard）

【例】Get the special drill bit to *bore* a hole in the block of wood.

stab [stæb] *v.* 刺伤，戳（to kill or hurt someone by pushing a knife or other sharp objects into their bodies）

【例】Somebody *stabbed* the mayor in the stomach.

【用】stab sb. in the back 背地里中伤…

prick [prik] *v.* 刺，扎（to make a very small hole in the surface of something）

【例】Jack *pricked* holes in the foil with a pin.

【用】prick sth.（with sth.）（用…）刺…；prick the bubble（of sth.）使对…的幻想破灭

粗鲁的（rude, rough, coarse, crude, vulgar, disrespectful, uncivil）

rude [ru:d] *a.* 粗鲁的，粗野的（not polite）

【例】*Rude* behavior will not be tolerated.

【用】It is rude to do sth. 做…是很不礼貌的。

rough [rʌf] *a.* 粗野的，粗暴的（not gentle）

【例】Don't be so *rough* with her, James, she's only a baby.

【用】be rough with sb. 粗暴地对待…

coarse [kɔ:s] *a.* 粗俗的（rude and offensive）

【例】They objected to the councilor's *coarse* language.

crude [kru:d] *a.* 粗俗的（not showing taste or refinement）

【例】I've never appreciated Ralph's *crude* sense of humor.

vulgar ['vʌlgə] *a.* 粗俗的（lacking in cultivation, perception, or taste）

【例】Martin's *vulgar* jokes shocked everyone.

disrespectful [,disri'spektful] *a.* 无礼的（having or exhibiting a lack of respect; rude）

【例】Most people often criticize the government, but they are never *disrespectful* towards the Royal Family.

uncivil ['ʌn'sivil] *a.* 粗鲁的，不礼貌的（lacking in courtesy）

【例】Mike was often *uncivil* to other members of his family.

错误 (mistake, error, misdeed, flaw, defect, wrongdoing, shortcoming)

mistake	[mi'steik] *n.* 错误，过失 (something that you have not done correctly) 【例】The officer's decision to invade was a costly ***mistake***.
error	['erə] *n.* 错误，差错 (a mistake, for example in a calculation or a decision) 【例】The report contains many ***errors***.
misdeed	[ˌmis'di:d] *n.* 错误行为 (an action that is wrong or illegal) 【例】You should feel shameful for that ***misdeed***.
flaw	[flɔ:] *n.* 瑕疵，缺点 (a mistake or fault in something that makes it useless or less effective) 【例】There are serious ***flaws*** in the way we train the new employees.
defect	['di:fekt] *n.* 缺点，不足之处 (a fault in someone or sth.) 【例】There are a few minor design ***defects*** in that plan.
wrongdoing	['rɒŋˌdu:iŋ; ˌrɔ:ŋ'du:iŋ] *n.* 不道德行为，坏事 (behavior that is illegal or not moral) 【例】The captain issued a denial of any ***wrongdoing***.
shortcoming	['ʃɔ:t'kʌmiŋ] *n.* 短处，缺点 (a fault or problem that makes someone or something less effective) 【例】Despite her ***shortcomings*** as a cook, she was still the best mother you could ever hope for.

打破，折断 (break, fracture, crack, rupture, shatter, breach, fall apart, smash, splinter, mangle)

break	[breik] *v.* 打破，折断 (to separate into pieces) 【例】The window ***broke*** into pieces.

【用】break away (from) 离开；断绝关系

fracture　[ˈfræktʃə] *v.* （使）断裂，（使）折断（to cause to break; to damage or destroy as if by rupturing）

【例】You've *fractured* a rib，maybe more than one.

crack　[kræk] *v.* （使）破裂（to break or snap apart）

【例】The windowpane was *cracked* but not broken.

rupture　[ˈrʌptʃə] *v.* （使）破裂（to part by violence）

【例】Most truck gasoline tanks can *rupture* and burn in a collision.

shatter　[ˈʃætə] *v.* 使…粉碎，破碎（to break at once into pieces; to damage badly）

【例】A bolt of lightning *shattered* the oak tree.

【用】shatter the peace/silence 打破寂静；shatter sb.'s confidence/hopes/illusions 使…失去自信/丧失希望/梦想幻灭

breach　[briːtʃ] *v.* 打破，裂开（to make a gap in）

【例】Fire *breached* the cargo tanks and set the oil ablaze.

【用】breach security 突破安全警戒

fall apart　破裂；破碎（become separated into pieces or fragments）

【例】The work was never finished and the building *fell apart* bit by bit.

smash　[smæʃ] *v.* 粉碎，打烂（violently break sth. into pieces）

【例】The thief *smashed* the window to get into the car.

【用】smash sth. down 击倒…

splinter　[ˈsplintə] *v.* 裂成碎片（to break something into small sharp pieces）

【例】The man *splintered* the locked door with an axe.

【用】splinter sth. off 使…裂成碎片

mangle　[ˈmæŋgl] *v.* 撕裂，毁坏（to damage or hurt someone or something seriously by twisting or crushing them）

【例】His body was crushed and *mangled* beyond recognition.

打扫，把…弄干净 (clean, cleanse, launder, scrub, scour, purify)

clean　[kliːn] *v.* 打扫，把…弄干净（to remove the dirt from something）

【例】*Clean* off the table when you finish your meal.

【用】clean off 打扫，扫除；clean out 清除，打扫干净

cleanse ［klenz］ v. **清洗，清除**（to clean the impurities by using a special liquid or cream）

【例】The nurse *cleansed* the wound before stitching it.

【用】cleanse sb. /sth. of sth. 使···彻底清洁；使···消除···

launder ［'lɔ:ndə］ v. **清洗，洗涤**（to wash (as clothes) in water）

【例】Anna wore a freshly *laundered* and starched white shirt.

scrub ［skrʌb］ v. **用力擦洗，把···擦净**（to wash or clean something by rubbing it hard，especially with a brush）

【例】Kirk *scrubbed* off the dirt from his shoes.

【用】scrub off 洗掉，擦除；scrub away 擦洗

scour ［'skauə］ v. **擦洗，擦亮**（to clean something thoroughly by rubbing it hard with something rough）

【例】It is hard work to *scour* a dirty oven.

【用】scour off sth. 擦掉，洗去···

purify ［'pjuərifai］ v. **使洁净，净化**（to make something clean by removing dirty or harmful substances from it）

【例】They went to church to *purify* their spirits of evil thoughts.

大步走（stride，step，swagger，strut，tread，trudge，march）

stride ［straid］ v. **大步走(过)；跨过**（to move with or as if with long steps）

【例】The teacher turned abruptly and *strode* off down the corridor.

【用】stride over/across sth. 一步跨越···

step ［step］ v. **行走，跨步**（to go on foot）

【例】Trevor *stepped* across the road.

【用】step aside 让位；让开；step down 辞职，让位；step in 介入

swagger ［'swægə］ v. **大摇大摆地走**（to walk with an air of overbearing self-confidence）

【例】The tall boy *swaggered* down the street after winning the fight.

strut　〔strʌt〕 v. 趾高气扬地走 (to walk with a proud gait)

【例】Jimmy *strutted* around the town as if he owned the place.

tread　〔tred〕 v. 踏，行走 (to step or walk on or over)

【例】Bean accidentally *trod* on the foot of the man behind him.

【用】tread sth. down 把…踩实；tread on sb.'s corns 冒犯…，得罪…

trudge　〔trʌdʒ〕 v. 跋涉 (to walk or march steadily and usually laboriously)

【例】Explorers *trudged* through deep snow.

march　〔mɑːtʃ〕 v. 行军；前进 (to move along steadily usually with a rhythmic stride and in step with others)

【例】Children were *marching* in the parade to the beat of the drums.

耽搁，推迟 (delay, postpone, put off, defer, stall, suspend)

delay　〔diˈlei〕 v. 耽搁，推迟 (to stop, detain, or hinder for a time; to put off)

【例】The train was *delayed* two hours because of the accident.

【用】delay doing sth. 推迟做…

postpone　〔ˌpəustˈpəun〕 v. 使延期，推迟 (to decide that something will not be done at the time when it was planned for, but at a later time)

【例】We've decided to *postpone* our holiday until September.

【用】postpone the evil hour/day 缓做一件终须做的厌恶事

put off　推迟，拖延 (to delay doing something, especially because you do not want to do it)

【例】Women who *put off* having a baby often make the best mothers.

defer　〔diˈfəː〕 v. （使）拖延，（使）推迟 (to arrange for something to happen at a later time than one had planned)

【例】Billy's military service was *deferred* until he finished college.

【用】deferred payment 延期付款

stall　〔stɔːl〕 v. 支吾，拖延 (to employ delaying tactics against)

【例】She *stalled* for time to think.

suspend ［sə'spend］ *v.* 推迟，暂缓（to put off something；to officially stop something for a short time）

【例】Parliament has been ***suspended*** because of the civil unrest.

【用】suspend payment 停止付款

导致（result, lead to, bring about/on, conduce, induce, generate）

result ［ri'zʌlt］ *v.* 导致，结果是（to be caused directly by something that has happened previously）

【例】An accident could ***result*** if you don't use the bolt.

【用】result from sth. 由…导致；result in sth. 导致…

lead to 导致，通向（to begin a process that causes something to happen）

【例】Excessive spending can ***lead to*** terrible bankruptcy.

bring about/on 导致，引起（to make something happen, especially to cause changes in a situation）

【例】The attack ***brought about*** a slaughter of the unarmed villagers.

conduce ［kən'dju:s］ *v.* 导致（help to bring about a particular situation or outcome）

【例】Daily exercise ***conduces*** to good health.

【用】conduce to/towards sth. /doing sth. 导致…

induce ［in'dju:s；in'du:s］ *v.* 引发，导致（to cause something, especially a mental or physical change）

【例】Alcohol can ***induce*** a loosening of the tongue.

【用】induce sb. to do sth. 诱使…做…

generate ［'dʒenəreit］ *v.* 引起，导致（cause something, especially an emotion or situation to come about）

【例】The divarication between the two parties ***generated*** a discussion.

敌对的，敌意的（hostile, unfriendly, antagonistic, malevolent, enemy）

hostile ［'hɔstail］ *a.* 敌对的，敌意的（behaving in a very unfriendly or threatening way toward someone）

【例】The Governor faced *hostile* crowds when he visited the town yesterday.

【用】be hostile to/towards sth. 对…怀有敌意，对…极不友好

unfriendly　[ˌʌnˈfrendli] *a.* 不友善的，不利的（not friendly）

【例】The courtroom was filled with an *unfriendly* atmosphere.

antagonistic　[ænˌtægəˈnistik] *a.* 对抗的，敌对的（disliking someone or something very much and behaving in a very unfriendly way toward them）

【例】Anthony was not only indifferent but *antagonistic* to labor.

【用】be antagonistic to/towards sth. 与…敌对，与…对抗

malevolent　[məˈlevələnt] *a.* 有恶意的（having, showing, or arising from intense, often vicious, ill will, spite, or hatred）

【例】The *malevolent* look on his face made us tremble.

【用】be malevolent to/towards sth. 对…不怀好意

enemy　[ˈenəmi] *a.* 敌人的，敌方的（of, relating to, or being a hostile power or force）

【例】Our air defense system has brought down all the *enemy* aircrafts.

抵消（offset, counteract, compensate, balance, neutralize, equalize, cancel out）

offset　[ˈɔfset] *v.* 补偿；抵消（to counterbalance, counteract, or compensate for）

【例】Donations to charities can *offset* taxes.

【用】offset sth. by sth. /doing sth. 用…来补偿或抵消…

counteract　[ˌkauntəˈrækt] *v.* 消除，抵消（to reduce the negative effect of something）

【例】Schools are taking action to *counteract* bullying.

compensate　[ˈkɔmpenseit] *v.* 补偿，赔偿（to change or remove the bad result of something）

【例】This payment *compensates* more than what we've lost.

【用】compensate for sth. 补偿…，赔偿…

balance　[ˈbæləns] *v.* 平衡，均衡（to reduce the effect, strength, or amount of something, and as a result make it better）

【例】The dark colors are *balanced* by the brightness of the walls.

neutralize ['nju:trəlaiz] *v.* 使无效，中和（to take away the effect or special quality of something by using something with the opposite effect or quality）

【例】Acids ***neutralize*** alkalis and vice versa.

equalize ['i:kwəlaiz] *v.* 使平衡，使均衡（to make equal, uniform, corresponding or matching）

【例】A nuclear deterrent ***equalizes*** the gap in conventional weapons between the two countries.

cancel out 抵消，偿还（of a factor or circumstance neutralize or negate the force or effect of another）

【例】That won't ***cancel out*** his crime.

调查（examine, probe, inspect, explore, investigate）

examine [ig'zæmin] *v.* 检查，调查（to look at something carefully in order to find out about it or see what it is like）

【例】The detective opened the suitcase and ***examined*** the contents carefully.

probe [prəub] *v.* 查究，调查（to try to find out the truth about something）

【例】Investigators have ***probed*** the causes of the plane crash for two years.

【用】probe into sth. 调查…

inspect [in'spekt] *v.* 检查，视察（to look at something carefully in order to check that it is correct or good enough）

【例】The young plants are regularly ***inspected*** for disease and insects.

【用】inspect sth. (for sth). 检查某物（某事）

explore [ik'splɔ:] *v.* 仔细检查，探索（to examine or discuss a subject, idea, etc. thoroughly）

【例】We are ***exploring*** the possibility of taking legal action against the opponent company.

investigate [in'vestigeit] *v.* 调查，调查研究（to try to find out the facts about something in order to learn the truth about it）

【例】All complaints from our customers are ***investigated*** quickly and efficiently.

丢弃，遗弃 (abandon, desert, discard, forsake, quit, dump, cast off, reject, renounce)

abandon	[ə'bændən] *v.* 丢弃，遗弃 (to give up by leaving or ceasing to operate or inhabit，especially as a recults of danger or other impending threat) 【例】The captain gave orders to ***abandon*** the ship when it was sinking. 【用】abandon oneself to sth. 完全屈从于…（某种情感）
desert	[di'zə:t] *v.* 抛弃，舍弃 (to withdraw from or leave a place; to leave someone in a difficult situation) 【例】The man ***deserted*** his wife.
discard	[dis'kɑ:d] *v.* 扔掉，丢弃 (to get rid of something that you no longer want or need) 【例】My father repaired the toy that I had ***discarded***.
forsake	[fə'seik] *v.* 遗弃，抛弃 (to leave someone or stop helping or taking care of them; to stop doing, using, or having something) 【例】Monica pleaded with her husband not to ***forsake*** her. 【用】forsake one's former habits 抛弃旧习惯
quit	[kwit] *v.* 停止，放弃 (to stop doing something; to leave a place) 【例】We encourage younger people to ***quit*** smoking. 【用】quit doing sth. 停止做…
dump	[dʌmp] *v.* 随便抛弃，扔掉 (to get rid of someone or something unceremoniously or irresponsibly) 【例】Over 250,000 tons of waste are ***dumped*** annually along the coastline.
cast off	抛弃，丢弃 (to get rid of someone or something) 【例】It took many years for this city to ***cast off*** its reputation as the home of violent gangsters.
reject	[ri'dʒekt] *v.* 抛弃，丢弃 (to throw away something) 【例】The cat ***rejected*** her ailing baby and refused to nurse it.
renounce	[ri'nauns] *v.* 声明放弃(信仰、主义、权力等) (to state formally that you want to give up a right，title，position，etc.)

【例】After a period of imprisonment，she **renounced** terrorism.

【用】renounce sb. /sth. for sth. 为…摒弃或背弃…

赌博；投机 (gamble, bet, wager, chance, speculate, risk, hazard)

gamble	['gæmbl] *v.* 赌博；投机 (to stake something on a contingency)
	【例】You are **gambling** with your health by continuing to smoke.
	【用】gamble away 赌掉，输光；gamble on/in 投机，冒险

bet [bet] *v.* 以…打赌，打赌 (to stake on the outcome of an issue or the performance of a contestant)

【例】I **bet** them that we would be first.

【用】You bet. 当然，的确

wager ['weidʒə] *v.* 打赌 (to agree to win or lose an amount of money depending on the result of a competition or other event)

【例】I'll **wager** you ＄500 that he's there.

【用】wager sth. on sth. 在…上打赌

chance [tʃɑ:ns；tʃæns] *v.* 冒…险 (to accept the hazard of)

【例】Andy knew the risks. I can't believe he would have **chanced** it.

speculate ['spekjuleit] *v.* 投机，做投机买卖 (to assume a business risk in hope of gain)

【例】Would Oscar be what he is if he hadn't **speculated** on the stock exchange?

【用】speculate in/on sth. 在…上做投机买卖

risk [risk] *v.* 冒…的危险，使遭受危险 (to do something although you know that something bad could happen as a result)

【例】Don't **risk** it. It isn't worth it.

hazard ['hæzəd] *v.* 冒…风险 (to expose to danger or harm, especially in order to gain something else)

【例】The cargo business is too risky to **hazard** money on.

短暂的 (temporary, transitory, transient, passing, fleeting, impermanent, momentary, short-lived, short-term)

temporary ['tempərəri] *a.* 短暂的，暂时的 (lasting for a limited time)

【例】The pain-killer can give you a **temporary** relief from pain.

transitory	['trænsitəri] *a.* 短暂的 (not permanent)
	【例】Most teenage romances are *transitory*.
transient	['trænziənt] *a.* 短暂的，转瞬即逝的 (passing especially quickly into and out of existence)
	【例】I don't want to seek *transient* happiness.
passing	['pɑːsiŋ; 'pæsiŋ] *a.* 短暂的，短促的 (having a brief duration)
	【例】I didn't give the matter even a *passing* thought.
fleeting	['fliːtiŋ] *a.* 短暂的，飞逝的 (passing swiftly)
	【例】The fans caught a *fleeting* glimpse of their idol as she ran into the car.
impermanent	[im'pəːmənənt] *a.* 暂时的 (not lasting or durable)
	【例】To meet the demands of workers，the boards of the company proposed an *impermanent* policy.
momentary	['məuməntəri] *a.* 片刻的，瞬间的 (continuing only a moment)
	【例】Nicholas hesitated in *momentary* confusion.
short-lived	['ʃɔːt'livd] *a.* 短命的，短暂的 (not living or lasting long)
	【例】Their opposition to the plan was *short-lived*.
short-term	['ʃɔːt'təːm] *a.* 短期的 (occurring over or involving a relatively short period of time)
	【例】The side-effects of the medicine was *short-term*.

发出，射出 (emit, discharge, emanate, expel, diffuse, outpour, secrete, excrete)

emit	[i'mit] *v.* 发出，射出 (to send something out into the air, especially gas，light，or heat)
	【例】Isotopes can *emit* radioactive particles.

| discharge | [dis'tʃɑːdʒ] v. 排放出（to allow liquid or gas to leave a place, especially when this has harmful effects）|

【例】The mercury had been **discharged** from a local chemical plant.

| emanate | ['eməneit] v. 散发，发出（to come or send forth, as from a source）|

【例】Wonderful smells **emanated** from the kitchen.

【用】emanate from 从…散发出来

| expel | [ik'spel] v. 喷出，排出（to force something out of a container or someone's body）|

【例】As you exhale, gas from your lung is **expelled** into atmosphere.

| diffuse | [di'fjuːz] v.（光等）漫射（to send out in all directions）|

【例】**Diffusing** a light will reduce its power.

| outpour | [aut'pɔː] v.（使）泻出；（使）流露（to stream out rapidly）|

【例】Water was **outpoured** from the broken tank.

【用】outpouring of 流露；outpour from 从…流出

| secrete | [si'kriːt] v. 分泌（to separate and expel a liquid）|

【例】Stomach **secretes** digestive juices.

| excrete | [ek'skriːt] v. 排泄，分泌（to separate and expel liquid or solid waste from your body）|

【例】The open pores **excrete** sweat and dirt.

发火，愤怒（fume, rage, rant, rave, seethe, boil, explode）

| fume | [fjuːm] v. 发火，愤怒（to feel or show great anger）|

【例】Rory was still **fuming** over the remark.

【用】fume over sth. 为…发火，愤怒

| rage | [reidʒ] v. 发怒，狂怒地说（to continue with a lot of force, violence, or angry arguments）|

【例】People **raged** at the mindless bureaucracy.

【用】rage at/against sb. /sth. 对…发怒

| rant | [rænt] v. 咆哮，口出狂言（to talk in a noisy, excited, or declamatory manner）|

【例】As the boss began to **rant**, I stood up and went out.

【用】rant and rave 咆哮

| rave | [reiv] v. 吼叫，发怒（to talk irrationally in or as if in delirium）|

【例】"It's all your fault!" Melissa *raved*.

【用】rave at sb. 向…吼叫，向…发怒

seethe	[siːð] *v.* 发怒，狂怒（to be extremely angry）

【例】I *seethed* with anger over the insult.

【用】seethe with 发怒

boil	[bɔil] *v.* 使激动（to feel something such as anger very strongly）

【例】He was *boiling* with rage.

【用】boil with rage/anger 因生气而激动

explode	[ikˈspləud] *v.* 勃然（大怒），大发（雷霆）（to suddenly become very angry）

【例】My neighbor *exploded* in rage at the trespassers.

【用】explode with lyric wrath 勃然大怒

发生（happen, occur, befall, take place, go on, come about, come to pass, break out）

happen	[ˈhæpən] *v.* 发生，产生（to take place, usually without being planned）

【例】It *happened* quite by chance.

【用】happen to sb. /sth. 降临到或发生在…上

occur	[əˈkəː] *v.* 发生，出现（to happen, especially unexpectedly）

【例】The clash between the armies *occurred* at dawn.

【用】occur to sb. 突然想起…

befall	[biˈfɔːl] *v.* 降临，发生（to happen, especially as if by fate）

【例】I'm afraid that some evil will *befall*.

take place	发生，进行（to happen；occur）

【例】The war *took place* seven years ago.

go on	发生（to take place；happen）

【例】Mr. Smith went outside to see what was *going on*.

come about	发生（to take place；happen）

【例】When Jill woke up, he was in the hospital and didn't know how that had *come about*.

come to pass	发生，实现（to occur）

【例】What Alice expected has now *come to pass*.

break out　发生，爆发（to develop or emerge with suddenness or force）

【例】A fire *broke out* yesterday.

发现（discover，dig out，root out，turn up）

discover　[dis'kʌvə] *v.* 发现，发觉（to find out something that you did not know before）

【例】Ponce de Leon *discovered* Florida in his quest for the fountain of youth.

dig out　发现，发掘（to find something that you have not used or seen for a long time）

【例】I *dug out* some old pictures of my father's.

root out　终于发现（to find sth. /sb. after searching for a long time）

【例】She tried to *root* the truth *out* of him.

turn up　找到，发现（to find out something by chance）

【例】The explorers *turned up* an inward passageway.

发现，觉察（detect，notice，perceive，sense，sniff out，stumble on）

detect　[di'tekt] *v.* 发现，觉察（to notice something, especially when it is not obvious）

【例】Arnold could *detect* a certain sadness in the old man's face.

notice　['nəutis] *v.* 注意到，察觉到（to become conscious of someone or something by seeing，hearing，or feeling them）

【例】Dirk *noticed* a bird sitting on the garage roof.

【用】get noticed 引起别人的注意

perceive　[pə'si:v] *v.* 感知，察觉（to notice or realize something）

【例】She *perceived* the truth quickly.

sense　[sens] *v.* 觉得，意识到（to know about something through a natural ability or feeling，without being told）

【例】Sonia probably *sensed* that I wasn't telling the whole story.

sniff out　看出，觉察出（to discover or find sth. /sb. by looking）

【例】The little girl left the house after she *sniffed out* the coming danger.

stumble on 无意中发现 (to find something by accident)

【例】Wherever I went, I *stumble on* people talking about the issue.

烦扰，困扰 (bother, annoy, pester, distress)

bother ['bɔðə] *v.* 烦扰，困扰 (to cause trouble or annoyance to somebody; to make someone feel worried or upset)

【例】The man is always *bothering* me to lend him money.

【用】bother about sb./sth. 为…操心；为…费心

annoy [ə'nɔi] *v.* 使烦恼，打搅 (to make someone feel slightly angry or impatient)

【例】I was *annoyed* by the way Jerry kept mumbling over and over to himself.

【用】be annoyed with sb. 对…感到恼火

pester ['pestə] *v.* 打扰，纠缠 (to keep disturbing someone, especially by asking them for something or to do something)

【例】I know he gets fed up with people *pestering* him for money.

【用】pester sb. for/with sth. 以…不断打扰…

distress [di'stres] *v.* 使痛苦，使忧虑 (to make someone feel unhappy, worried, or upset)

【例】I did not want to frighten or *distress* the horse.

繁荣 (prosper, thrive, flourish)

prosper ['prɔspə] *v.* 兴旺，繁荣 (to be successful, especially by making a lot of money)

【例】The business continues to *prosper* from last year.

thrive [θraiv] *v.* 兴旺，繁荣 (to gain in wealth or possessions)

【例】Now that the highway is finished, the shopping center will *thrive* soon.

【用】thrive on sth. …蓬勃发展

flourish ['flʌriʃ; 'fləːriʃ] *v.* 昌盛，繁荣 (to be very successful)

【例】Mark's dry-cleaning business began to *flourish* this year.

反对 (object, disapprove, protest, oppose, demur, remonstrate)

object
[,əb'dʒekt] *v.* 反对，不赞成 (to present a dissenting or opposing argument or to express your opposition to it in words)
【例】I'll take care of this dog, if no one *objects*.
【用】object to sb. /sth. 反对…，不赞成…

disapprove
[,disə'pruːv] *v.* 不赞成，反对 (to have an unfavorable opinion)
【例】Why do you always *disapprove* of everything I do?
【用】disapprove of sth. 反对…

protest
[prəu'test] *v.* 抗议，反对 (to disagree strongly with something, often by making a formal statement or taking action in public)
【例】They are *protesting* against high unemployment and inflation.
【用】protest about/against/at sth. 抗议…，反对…

oppose
[ə'pəuz] *v.* 反对，反抗 (to disagree with a plan or policy; to speak against a proposal or law in a debate)
【例】These countries were unanimous in *opposing* NATO's bombing raids.

demur
[di'məː] *v.* 表示异议，反对 (to say you do not approve of something; to refuse to do something)
【例】Both teams *demurred* to accept the result.
【用】demur at sth. 反对…；对…表示怀疑

remonstrate
['remənstreit] *v.* 抗议，反对 (to make a protest or complain about somebody or something)
【例】Mary *remonstrated* with Bill about his rudeness.
【用】remonstrate with sb. /against sth. 对…提出抗议，反对…

反抗 (resist, repulse, repel, counter, refute, contradict)

resist
[ri'zist] *v.* 抵抗，反抗 (to remain firm against the actions, effects, or force of)
【例】A protestor was injured while *resisting* arrest.

repulse	[ri'pʌls] *v.* 击退，驱逐（to force an army or other group of people to move back and stop attacking you）

【例】Finally，we *repulsed* the enemy.

repel	[ri'pel] *v.* 抵抗，抗御（to keep something away）

【例】Everyone should try his best to *repel* the invasion of the enemy.

counter	['kaʊntə] *v.* 抵制，反抗（to take action in order to oppose or stop something or reduce its negative effects）

【例】How can we *counter* these rumors?

refute	[ri'fju:t] *v.* 反驳，否认（to say that a statement is not true or fair）

【例】She refutes any suggestion that she behaved unprofessionally.

contradict	[,kɔntrə'dikt] *v.* 抵触（to be contrary to）

【例】Sandy's account of the accident *contradicts* that of the others.

飞快移动（dash，zip，bolt，dart，rush，tear，zoom）

dash	[dæʃ] *v.* 飞奔，猛冲（to move with sudden speed）

【例】The robbers *dashed* out of the bank and ran away.

zip	[zip] *v.* 飞快移动（to travel with a sharp hissing or humming sound）

【例】The bullets *zipped* past.

【用】zip across/along/through 沿着某方向迅速地运动

bolt	[bəʊlt] *v.* 迅速逃跑（to dart off or away）

【例】The thief *bolted* out of his house.

dart	[dɑ:t] *v.* 猛冲（to thrust or move with sudden speed）

【例】The dog *darted* across the street.

【用】dart away 迅速跑掉

rush	[rʌʃ] *v.* （使）冲，（使）突进（to move forward, progress, or act with haste or eagerness or without preparation）

【例】Two dogs *rushed* at Mary, growling and baring their teeth.

【用】rush sb. into sth. /doing sth. 使…仓促行事

tear	[teə] *v.* 飞跑，疾驶（to move or act with violence, haste, or force）

【例】Many children are *tearing* about on the playground.

zoom ［zuːm］ v. 急速移动（to go speedily）
【例】A police car *zoomed* very close to them.

废止，废除（abolish, annul, quash, repeal, extinguish）

abolish ［ə'bɔliʃ］ v. 废止，废除（to officially get rid of a law, system，practice，etc.）
【例】Congress should *abolish* the estate tax.

annul ［ə'nʌl］ v. 宣告（婚姻、合同、选举结果等）无效（to state officially that something has no legal authority）
【例】The court *annulled* this marriage.
【用】annul an agreement 宣告协议无效

quash ［kwɔʃ］ v. 取消（to say officially a decision made by another court is wrong and no longer has legal force）
【例】The Appeal Court has *quashed* the convictions of all eleven people.
【用】quash a verdict 宣布裁决无效

repeal ［ri'piːl］ v. 废除，废止（法律）（to state officially that a law no longer has legal authority and has ended）
【例】The government has just *repealed* the law segregating public facilities.

extinguish ［ik'stiŋgwiʃ］ v. 熄灭；消灭（to make a fire or cigarette stop burning；to stop a feeling or idea from continuing to exist）
【例】Firemen fought for hours to *extinguish* the blaze.

分等，归类（classify, categorize, catalog, grade, sort, label, rank）

classify ［'klæsifai］ v. 分类，归类（to put people or things into particular groups according to the features that they have）
【例】In the library，books are usually *classified* by subjects.
【用】classify sth. into sth. 把…归类

categorize ［'kætigəraiz］ v. 将（某事物）分类（to put people or things into groups according to their qualities）
【例】Make a list of your child's toys and then *categorize* them.

catalog [ˈkætəlɔg] *v.* 分类，编目录（to make a list of things that includes details about each one）

【例】He *cataloged* all the insects in his collection.

grade [greid] *v.* 分等级（to separate things into different groups according to quality, size, importance, etc.）

【例】In this country, schools are *graded* by certain standards for equipment and teaching.

【用】grade sth./sb. by/according to sth. 按照…给…分类

sort [sɔːt] *v.* 分类，整理（to arrange things in groups or in a particular order, for example by date, importance, size, or color）

【例】Mother *sorted* old papers to see what could be thrown away.

【用】sort out 挑选出

label [ˈleibəl] *v.* 把…归类（to divide people or things into groups according to their features）

【例】People *labeled* them bad boys.

【用】label sth. as sth. 将…归类

rank [ræŋk] *v.* 将…归类（to put someone or something into a position according to their success, importance, size, etc.）

【例】This town *ranks* among the English beauty spots.

【用】rank sb./sth. as sth. 将…分等级

分配 (share, distribute, assign, allot, allocate, apportion, dispense)

share [ʃeə] *v.* 分配，分摊（to divide sth. between two or more people）

【例】We *shared* the pizza between the four of us.

【用】share sth. with sb. 与…分享

distribute [diˈstribjuːt] *v.* 分配；分发（give a share or a unit of something to each of a member of recipients）

【例】The organization *distributed* food and blankets to the earthquake victims.

【用】distribute sth. to sb. 将…分配给…

assign [əˈsain] *v.* 分配（to give someone money or equipment so that they can use it for a particular purpose）

【例】I was *assigned* a car for my personal use.

【用】assign sb. sth. 分配…给…

allot	[ə'lɔt] v. 分配，拨给 (to give someone part of an amount of something that is available)

【例】We **allot** half an hour a day for recreation.

allocate	['æləukeit] v. 配给，分配 (to officially give something to someone)

【例】No agreement was reached on how much food should be **allocated**.

【用】allocate sb. sth. 给…分配…；allocate sth. to sb./sth. 将…分配给…；allocate sth. for sth. 分配…用于…

apportion	[ə'pɔːʃən] v. 分配；分派 (to divide something such as payments between two or more people, organizations, etc.)

【例】The profit will be **apportioned** between the factory and the company.

【用】apportion sth. among/between 把…在…之间分配

dispense	[dis'pens] v. 分配，施与 (distribute or provide a service or information to a number of people)

【例】Orderlies went round **dispensing** food and drink.

丰富的 (profuse, abundant, lush)

profuse	[prəu'fjuːs] a. 很多的，丰富的 (exhibiting great abundance)

【例】This field was **profuse** with wildflowers.

【用】profuse in sth. 在…上一再表示；在…上滥施

abundant	[ə'bʌndənt] a. 丰富的，富裕的 (marked by great plenty)

【例】This country is **abundant** in petroleum deposits.

【用】abundant in sth. 富有…，富于…

lush	[lʌʃ] a. 繁茂的，茂盛的 (produced or growing in extreme abundance)

【例】A lot of animals are nestling amongst this **lush** rainforest.

风 (wind, breeze, gust, blast, gale, hurricane, typhoon, tornado)

wind	[wind] n. 风 (a natural current of air that moves fast enough for you to feel it)

【例】The sailors are battling with the *wind* and the waves.

【用】a gust of wind 一阵大风

breeze ［briːz］*n.* 微风，轻风 (a light wind)

【例】A cool *breeze* from the window made Roger shiver.

gust ［gʌst］*n.* （突然的一阵）狂风，阵风 (a sudden strong wind)

【例】A *gust* of wind blew through the branches of trees.

blast ［blɑːst；blæst］*n.* 一阵强烈的气流，一阵风 (a strong current of air，wind，heat，etc.)

【例】An icy *blast* of wind hit them as they opened the door.

【用】a blast of sth. 一阵（强烈的气流等）

gale ［geil］*n.* 大风，风暴 (a very strong wind)

【例】The *gale* blustered a whole day.

hurricane ［'hʌrikən］*n.* 飓风 (a violent storm with extremely strong winds and heavy rain)

【例】The violence of the *hurricane* caused widespread damage.

typhoon ［tai'fuːn］*n.* 台风 (a tropical storm with strong winds that move in circles)

【例】The southern part of Japan was attacked by a *typhoon* again.

tornado ［tɔː'neidəu］*n.* 龙卷风 (a very strong wind that goes quickly around in a circle or funnel)

【例】Many houses were leveled to the ground because of the *tornado*.

风景（view, scene, scenery, sight, landscape, prospect）

view ［vjuː］*n.* 景色，风景 (what can be seen from a particular place)

【例】This set of postcards shows ten *views* of Beijing.

scene ［siːn］*n.* 景色，景象 (a view that you can see in a picture or from the place where you are)

【例】The birds in the sky make a beautiful *scene*.

scenery ［'siːnəri］*n.* 风景，景色 (natural things such as trees，hills，and lakes that you can see in a particular place)

【例】Mexico has some spectacular *sceneries*.

【用】admire the scenery 欣赏风景

sight	[sait] *n.* [常用复] 风景，名胜 (interesting buildings, places etc. of a place or district)
	【例】Come and see the *sights* of Shanghai!
landscape	['lændskeip] *n.* 风景 (an expanse of scenery that can be seen in a single view)
	【例】Philip abandoned himself to the desert *landscape*.
prospect	['prɔspekt] *n.* 景象，景色 (a view of a wide area of land or water，especially from a high place)
	【例】The tourist is enjoying a pleasant *prospect* with a telescope.

疯狂的；残忍的 (wild, fierce, vicious, brutal, cruel, ruthless, bloodthirsty)

wild	[waild] *a.* 疯狂的，狂热的 (full of，marked by，or suggestive of strong，uncontrolled emotion)
	【例】She is totally *wild* about him.
fierce	[fiəs] *a.* 凶狠的，凶残的 ((especially of people or animals) angry and aggressive in a way that is frightening)
	【例】Who was that *fierce* old lady?
vicious	['viʃəs] *a.* 残酷的，危险的 (wild and dangerous to people)
	【例】You're a *vicious* killer.
brutal	['bru:təl] *a.* 无情的，冷酷的 (extremely violent)
	【例】He launched a *brutal* kick in his wife's face.
cruel	['kru:əl] *a.* 残忍的，残暴的 (causing pain or suffering)
	【例】I hate those people who are *cruel* to animals.
ruthless	['ru:θlis] *a.* 无情的，冷酷的 (willing to make other people suffer so that you can achieve your goals)
	【例】It's obvious from his *ruthless* behavior that he is underbred.
bloodthirsty	['blʌdθə:sti] *a.* 残忍的，嗜杀的 (involving violence and killing)
	【例】Hitler was a *bloodthirsty* dictator.

奉承 (flatter, adulate, toady, cajole, fawn, blandish)

flatter	['flætə] *v.* 奉承 (to praise somebody in order to get something you want)

【例】Are you trying to *flatter* me?

adulate	['ædjuleit] *v.* 谄媚，奉承 (to praise or admire excessively)

【例】Mike respected science without ***adulating*** it.

toady	['təudi] *v.* 谄媚，拍马屁 (to pretend to like a rich or important person in order to get some advantage from him/her)

【例】Roger got good grades only because he ***toadied*** to the teacher.

【用】toady to sb. 向…谄媚，奉承

cajole	[kə'dʒəul] *v.* （以甜言蜜语）哄骗 (to persuade somebody to do something by encouraging them gently or being nice to them)

【例】It was no use trying to ***cajole*** me into silence.

【用】cajole sb. into/out of sth. /doing sth. 哄骗…做…

fawn	[fɔːn] *v.* 巴结，奉承 (to seek favor or attention by flattery and obsequious behavior)

【例】The man ***fawned*** his boss, but sneered at him underneath.

【用】fawn over/on sb. 巴结…

blandish	['blændiʃ] *v.* 谄媚，奉承 (to coax by flattery or wheedling)

【例】Jack ***blandished*** Lucy out of her black mood.

服从 (obey, comply, submit, defer, yield, abide)

obey	[ə'bei] *v.* 服从，听从 (to do what a law or person says you must do, to carry out a command)

【例】Tom told the dog to sit and it immediately ***obeyed***.

comply	[kəm'plai] *v.* 服从，依从 (to obey a rule or law, or to do what someone asks you to do)

【例】If you don't ***comply***, you could face a penalty of $100.

【用】comply with sth. 按…的要求做，服从…

submit	[səb'mit] *v.* 屈服，听从 (to agree to obey a rule, a law, or the decision of someone in authority)

【例】In the end, they ***submitted*** to the Americans.

【用】submit to sb. /sth. 屈服或顺从…

defer	[di'fəː] *v.* 听从，服从 (to submit to another's wishes, opinion, or governance usually through deference or respect)

【例】I will **defer** to Mr. White on this point.

【用】defer to sb. /sth. 服从…的意愿等

yield [ji:ld] *v.* 屈服，顺从（to allow oneself to be overcome by pressure）

【例】The central government has not **yielded** to public opinion.

【用】yield to sb. /sth. 向…屈服

abide [ə'baid] *v.* 遵守，服从（to follow a rule，decision，or an instruction）

【例】They promised to **abide** by the rules of the contest.

【用】abide by sth. 遵守…，忠于…

腐烂（decay，rot，decompose）

decay [di'kei] *v.* 腐烂（to be gradually destroyed as a result of a natural process of change）

【例】Bruised apples **decay** quickly.

rot [rɔt] *v.* （使）腐烂，（使）腐朽（to undergo decomposition）

【例】The rain **rotted** the wood.

【用】rot away 腐烂

decompose [,di:kəm'pəuz] *v.* 分解，（使）腐烂（to separate into components or basic elements；to be destroyed by a slow natural process）

【例】The chemical compound was **decomposed**.

复杂的（complex，complicated，intricate，involved）

complex ['kɔmpleks] *a.* 复杂的，难懂的（with many details or small parts，which makes something difficult to understand or deal with）

【例】No one could make clear the **complex** web of relationships between the two families.

complicated ['kɔmplikeitid] *a.* 复杂的，难懂的（difficult to do，deal with，or understand）

【例】The situation seems to be getting more and more **complicated**.

intricate ['intrikət] *a.* 复杂的，难懂的（very complicated and difficult to understand or learn）

【例】The *intricate* computer requires more than one skilled operator.

involved [in'vɔlvd] *a*. 复杂的 (complicated and difficult to understand)

【例】The professor gave a long *involved* explanation that no one could follow.

复制 (duplicate, copy, reproduce, replicate, clone, counterfeit)

duplicate ['djuːplikeit] *v*. 复制 (to make an exact copy of something such as a document)

【例】Toni found that Ned alone was *duplicating* some articles in the photocopy room.

copy ['kɔpi] *v*. 抄写，复印 (to make a copy of a piece of information by writing it somewhere)

【例】Susan never participated in *copying* any classified documents for anyone.

【用】copy from 抄写

reproduce [ˌriːprə'djuːs] *v*. 复制；再现 (to make a copy of something; to cause something to be heard or seen again)

【例】The effect has proved hard to *reproduce*.

【用】reproduce something accurately/faithfully/exactly 精确/如实再现…

replicate ['replikit] *v*. 重复，复制 (to do or make something again in the same way as before)

【例】Alf invited Wendy to his laboratory to see if she could *replicate* the experiment.

clone [kləun] *v*. (使)无性繁殖，克隆 (to create an animal or plant in a laboratory that is an exact copy of another using the original animal's or plant's DNA)

【例】Scientists successfully *cloned* a sheep a few years ago.

counterfeit ['kauntəfit] *v*. 伪造 (to make an illegal copy of money, products, tickets, etc.)

【例】These were the coins Davies alleged to have *counterfeited*.

改编，修改（adapt，modify）

adapt　[ə'dæpt] v. 改编（to change a book or play so that it can be made into a movie，TV program，etc.）
【例】The film is *adapted* from a play of the same title.
【用】adapt sth. for sth. 为…改写…

modify　['mɔdifai] v. 修改，变更（to change something slightly，especially in order to improve it or to make it less extreme）
【例】The two governments will never reach an agreement if one or the other does not *modify* its demands.

改变，变化（alter，change，transform，vary，shift，remodel，reform）

alter　['ɔːltə] v. 改变，改动（to make something or someone different；to make small changes to a piece of clothing so that it fits better）
【例】The tailor could *alter* the size of a coat without changing its style.

change　[tʃeindʒ] v. 改变，变化（to become different or to make someone or something different）
【例】Some things never *change*.
【用】change off 换班，轮流

transform　[træns'fɔːm] v. 转变（to make someone or something completely different，usually to make them more attractive，easier，etc.）
【例】A smile *transformed* her face.
【用】transform sth. into sth. …转变为…；把…变成…

vary	['veəri] *v.* 变化，（使）不同（to be different in different situations; to change something） 【例】Old people don't like to **vary** their habits. 【用】vary from sth. to sth. 从…到…变动；从…到…不等
shift	[ʃift] *v.* 改变，转变（to cause someone or something to change） 【例】Attitudes to mental illness have **shifted** in recent years. 【用】shift about 搬来搬去；改变方向
remodel	[ˌriːˈmɔdəl] *v.* 改变（to change the structure or appearance of something） 【例】The house was **remodeled** by its present owner.
reform	[riˈfɔːm] *v.* 改革，改造（to improve a situation by correcting things that are wrong or unfair） 【例】The **reformed** party was still a force to be reckoned with. 【用】reform oneself 改过自新

概述 (outline, rough out, sketch, delineate, summarize, draft, abstract, synopsize)

outline	[ˈautlain] *v.* 略述，概述（to give the main ideas of a plan or a piece of writing without giving all the details） 【例】Please **outline** the article with four sentences.
rough out	拟定草案，拟出梗概（prepare in preliminary or sketchy form） 【例】The secretary got the memos **roughed out** quickly.
sketch	[sketʃ] *v.* 概述，草拟（to give a general description or account of something） 【例】Please **sketch** out what you intend to do next. 【用】sketch out 简要地叙述
delineate	[diˈlinieit] *v.* 记述；画出…的轮廓（describe or portray sth. precisely） 【例】The law should **delineate** and prohibit behavior which is socially abhorrent.
summarize	[ˈsʌməraiz] *v.* 概括，总结（to provide a short account of the most important facts or features of something） 【例】most important facts or features of something）

— 153 —

【例】Basically，the article can be **summarized** in three sentences.

draft [drɑːft；dræft] *v.* 起草，草拟（to draw up a preliminary version of or plan for）

【例】In many countries，laws are **drafted** by special committees of their parliament.

abstract [æb'strækt] *v.* 概括，归纳（to write a short summary of a speech，report，or other piece of writing）

【例】The writer spent two days **abstracting** the story for a book review.

synopsize [si'nɔpsaiz] *v.* 做…的提要，概述…的大意（to make a brief summary or general survey of something）

【例】The teacher wanted students to **synopsize** the text they learned today.

感染（taint，infect，affect）

taint [teint] *v.* 感染（to touch or affect slightly with something bad）

【例】All the poultry in this small town were **tainted** with bird flu.

【用】taint sth. with sth. 用…给…带来坏的影响

infect [in'fekt] *v.* 传染，感染（to contaminate with a disease-producing substance or agent）

【例】People who were **infected** by SARS have been quarantined.

【用】infect sb. /sth. with sth. 使…感染…

affect [ə'fekt] *v.* 影响，感染（to produce an effect upon）

【例】The left lung was **affected** by tuberculosis.

隔离，分开（separate，segregate，isolate，insulate，dissociate，quarantine，set apart，split up）

separate ['sepəreit] *v.* 使分离，使分开（to keep people or things apart from each other）

【例】The channel **separates** the small island from the mainland.

【用】separate the sheep from the goats 把好人同坏人分开

segregate ['segrigeit] *v.* 隔离，分开（to separate groups of people or things, especially because of race, gender, or religion）
【例】They *segregate* you from the rest of the community.
【用】segregate sb. /sth. from sb. /sth. 将…与…隔离

isolate ['aisəleit] *v.* 使隔离（to keep someone in a place away from other people）
【例】The infected people should be *isolated* from others.
【用】isolate sb. /sth. from sb. /sth. 将…与…隔离

insulate ['insjuleit; 'insəleit] *v.* 隔离；使绝缘（to cover something to prevent heat, cold, noise, or electricity from passing through it）
【例】Is there any way that we can *insulate* our home from the noise?
【用】insulate sth. from/against sth. （with sth. ）（用…）将…与…隔开；insulate sb. /sth. from/against sth. 使…与不良影响隔绝

dissociate [di'səuʃieit] *v.* 分离；分裂（to consider two people or things to be separate, different, or not connected to each other）
【例】Marx never *dissociated* man from his social environment.
【用】dissociate sb. /sth. from sth. （在感情方面）将…分开

quarantine ['kwɔrəntiːn] *v.* 隔离（impose isolation on a person, animal, or place）
【例】The man was *quarantined* because of SARS.

set apart 使分离，使分开（to isolate）
【例】The dormitory is *set apart* from other school buildings and surrounded by tall trees.

split up 分裂（to separate into parts or portions）
【例】The constant civil war *split up* the country.

根本的，基础的（basic, elementary, fundamental, primary）

basic ['beisik] *a.* 基本的，基础的（forming the main or most important part of something）
【例】We have the *basic* framework for an agreement.
【用】be basic to sth. 是…的基础或依据

elementary [ˌeliˈmentəri] *a.* 基本的，基础的（relating to the most basic and important part of something）

【例】They clearly failed to take even the most ***elementary*** precautions.

【用】elementary particle 基本粒子

fundamental [ˌfʌndəˈmentəl] *a.* 根本的（relating to the basic nature or character of something）

【例】We'll have to make some ***fundamental*** changes in the way we do business.

【用】be fundamental to sth. 是…的根本

primary [ˈpraiməri] *a.* 根本的（most important）

【例】The ***primary*** objective is to ensure improvements in people's welfare.

工具，设备 (tool, instrument, device, implement, apparatus, facility)

tool [tuːl] *n.* 工具，用具（a piece of equipment or something used to perform a job or achieve an goal）

【例】Words are essential ***tools*** for formulating and communicating thoughts.

【用】tool for doing sth. 做…的工具

instrument [ˈinstrumənt] *n.* 工具，器械，仪器（a piece of equipment used in science, medicine, or technology）

【例】All surgical ***instruments*** must be sterilized.

device [diˈvais] *n.* 装置，设备（a machine or piece of equipment that does a particular thing）

【例】Justin invented a ***device*** that automatically closes windows when it rains.

【用】device for 做…的设备

implement [ˈimplimənt] *n.* [常用复] 工具，器具（a tool or simple piece of equipment used in doing work）

【例】What ***implements*** are needed for gardening?

【用】farm implements 农具

apparatus　[ˌæpəˈreitəs] *n.* 器械，仪器（machines and equipment needed for doing something，especially something technical or scientific）

【例】The scientists were setting up the **apparatus** for the experiment.

facility　[fəˈsiləti] *n.* ［常用复］（使事情便利的）设备、工具（something that makes an action，operation，or course of conduct easier）

【例】This hotel has excellent recreational **facilities**.

公正的 (fair, unbiased, equitable, evenhanded, impartial, neutral, nondiscriminatory, objective, unprejudiced)

fair　[feə] *a.* 公平的，公正的（marked by impartiality and honesty）

【例】Independent observers say the campaign has been much **fairer** than expected.

【用】be fair to/on sb. 公平地对待…；by fair means or foul 千方百计；fair play 尊重规则；公平地对待双方

unbiased　[ˌʌnˈbaiəst] *a.* 没有偏见的（showing no prejudice for or against something）

【例】There is no clear and **unbiased** information available for consumers at present.

equitable　[ˈekwitəbl] *a.* 公正的，合理的（having or exhibiting equity）

【例】Ken could distribute this money in an **equitable** way to the poor.

evenhanded　[ˈivənˈhændid] *a.* 公平的，不偏不倚的（fair，impartial）

【例】The administration wants to ensure the meetings appear **evenhanded**.

impartial　[imˈpɑːʃəl] *a.* 不偏不倚的，公正的（treating all rivals or disputants equally）

【例】As an **impartial** observer，my analysis is supposed to be objective.

neutral　[ˈnjuːtrəl] *a.* 中立的（not engaged on either side）

【例】Those who had decided to remain **neutral** in the struggle now found themselves required to take sides.

nondiscriminatory [ˌnɔndiˈskrimineteri] *a.* 一视同仁的，不歧视的（not showing or making any unfair or prejudicial distinction between different people or things）

【例】People call for a **nondiscriminatory** negotiation on a government level to solve the conflict.

objective [ɔbˈdʒektiv] *a.* 客观的，无个人偏见的（expressing or dealing with facts or conditions as perceived without distortion）

【例】A jury's decision should be absolutely **objective**.

unprejudiced [ˌʌnˈpredʒudist] *a.* 没有偏见的，公正的（impartial；not having or showing a dislike or distrust based on fixed or preconceived ideas）

【例】The **unprejudiced** view of the judge was supported by the jury.

攻击 (attack, raid, invade, storm, strike, assail)

attack [əˈtæk] *v.* 攻击，进攻（to use violence to harm a person, animal, or place）

【例】The enemy **attacked** during the night.

raid [reid] *v.* 奇袭（to suddenly attack a place and cause a lot of damage）

【例】Police **raided** the hidden house and arrested the murder.

invade [inˈveid] *v.* 侵犯，侵袭（to take or send an army into another country in order to get control of it）

【例】In autumn 1944, the allies **invaded** the Italian mainland at Salerno.

【用】invade sth. with sth. 以…侵犯…

storm [stɔːm] *v.* 猛攻（to use force to enter a place and take control of it）

【例】The attackers **stormed** ashore at zero hour.

【用】storm one's way across/in/through 猛攻而强行穿越、经过…

strike [straik] *v.* 侵袭（make violent attack）

【例】The enemy **struck** our town at dawn.

assail [əˈseil] *v.* 攻击（to attack with or as if with violent blows）

【例】Maggie's husband was *assailed* by a young man with a knife in the park.

【用】assail sb. with sth. 用…猛击…

孤独的 (lone, alone, lonely, lonesome, separate, solo, isolated, secluded)

lone	[ləun] *a.* 孤独的，无伴的 (having no company) 【例】There was a *lone* figure trudging through the snow. 【用】a lone wolf 好孤独自处、工作的人
alone	[ə'ləun] *a.* 单独的，孤独的 (being without anyone or anything else) 【例】When she's *alone*, Mary prefers reading. 【用】leave sb. /sth. alone 不干涉…；let alone 更不用说
lonely	['ləunli] *a.* 孤独的，寂寞的 (being without company, sad from being alone) 【例】The old lady lives a *lonely* life in a big house. 【用】plough a lonely furrow 孤立无援地工作
lonesome	['ləunsəm] *a.* 极为孤单寂寞的 (sad or dejected as a result of lack of companionship or separation from others) 【例】I get *lonesome* when you're out.
separate	['sepəreit] *a.* 分开的；单独的 (solitary, secluded) 【例】The couple lived in two *separate* houses. 【用】be separate from 与…分开
solo	['səuləu] *a.* 单独的 (done by one person alone, without any help) 【例】Bruce is a little excited about his first *solo* flight.
isolated	['aisəleitid] *a.* 分离的；孤独的 (separated from others) 【例】There was an *isolated* island in the sea.
secluded	[si'klu:did] *a.* 与人隔绝的，隐退的 (of a place not seen or visited by many people；sheltered and private) 【例】The old lady led a *secluded* life.

固定的 (stationary, fixed, immobile, motionless, static, rooted, stable)

stationary	['steiʃənəri] *a.* 固定的 (fixed in a station, course, or mode) 【例】The bus remained *stationary*.

fixed	[fikst] *a.* 固定的（not subject to change or variation） 【例】He is a pensioner on a *fixed* income. 【用】fixed assets 固定资产；fixed costs 固定成本
immobile	[i'məubail] *a.* 固定的，静止的（incapable of being moved，not moving） 【例】Sophie sat *immobile* for a long time.
motionless	['məuʃənlis] *a.* 不动的，静止的（not moving at all） 【例】The man stood *motionless* against the wall.
static	['stætik] *a.* 静的，静止的（standing or fixed in one place） 【例】Property prices remained *static* between February and April. 【用】static electricity 静电
rooted	['ru:tid] *a.* 固定的，根深蒂固的（strong and difficult to destroy） 【例】There is a deeply *rooted* belief in a mystical power that derives from God.
stable	['steibl] *a.* 稳定的，稳固的（not changing or fluctuating） 【例】The government tried to establish a *stable* political environment to develop its economy.

故意地（intentionally, deliberately, advisedly, purposely, on purpose, by design）

intentionally	[in'tenʃənəli] *ad.* 故意地，特意地（not accidentally） 【例】You did that *intentionally*, just to annoy me.
deliberately	[di'libərətli] *ad.* 故意地，蓄意地（with a definite intention，not by chance or by accident） 【例】It was reported that the fire was started *deliberately*.
advisedly	[əd'vaizidli] *ad.* 故意地（to do something not by chance but with a definite intention） 【例】I'm quite sure that she used these words *advisedly*.
purposely	['pə:pəsli] *ad.* 故意地，有意地（to do something with a definite and deliberate purpose） 【例】Don't close the door. Jeff *purposely* left it open.
on purpose	故意地（intentionally） 【例】Little Tom broke the window *on purpose*.

by design

故意地（on purpose, intentionally）

【例】They didn't know whether it was done by chance or **by design**.

雇用（employ, hire, engage, take on）

employ

［im'plɔi］ v. 雇用（to pay someone regularly to do a job for you or work as a member of your organization）

【例】Bill was **employed** by the company as a computer programmer.

【用】employ sb. as sth. 雇用…作为…；employ sb. to do sth. 雇用…做…

hire

［'haiə］ v. 雇用（to pay someone to work for you）

【例】We should **hire** someone to paint the house.

【用】hire sb. to do sth. 雇用…做…

engage

［in'geidʒ］ v. 雇用，聘用（to arrange to pay someone to do a job）

【例】Andy was **engaged** to decorate the house.

【用】engage sb. to do sth. 雇用…做…

take on

雇用，聘用

【例】Dean was **taken on** as a graduate trainee.

害羞的（timid, sheepish, cowardly, bashful）

timid

［'timid］ a. 胆小的，羞怯的（shy and nervous）

【例】She is as **timid** as a rabbit.

【用】be timid about sth. 对…羞于启齿

sheepish	['ʃiːpiʃ] *a.* 羞怯的；局促不安的（ashamed or embarrassed about something you have done） 【例】The young lady nodded with a **sheepish** smile. 【用】feel/be sheepish about sth. 对…感到局促不安
cowardly	['kauədli] *a.* 胆小的，怯懦的（not brave enough to do something difficult or dangerous） 【例】He is **cowardly** to make a speech in public.
bashful	['bæʃful] *a.* 害羞的，难为情的（easily embarrassed when you are with other people） 【例】Don't be **bashful** about showing the manager what you can do. 【用】be bashful about sth. 为…感到难为情

合法的（legal, lawful, licit, allowable, sanctioned, constitutional, just, legitimate, judicial）

legal	['liːgəl] *a.* 合法的（permitted by law） 【例】I have **legal** access to those files.
lawful	['lɔːful] *a.* 合法的（not against the law） 【例】It is not **lawful** to park here.
licit	['lisit] *a.* 合法的（conforming to the requirements of the law） 【例】Can you tell the **licit** drugs from these drugs?
allowable	[ə'lauəbl] *a.* （法律、规则等）可容许的（allowed by a particular set of rules or by the law） 【例】Food expenses are **allowable**.
sanctioned	['sæŋkʃənd] *a.* 批准的，同意的（giving official approval or permission for an action） 【例】The doctor and his men carry out all sorts of **sanctioned** experiments in the lab.
constitutional	[ˌkɔnsti'tjuːʃənəl] *a.* 宪法的，法规的（allowed by the constitution of a country or organization） 【例】There are severe **constitutional** limits on the King's power.
just	[dʒʌst] *a.* 正义的，公正的（morally right or supported by a good reason） 【例】The judge made a **just** but not generous decision. 【用】sleep the sleep of the just 能安稳睡觉，问心无愧

legitimate

[li'dʒitimət] *a.* 合法的（allowed by the law or correct according to the law）

【例】This man is not the real king. He has usurped the throne from the *legitimate* heir.

judicial

[dʒu:'diʃəl] *a.* 司法的（relating to the judges and courts that are responsible for justice in a country or state）

【例】One of the foundations of our *judicial* system is that any citizen has access to the courts.

和蔼的，仁慈的（kind, humane, compassionate, sympathetic, merciful, understanding, forgiving, tolerant, magnanimous）

kind

[kaind] *a.* 和蔼的，仁慈的（of a sympathetic or helpful nature）

【例】Human beings should be more *kind* to animals.

humane

[hju:'mein] *a.* 仁慈的，慈悲的（marked by compassion, sympathy, or consideration for humans or animals）

【例】A *humane* man will feel for others in their suffering.

compassionate

[kəm'pæʃənət] *a.* 有同情心的（understanding and caring about someone who is in a bad situation）

【例】Bill is *compassionate* and likes to help those who are miserable.

【用】compassionate leave 特殊私事假

sympathetic

[ˌsimpə'θetik] *a.* 同情的，体谅的（kind to someone who has a problem and willing to understand how they feel）

【例】When I told her why I was late, she was very *sympathetic*.

【用】be sympathetic to/towards/with sb. 对⋯表示同情

merciful

['mə:siful] *a.* 仁慈的，慈悲的（showing kindness toward someone, even when other people might punish or be cruel to them）

【例】The *merciful* king saved Jim from death.

【用】be merciful to/towards sb. 对⋯是宽容的，仁慈的

understanding

[ˌʌndə'stændiŋ] *a.* 体谅的，通情达理的（willing to forgive other people or be sympathetic because you understand how they feel）

【例】I appreciated my manager's *understanding* view of my personal problems.

forgiving [fə'givin] *a.* 宽容的，仁慈的（willing to forget bad feelings toward someone who has offended or harmed you）
【例】The girl has a gentle *forgiving* nature.

tolerant ['tɔlərənt] *a.* 宽容的，容忍的（willing to accept other people's beliefs, way of life, etc. without criticizing them, even if you disagree with them）
【例】We should be *tolerant* about other people's hobbies.
【用】be tolerant of/towards sb./sth. 对…容忍的，宽容的

magnanimous [mæg'næniməs] *a.* 宽宏大量的（willing to forgive people or willing to be kind and fair）
【例】She should be *magnanimous* in victory.

忽视（neglect, disregard, ignore, overlook, pass over, discount, brush aside）

neglect [ni'glekt] *v.* 忽视（to fail to take care of someone when you are responsible for them）
【例】No matter how busy you are, you cannot *neglect* your child.
【用】neglect to do sth. 忘了做…

disregard [,disri'gɑːd] *v.* 不理会（not to consider something important or pay any attention to it）
【例】Please *disregard* my previous message.

ignore [ig'nɔː] *v.* 不顾，忽视（not to consider something or not let it influence you）
【例】You have been always *ignoring* me!
【用】ignore sb.'s advice 不顾…的建议

overlook [,əuvə'luk] *v.* 忽略（to fail to notice or do something）
【例】Accidents happen when safety checks are *overlooked*.

pass over 对…不加考虑（to pay no attention to）
【例】Bill was upset about being *passed over* for the marketing job.

discount ['diskaunt] *v.* 不重视（to consider that something is not important, possible, or likely）
【例】You'd better *discount* what Jack said.

| brush aside | 不理会（to refuse to accept that something is important or true）
【例】The defendant **brushed aside** accusations that he had lied. |

花费（disburse, squander, expend, consume, outlay, splurge）

disburse	[dis'bə:s] *v.* 支付，支出（to pay out） 【例】This project was **disbursed** by the government.
squander	['skwɔndə] *v.* 浪费，挥霍（时间、金钱等）（to spend extravagantly or foolishly） 【例】The rich man **squandered** all his money on lottery tickets. 【用】squander sth.（on sth. /sb.）把…挥霍或浪费（在…上）
expend	[ik'spend] *v.* 花费（to use time，energy，money，etc. doing something） 【例】Much thought had been **expended**，but little achieved. 【用】expend sth.（on/upon sth. /doing sth.）花…（做…）
consume	[kən'sju:m；kən'su:m] *v.* 消耗，消费（to use a supply of something such as time，energy，or fuel） 【例】A computer **consumes** a tiny amount of electricity.
outlay	['autlei] *v.* 支出，花费（to spend an amount of money on something） 【例】The company has **outlaid** thirty thousand dollars on advertisements. 【用】outlay sth. on sth. 在…上花费…
splurge	[splə:dʒ] *v.* 挥霍（to spend extravagantly or ostentatiously） 【例】The girl **splurged** the extra money on a diamond ring. 【用】splurge sth.（on sth.）（在…上）无节制地挥霍…

唤起；引起（evoke, summon, call forth, elicit, rouse, awaken）

| evoke | [i'vəuk] *v.* 唤起；引起（to bring a particular emotion，idea，or memory into your mind）
【例】The enchanting music **evoked** the beautiful memories of the past. |
| summon | ['sʌmən] *v.* 召唤；召集（to officially order somebody to come to a place；to call together） |

【例】The teacher **summoned** all the children to the room.

【用】summon sb. to 召唤…到…; summon sb. to do sth. 召集…做…

call forth

使产生，引起

【例】April showers **call forth** May flowers.

elicit

[i'lisit] *v.* 诱出，引出（to manage to get information from somebody）

【例】The teacher **elicited** the truth at last，by questioning all the boys in the school.

【用】elicit sth. from sb. 从…处探出…

rouse

[rauz] *v.* 唤起，唤醒（to produce an emotion or feeling in someone；to wake somebody up）

【例】This **roused** my interest in politics.

【用】rouse oneself 激动；激励

awaken

[ə'weikən] *v.* 弄醒；引起（to wake up or wake somebody up；to make someone experience a feeling or emotion）

【例】We must **awaken** the people to the dangers facing our country.

【用】awaken sb. to sth. 使…意识到…

会议 (meeting, conference, assembly, congress, convention, session, gathering)

meeting

['mi:tiŋ] *n.* 会议，集会（an occasion when people gather to discuss things and make decisions）

【例】Many people attended the **meeting** in the hall.

【用】meeting on sth. 关于…的会议

conference

['kɔnfərəns] *n.* （正式）会议，讨论会（a large meeting, often lasting a few days for discussing matters of common concern）

【例】More and more international **conferences** are held in China.

【用】conference on sth. 有关…的讨论会

assembly

[ə'sembli] *n.* 集会；议会（coming together of a group of people for a specific purpose；a legislative body）

【例】All important announcements will be made during morning **assembly**.

| congress | ['kɔŋgres] *n.* 代表大会 (a formal meeting of delegates for discussion and usually action on some question)
【例】 The Eighth National People's *Congress*（NPC) was held in March, 1993. |

| convention | [kən'venʃən] *n.* （某一职业或政党等人士的）会议，大会 (a meeting of members of a profession, organization etc.)
【例】 Paris was chosen as the site for an international dentists' *convention*. |

| session | ['seʃən] *n.* 会议 (a formal meeting of an institution such as a legislature or a court of law)
【例】 This issue will be dealt with during the last *session* of Congress.
【用】 in session 开会 |

| gathering | ['gæðəriŋ] *n.* 聚会，集会 (meeting or coming together of people)
【例】 Welcome to my family *gathering*! |

混合，合并 (mix, blend, compound, mingle, combine, merge, meld)

| mix | [miks] *v.* 使混合 (to combine two or more substances so that they become a single substance)
【例】 You can *mix* blue paint with yellow to produce the green color.
【用】 be mixed up in sth. 介入…；与…有牵连；mix sth. with sth. 将…和…混合 |

| blend | [blend] *v.* 混合，合并 (to combine or associate so that the separate constituents or the line of demarcation cannot be distinguished)
【例】 Water and oil do not *blend*.
【用】 blend sth. with sth. 将…与…混合；blend sth. into sth. 把…混入… |

| compound | [kəm'paund] *v.* 使化合，使合成 (to mix two or more substances together in order to make a new substance or product)
【例】 The doctor is *compounding* a medicine.
【用】 compound sth. from sth. 用…混合制出 |

mingle	['miŋgl] v. （使）混合（to bring or mix together or with something else usually without fundamental loss of） 【例】Now the cheers and applause *mingled* in a single sustained roar. 【用】mingle with sb. /sth. 混进…中
combine	[kəm'bain] v. 联合，结合（to cause things to join or mix together to form a whole） 【例】*Combine* the eggs with a little flour and heat the mixture gently. 【用】combine sth. with sth. （使）…和…结合
merge	[mə:dʒ] v. 合并，并入（to cause two things to come together） 【例】Jeff showed me how to *merge* graphic with text on the same screen. 【用】merge into （使）合并，（使）结合
meld	[meld] v. （使）混合；（使）合并（blend；combine） 【例】Clouds and grey sea *melded* and a steady rain began.

混杂，掺杂（jumble, mixture, hodgepodge, mishmash, medley, tangle, miscellany, mess）

jumble	['dʒʌmbl] n. 混杂，掺杂（a collection of different things mixed together） 【例】The little town is a charming *jumble* of brick and wooden buildings. 【用】jumble of sth. 杂乱的一堆…
mixture	['mikstʃə] n. 混合（a combination of two or more different things，people，qualities） 【例】James uses a *mixture* of English and occasionally Italian.
hodgepodge	['hɔdʒpɔdʒ] n. 相混（a collection of things that do not belong together or have been put together carelessly） 【例】My garden was simply a *hodgepodge* of herbs，flowers and shrubs.
mishmash	['miʃmæʃ] n. 混杂物（a messy or confused collection of different things） 【例】This floor was covered with a *mishmash* of broken china and goblets. 【用】a mishmash of sth. 杂乱的一堆…

medley	['medli] *n.* 混杂 (a mixture of things such as different types of food)

medley　['medli] *n.* 混杂 (a mixture of things such as different types of food)
【例】This country seemed to be a *medley* of all the countries he'd ever been to.

tangle　['tæŋgl] *n.* 混乱 (the messy shape that things make when they are twisted around each other or around something else)
【例】The wire was in a *tangle*.

miscellany　[mi'seləni; 'meisəleini] *n.* 混合物 (a collection of things of various kinds)
【例】Their present religion is nothing but a kind of *miscellany* of Jewish and Mohammedan superstitions.

mess　[mes] *n.* 凌乱(或肮脏)的一堆 (a situation in which a place is dirty or not neat)
【例】Their room is in a *mess*. Please tidy it for them.
【用】What a mess! 简直乱七八糟!

获得，取得 (get, acquire, obtain, gain, procure, purchase, earn)

get　[get] *v.* 获得，弄到 (to obtain, receive, or be given something)
【例】After two years' pursuing, the boy finally *got* her heart.
【用】get sth. for oneself/sb. 为…得到…

acquire　[ə'kwaiə] *v.* 取得，获得 (to get something)
【例】John *acquired* a fortune in the oil business.
【用】acquire a good knowledge of 学好…

obtain　[əb'tein] *v.* 获得，得到 (to get something you want or need, especially by going through a process that is difficult)
【例】Where did you *obtain* your knowledge of Chinese history?
【用】obtain sth. for sb. 为…得到…

gain　[gein] *v.* 获得，赢得 (to win or get something, especially things are wanted and needed)
【例】If nothing more, you will *gain* experience in that job.
【用】gain by/from sth./doing sth. 从…中获益

procure　[prə'kjuə] *v.* 取得，获得 (to get something, especially with effort or difficulty)

【例】Dean was able to ***procure*** Rembrandt's etching from the art dealer.

【用】procure sth. for sb. 为…取得，获得…；procure sth. from sb. 从…获得

purchase　　['pə:tʃəs] *v.* 买；（以努力、受苦）换得（to buy something; to get or achieve something at a cost or with sacrifice)

【例】The freedom of the people was ***purchased*** with our soldiers' blood.

【用】purchase sth. with sth. 以…（代价等）换来…

earn　　[ə:n] *v.* 赚得，挣得（to receive money from work that you do; to get something as a result of your efforts or your behavior)

【例】The average skilled worker now ***earns*** 2,000 RMB a month.

【用】earn one's living 谋生

积极的(active, energetic, brisk, animated, vigorous, spirited, vivacious)

active　　['æktiv] *a.* 积极的，活跃的（very involved in the work or with a particular activity)

【例】The lady continues to be ***active*** in politics.

【用】be active in sth. 积极从事或参加…

energetic　　[,enə'dʒetik] *a.* 充满活力的；精力充沛的（full of or done with energy)

【例】Her grandpa, now an ***energetic*** 80-year-old man, was also present.

brisk　　[brisk] *a.* 活泼的，敏捷的（moving or acting quickly)

【例】My uncle goes for a ***brisk*** walk every morning.

animated　　['ænimeitid] *a.* 活跃的；活泼的（full of life or excitement; lively)

【例】I have never seen him so ***animated*** before.

vigorous ['vigərəs] *a.* 积极的；有力的 (full of energy, enthusiasm, or determination)

【例】We need a *vigorous* campaign to reduce accidents on the roads.

spirited ['spiritid] *a.* 活跃的；精神饱满的 (full of energy)

【例】The girl is having a *spirited* conversation with her colleagues.

vivacious [vi'veiʃəs] *a.* 活泼的，快活的 (lively or high-spirited)

【例】He gave a *vivacious* laugh when he heard the joke.

激发 (excite, arouse, stir, provoke, incite, stimulate)

excite [ik'sait] *v.* 引起，激起 (to bring out or give rise to)

【例】Everybody was *excited* by the news of the victory.

【用】excite sb. to sth. 刺激…做…；excite sth. in sb. 激起…的…（感情等）

arouse [ə'rauz] *v.* 激起，唤醒 (to cause an emotion or attitude)

【例】Mary's story got my curiosity *aroused*.

【用】arouse sb. from sth. 将…从…中唤醒

stir [stə:] *v.* 激起，打动 (to make someone feel enthusiastic about something)

【例】The professor's emotional pep talk *stirred* the students.

【用】stir sb. to sth. 激起…的…（感情等）；激励…做…

provoke [prə'vəuk] *v.* 引起，产生 (to cause a reaction, especially an angry one)

【例】The match *provoked* his spirit of competition.

incite [in'sait] *v.* 激发，鼓动 (to encourage people to be violent or commit crimes by making them angry or excited)

【例】His rude announcement was accused of *inciting* racial hatred.

【用】incite sb. to sth. 鼓动…做…

stimulate ['stimjuleit] *v.* 激发，鼓舞 (to encourage something to happen, develop, or improve)

【例】The government should take new measures to *stimulate* the economy.

【用】stimulate sb. /sth. to sth. 刺激或激励…

极端的 (ultra, extreme, excessive, radical, extravagant, inordinate, extraordinary, drastic)

ultra	［'ʌltrə］ a. 极端的，过激的 (going beyond others or beyond due limit) 【例】The leader of the party pursued an **ultra** political individualism.
extreme	［ik'striːm］ a. 偏激的，极端的 ((of people and their opinions) far from moderate) 【例】Henry is a supporter of the **extreme** right.
excessive	［ik'sesiv］ a. 过分的，极度的 (exceeding what is usual, proper, necessary, or normal) 【例】The boy took an **excessive** interest in video games.
radical	［'rædikəl］ a. 激进的 (marked by a considerable departure from the usual or traditional) 【例】The country needs a period of calm without more surges of **radical** change.
extravagant	［ik'strævəgənt］ a. 过度的，过分的 (exceeding the limits of reason or necessity) 【例】The new manager made the most **extravagant** claims for his new plan.
inordinate	［i'nɔːdinət］ a. 无节制的，过度的 (exceeding reasonable limits) 【例】They have **inordinate** demands for higher wages.
extraordinary	［ik'strɔːdənəri］ a. 不同寻常的，非常的 (going beyond what is usual, regular, or customary) 【例】Bob's father's courage was **extraordinary**.
drastic	［'dræstik］ a. 猛烈的，激烈的 (acting rapidly or violently) 【例】Foreign food aid has led to a **drastic** reduction in the number of people who died of starvation.

极好的 (noble, preeminent, sublime, unsurpassed, superexcellent, unexceptionable)

noble	［'nəubl］ a. 卓越的，光辉的 (possessing very high or excellent qualities or properties or very good or excellent)

【例】This is a **noble** poem in the history of literature.

preeminent ［prie(:)'eminənt］*a.* 卓越的（surpassing all others；very distinguished in someway）

【例】He's the world's **preeminent** expert on asbestos.

sublime ［sə'blaim］*a.* 伟大的，崇高的（lofty, grand，or exalted in thought，expression，or manner）

【例】Kate's husband is a man of **sublime** taste.

unsurpassed ［,ʌnsə'pɑːst］*a.* 无与伦比的，卓绝的（better than everything or everyone else in a particular way）

【例】Twenty miles north you'll find a coastline **unsurpassed** in its beauty.

superexcellent ［sjuːpər'eksələnt］*a.* 卓越的，极好的（extremely good，very good）

【例】The manager sent the guest some **superexcellent** tobacco as present.

unexceptionable ［,ʌnik'sepʃənəbl］*a.* 无可挑剔的，无懈可击的（satisfactory and not deserving any criticism，but often also without any special qualities）

【例】Lucy's work is **unexceptionable**.

极小的（tiny, minute, slight, miniature, undersized）

tiny ['taini］*a.* 极小的，微小的（extremely small）

【例】The table was covered with **tiny** pieces of paper.

minute ［mai'njuːt］*a.* 微细的，极少的（exceptionally small）

【例】My apartment is quite **minute**.

slight ［slait］*a.* 轻微的，不足道的（small in size, amount or degree）

【例】Our headmaster is a perfectionist. He won't overlook even the **slightest** mistake.

miniature ['miniətʃə］*a.* 小型的，微小的（much smaller than things of the same kind）

【例】This **miniature** camera is of very bright color.

undersized ['ʌndə'saizd］*a.* 小的，不够大的（too small，or smaller than normal）

【例】His girlfriend has **undersized** feet.

棘手的，困难的 (knotty, puzzling, baffling, perplexing, troublesome, thorny)

knotty
['nɔti] *a.* 棘手的，困难的 (difficult to solve or understand)

【例】We have a *knotty* case in hand.

puzzling
['pʌzliŋ] *a.* 令人费解的 (confusing or difficult to understand or solve)

【例】The universe is filled with *puzzling* materials.

baffling
['bæfliŋ] *a.* 困惑的，不可理解的 (confusing)

【例】The apparition watched him with a *baffling* expression，but did not answer.

perplexing
[pə'pleksiŋ] *a.* 令人困惑的 (unable to grasp something clearly or to think logically and decisively about something)

【例】You're *perplexing* to me these days.

troublesome
['trʌblsəm] *a.* 麻烦的 (causing problems or difficulties，especially in an annoying way)

【例】Highway maintenance is a *troublesome* problem.

thorny
['θɔːni] *a.* 困难的 (difficult to deal with)

【例】I can find a solution to this *thorny* problem.

加强 (strengthen, fortify, reinforce, buttress, harden, steel, intensify, beef up)

strengthen
['streŋθən] *v.* 加强，巩固 (to make stronger)

【例】Cycling *strengthens* all the muscles of the body.

fortify
['fɔːtifai] *v.* 增强；筑防御工事于 (to strengthen and secure (as a town) by forts or batteries)

【例】Our soldiers were working day and night to *fortify* the airbase.

【用】fortify sth. (against sth.) 防卫… (以抵御…)

reinforce
[ˌriːin'fɔːs] *v.* 加强；增援 (to strengthen by additional assistance，material，or support)

【例】The rescue effort was *reinforced* by 12 experienced miners.

buttress ['bʌtris] v. 加固，支持（to support，to strengthen）

【例】As always，his argument is **buttressed** by facts and quotations.

【用】buttress sth. up 支持或加强…

harden ['hɑːdən] v.（使）变硬（to make hard or harder）

【例】Give the cardboard two or three coats of varnish to **harden** it.

【用】harden sb. to sth. 使…对…麻木不仁或毫不在乎

steel [stiːl] v. 使坚强（to fill with resolution or determination）

【例】Tom **steeled** his heart against her sorrow.

【用】steel oneself/sth.（for/against sth.）使…坚强起来去应付…

intensify [in'tensifai] v.（使）增强，（使）加剧（to make intense or more intensive）

【例】The scientists have **intensified** their search for the new gene by working harder.

beef up 加强，补充

【例】The hotel plans to **beef up** security.

假如（provided, providing, supposing, in case, on condition）

provided [prəu'vaidid] conj. 倘若（only if a particular thing happens or is done）

【例】You can go out to play **provided** that you finish your homework first.

providing [prə'vaidiŋ] conj. 倘若（only if a particular thing happens or is done）

【例】Financiers are prepared to be generous，**providing** that it is not their own money they are spending.

supposing [sə'pəuziŋ] conj. 假使，假如（on the assumption that）

【例】**Supposing** that you won the lottery，what would you do with the money?

in case 假使（if）

【例】**In case** you can't come，give me a call before I leave for work.

on condition 倘若（only if）

【例】You can go home **on condition** that you finish your work on time.

假装 (pretend, simulate, fake, pose, feign, affect, counterfeit, sham, put on)

pretend
[pri'tend] *v.* 假装，佯作 (to give a false appearance of being, possessing or performing)
【例】I waved at my friend but he **pretended** not to see me.
【用】pretend to do 假装做…

simulate
['simjuleit] *v.* 假装 (to pretend to feel or think of something)
【例】John lifted his hands in a gesture meant to **simulate** amazement.

fake
[feik] *v.* 伪装 (to pretend that something has happened when it has not)
【例】I leant against the glass partition and **faked** a yawn.

pose
[pəuz] *v.* 假装 (to affect an attitude or character usually to deceive or impress)
【例】The team **posed** as drug dealers to trap the ringleaders.
【用】pose as sb. /sth. 自称或装成…

feign
[fein] *v.* 假装，冒充 (to give a false appearance of)
【例】Duane **feigned** death to escape the manhunt.

affect
[ə'fekt] *v.* 假装 (to put on a pretense of)
【例】The Australian man **affected** a British accent.

counterfeit
['kauntəfit] *v.* 伪造，假冒 (to imitate or feign especially with intent to deceive)
【例】Police recently detected a factory that had **counterfeited** a great amount of money.

sham
[ʃæm] *v.* 伪装，假冒 (to act intentionally so as to give a false impression)
【例】The little boy **shammed** sleeping.

put on
假装
【例】The boy **put on** a silly face.

监禁，拘留 (jail, imprison, lock up, cage, confine, intern, impound)

jail
[dʒeil] *v.* 监禁，拘留 (to detain in custody)
【例】Tom and Jack are both **jailed** as the murders.

imprison	[im'prizən] *v.* 关押（to put in a cage or as if in prison）

【例】The king captured and subsequently *imprisoned* his enemies.

【用】imprison sb. in sth. 把…关在…

lock up　监禁

【例】The soldiers are going to be *locked up*, if they don't get back to barracks on time.

cage　[keidʒ] *v.* 关入笼中（to confine in a cage）

【例】I shall not be *caged* like some animals.

【用】cage sb. in 使…困于笼中

confine　[kən'fain] *v.* 禁闭（to force someone to stay in a place and prevent them from leaving）

【例】His mother *confined* him to his room for the weekend.

【用】confine sb. /sth. in. /to sth. 将…限制在某空间内

intern　[in'tə:n] *v.* 拘禁（to put someone in a prison without officially accusing them of a crime, especially for political reasons）

【例】The reporter was *interned* in the police office for a week.

【用】intern sb. in sth. 将…扣押在…

impound　[im'paund] *v.* 没收；拘留（to seize and take legal custody of something）

【例】The police *impounded* Tom's car for some investigations.

减少（abate, slacken, dwindle, fall off, downsize, pare, subtract）

abate　[ə'beit] *v.* （指风力、声音、痛苦等）减小，减轻（to gradually become less serious or extreme）

【例】Age *abated* my strength.

slacken　['slækən] *v.* 放松，放慢（to become slower or less active, or make something become slower or less active）

【例】Steve's horse stumbled and injured, and they were obliged to *slacken* their pace.

【用】slacken sth. off/up 使…放慢，迟缓

dwindle　['dwindl] *v.* 变小（to become gradually less or smaller over a period of time until almost nothing remains）

【例】Jeff watches the truck *dwindle* in the distance.

【用】dwindle away 逐渐变少或变小

fall off	减少 (to reduce in the amount or level of something)
	【例】Our sales have begun to ***fall off*** this year.
downsize	[daun'saiz] *v.* (公司等)削减员工 (to make a company or organization smaller by reducing the number of workers)
	【例】Firms would claim that they ***downsize*** for economic reasons.
pare	[peə] *v.* 削减，缩减 (to reduce the total number or amount of something)
	【例】The candidates were ***pared*** from 660 to 160.
	【用】pare sth. down 大量削减…
subtract	[səb'trækt] *v.* 减(去) (to take a number or amount from another number or amount)
	【例】If you ***subtract*** 4 from 9，you get 5.
	【用】subtract sth. from sth. 从…里减去…

讲述 (report, portray, detail)

report	[ri'pɔːt] *v.* 叙述，讲述 (to give an account of)
	【例】Roger ***reported*** he saw the murderer.
	【用】report sth. to sb. 向…讲述…
portray	[pɔː'trei] *v.* 描写，描绘 (to describe in words)
	【例】Opponents ***portray*** the president as weak and ineffectual.
detail	['diːteil；di'teil] *v.* 详述 (to list all the facts or aspects of a situation)
	【例】In a special report the reporter ***detailed*** the fighting.
	【用】detail sth. to/for sb. 向…详述…

奖品，奖金 (prize, reward, award, bounty, premium)

prize	[praiz] *n.* 奖赏，奖品 (something offered or striven for in competition or in contests of chance)
	【例】There's a chance to win a ***prize*** if you can answer this question.
	【用】win a prize 赢得奖赏
reward	[ri'wɔːd] *n.* 奖赏 (something that is given in return for good or evil done or received or that is offered or given for some service or attainment)

【例】*Rewards* for appropriate behavior can be successful in teaching children.

【用】reward for 对…的奖励；as a reward 把…作为奖励

award　[ə'wɔːd] *n.* 奖，奖品 (a prize or other reward that is given to someone who has achieved something)

【例】The *award* for outstanding services to the industry will be issued on this meeting.

【用】award for 对…的奖励

bounty　['baunti] *n.* 奖金，赏金 (a reward, premium, or subsidy especially when offered or given by a government)

【例】Mason worked as a *bounty* hunter.

【用】bounty hunter 为领赏而追捕逃犯者

premium　['priːmiəm] *n.* 奖金，奖赏 (a reward or recompense for a particular act)

【例】A *premium* of 5 percent is paid on long-term investors.

狡猾的 (artful, sly, foxy, cunning, tricky, wily, crafty)

artful　['ɑːtful] *a.* 狡猾的，诡诈的 (adroit in attaining an end usually by insinuating or indirect means)

【例】Morris was very *artful* and usually succeeded in getting what he wanted.

sly　[slai] *a.* 狡猾的，狡诈的 (clever at tricking people or at secretly doing unfair or dishonest things)

【例】The dealer won the bid with a *sly* maneuver.

foxy　['fɔksi] *a.* 狡猾的 (good at tricking or cheating people)

【例】Robin's father was a *foxy* old man.

cunning　['kʌniŋ] *a.* 狡猾的 (having or showing skill in achieving one's ends by deceit or evasion)

【例】Every man wishes to be wise, and those who can't be wise are always *cunning*.

tricky　['triki] *a.* 狡猾的 (inclined to or marked by trickery)

【例】Most people fear a *tricky* opponent more than a skillful one.

wily　['waili] *a.* 狡猾的，老谋深算的 (clever and willing to trick people in order to get what you want)

【例】 Joanna finally fell a victim to an unscrupulous *wily* rogue.

crafty	['krɑːfti; 'kræfti] *a.* 狡猾的，狡诈的 (good at getting what you want, especially in a slightly dishonest way) **【例】** That old businessman was as *crafty* as a fox.

教育，培养 (educate, train, enlighten, school, edify, tutor, coach, cultivate)

educate	['edjuːkeit] *v.* 教育，培养 (to teach someone, usually for several years, especially at a school, college, or university) **【例】** Hugh was born in England but was *educated* in China. **【用】** educate sb. in sth. 培养…的相关知识; educate sb. about sth. 教育…; educate sb. to do sth. 教育…做…
train	[trein] *v.* (受)训练; (受)培养 (to teach someone to do a particular job or activity) **【例】** These dogs were *trained* to detect explosives. **【用】** train sb./sth. to do sth. 训练…做…
enlighten	[in'laitən] *v.* 启发; 教导 (to give someone information about something so that they understand more about it) **【例】** Father *enlightened* me as to learning English. **【用】** enlighten sb. as to/on/about sth. 启发或启迪…
school	[skuːl] *v.* 教育 (to teach or train someone in a particular subject or skill) **【例】** Some of them have been *schooled* at Eton. **【用】** school sb. in sth. 在…（方面）教育…
edify	['edifai] *v.* 陶冶，启发 (to teach someone something that increases their knowledge or improves their character) **【例】** Gary was *edified* by the Catholicism.
tutor	['tjuːtə] *v.* 辅导 (to teach or guide usually individually in a special subject or for a particular purpose) **【例】** The parents are paying a graduate to *tutor* their son in his poorer subjects. **【用】** tutor sb. in sth. 在…（方面）教…
coach	[kəutʃ] *v.* 训练; 指导 (to teach or train someone especially in order to help them prepare for an examination or a sporting contest)

【例】Mr. Jones **coaches** the football team.

【用】coach sb. for/in sth. 辅导或训练…

cultivate ['kʌltiveit] *v.* 教养，培养（to develop something such as an attitude，ability，or skill）

【例】It will be a long time to **cultivate** a savage tribe.

揭露（reveal，disclose，expose，divulge，uncover，unmask，lay bare）

reveal [ri'vi:l] *v.* 揭露；揭示（to let something become known）

【例】Lydia refused to **reveal** the contents of the letter.

【用】reveal sth. to sb. 向…透露…

disclose [dis'kləuz] *v.* 公开，透露（to give information to people，especially information that was secret）

【例】Most of the people interviewed requested that their identity not be **disclosed**.

【用】disclose sth. to sb. 向…透露…

expose [ik'spəuz] *v.* （使）暴露；揭露（to allow something that is usually covered or hidden to be seen）

【例】Many of the soldiers had been **exposed** to radiation.

【用】expose to sth. 使处于…作用（或影响）之下；使暴露在…中

divulge [dai'vʌldʒ] *v.* 泄露（to give information about something，especially something that should be kept secret）

【例】I'm not allowed to **divulge** information about my clients.

【用】divulge sth. to sb. 向…透露…

uncover [ˌʌn'kʌvə] *v.* 揭露，暴露（to find out about something that has been hidden or kept secret）

【例】The Minister of Foreign Affairs **uncovered** a plot against the President.

unmask [ˌʌn'ma:sk] *v.* 露出真相，揭露（to discover the real truth about someone or something）

【例】The detective **unmasked** the culprit.

lay bare 暴露，揭发

【例】In this book，that period of history has been **laid bare**.

节省，节约 (economize, conserve, scrimp, cut corners, stint, cut back)

economize [i'kɔnəmaiz] v. 节省，节约 (to use something such as money or fuel very carefully, so that you waste as little as possible)
【例】*Economizing* on food is the only choice we have.
【用】economize on sth. 节约…

conserve [kən'sə:v] v. 节约 (to use very little of something such as electricity or water so that it is not wasted)
【例】People were forced to *conserve* water during the drought.

scrimp [skrimp] v. 节省或精打细算 (to spend money only on what is necessary and save as much as you can)
【例】Harold had to *scrimp* and save to pay for his tuition.

cut corners 节省(钱或人力、时间等) (to do something less carefully or thoroughly than you should because you are trying to save time or money)
【例】They finished the work in less an hour because they *cut corners*.

stint [stint] v. 节省 (to supply a very ungenerous or inadequate amount of something)
【例】Mike certainly doesn't *stint* on wine in his cooking.
【用】not stint on sth. 不吝惜…

cut back 削减 (to reduce something such as the amount of money available to spend)
【例】They *cut back* on production during the power cuts.

结合 (synthesize, assemble, combine, integrate, conglomerate)

synthesize ['sinθisaiz] v. 合成，综合 (combine a number of things into a coherent whole)
【例】Justin *synthesized* and analyzed the information to make a judgment.

assemble [ə'sembl] v. 集合，装配 (to bring together; to fit together the parts of)
【例】The shelves are sold in kits that you have to *assemble* by yourself.

combine

[kəm'bain] *v.* 联合，结合（to join or mix together to form a whole）

【例】Hydrogen *combines* with oxygen to form water.

【用】combine with sth. (使)…结合，联合

integrate

['intigreit] *v.* 使成整体，(使)成为一体（to form, coordinate，or blend into a functioning or unified whole）

【例】Little attempt was made to *integrate* the parts into a coherent whole.

【用】integrate into/with sth. (使)成为一体，(使)合并

conglomerate

[kən'glɔmərət] *v.* 聚合，聚集（to gather into a mass or coherent whole）

【例】Numbers of people *conglomerated* around the spot of the car accident.

解放（liberate, release, emancipate, loose, unshackle, deliver, manumit, unbind）

liberate

['libəreit] *v.* 解放；释放（to free from）

【例】I'm going to *liberate* him from his dismal life.

【用】liberate sb. /sth. from sth. 将…从…解放出来

release

[ri'li:s] *v.* 释放；解放（to let someone leave a place where they have been kept）

【例】Those prisoners were *released*.

【用】release sb. /sth. from sth. 将…从…释放出来

emancipate

[i'mænsipeit] *v.* 解放，解除（to give freedom and rights to someone）

【例】The king *emancipated* the slave from his slavery.

【用】emancipate sb. from sth. 将…从…中解放出来（尤指摆脱政治、法律或社会的束缚）

loose

[lu:s] *v.* 释放（to untie a person or animal）

【例】The man *loosed* the tiger from the cage.

【用】loose sth. off at sb. /sth. 朝…放枪，朝…发射导弹

unshackle

[ˌʌn'ʃækl] *v.* 解放，使自由（to free from shackles, chains, or other physical restrains）

【例】The knight *unshackled* the slave.

deliver ［di'livə］ *v.* 解救，释放（to free someone from an unpleasant situation）

【例】Nothing would *deliver* them from evil.

【用】deliver sb. from sth. 将某人从…中解放出来，将某人从…中拯救出来

manumit ［,mænju'mit］ *v.* 解放（奴隶）（to free from slavery）

【例】The teacher *manumitted* those boys from ignorance.

unbind ［,ʌn'baind］ *v.* 解开，松开（to free from fastenings）

【例】Her fingers slowly *unbound* her braids and the hair flew out around her shoulders.

解雇（fire，dismiss，lay off，discharge，expel）

fire ［'faiə］ *v.* 解雇，开除（to make someone leave their job, sometimes as a punishment）

【例】The salesgirl was *fired* for refusing to comply with safety regulations.

dismiss ［dis'mis］ *v.* 解雇，开除（to force someone to leave their job）

【例】Edwards claimed that he had been unfairly *dismissed*.

【用】dismiss sb. for sth. 因…而将…解雇；dismiss sb. from 将…从…解雇

lay off 解雇（to end someone's employment，especially temporarily）

【例】They've had to cut back production and *lay off* workers.

discharge ［dis'tʃɑːdʒ］ *v.* 解雇，开除（to force someone to leave an official job or position）

【例】Mr. Givens was *discharged* from the committee and replaced by Mr. Benton.

【用】discharge sb. from 将…从…开除

expel ［ik'spel］ *v.* 除名，驱逐（to officially force someone to leave a place or organization because of their bad behavior）

【例】Tom was *expelled* from school for threatening a teacher with a knife.

【用】expel sb. from 将…从…除名

解释 (translate, paraphrase, reword, restate, rephrase)

translate	['trænsleit] *v.* 解释，阐释 (to change something into a different form or to express something in a different way) 【例】I *translated* this as a desire to lock up every single person with HIV. 【用】translate sth. into sth. 把…译成…；translate sth. as sth. 把…解释成…
paraphrase	['pærəfreiz] *v.* 将…释义，解释 (to express what someone else has said or written by using different words) 【例】I *paraphrased* what the secretary had said.
reword	[ˌriː'wəːd] *v.* 改说，改变…的措辞 (to express something using different words) 【例】All right，I'll *reword* my question.
restate	[ˌriː'steit] *v.* 复述，重说 (to say or write something again or using different words in order to emphasize it or make it clearer) 【例】The letter merely *restated* the law of the land.
rephrase	[riː'freiz] *v.* 改述，改撰 (to say or write the same thing using different words) 【例】Again，the executive *rephrased* the question.

紧迫的 (urgent, pressing, exigent, imperative)

urgent	['əːdʒnent] *a.* 迫切的，紧急的 (calling for immediate attention) 【例】Refugees there are in *urgent* need of food. 【用】in urgent need of 急需
pressing	['presiŋ] *a.* 紧迫的，迫切的 (very important and urgent) 【例】The safety of the hostages is a matter of *pressing* concern.
exigent	['eksidʒənt] *a.* 紧急的，需要立即行动或补救的 (requiring immediate aid or action) 【例】Unemployment is the most *exigent* problem facing most countries today.
imperative	[im'perətiv] *a.* 紧急的 (extremely important and urgent)

【例】It was *imperative* to maintain peace and stability in the region.

紧张不安的，心惊肉跳的 (jumpy，restless，jittery，skittish，edgy，on edge，fidgety，tense)

jumpy	['dʒʌmpi] *a.* 紧张不安的，心惊肉跳的 (nervous) 【例】Carla knew that something was going to happen，and she was very *jumpy*.
restless	['restlis] *a.* 不安的，焦躁的 (not willing or able to keep still because you are nervous, bored, or impatient) 【例】Colin was too *restless* to sit still.
jittery	['dʒitəri] *a.* 神经过敏的 (feeling nervous, and sometimes being unable to keep still because of this) 【例】It was raining, and there would be a flood and everybody was *jittery*.
skittish	['skitiʃ] *a.* 不安定的；紧张的 (restlessly active or nervous) 【例】Being unsure of its footing and blinded by the light, the horse becomes *skittish*.
edgy	['edʒi] *a.* 急躁的；紧张的 (in a bad mood because you are worried or nervous) 【例】The boss has been a little *edgy* today.
on edge	紧张不安，烦躁 (anxious) 【例】Everybody is *on edge* until the performance is over.
fidgety	['fidʒiti] *a.* 坐立不安的 (inclined to move or act restlessly or nervously) 【例】Students became *fidgety* towards the end of the day.
tense	[tens] *a.* 紧张的 (making one feel nervous and not relaxed) 【例】The players felt *tense* at the beginning of the game.

紧张的 (nervous，anxious，stressed，uneasy，high-strung)

nervous	['nəːvəs] *a.* 神经紧张的 (feeling excited and worried, or slightly afraid) 【例】Driving on icy mountain roads makes me *nervous*. 【用】be nervous about 为…而担心

anxious	['æŋkʃəs] *a.* 焦虑的 (characterized by extreme uneasiness of mind or brooding fear about some contingency) 【例】I'm very ***anxious*** about my grandma's health. 【用】be anxious about/for sb. /sth. 为…焦虑，为…担忧
stressed	['strest] *a.* 紧张的 (feeling strained or tensive) 【例】I've been really ***stressed*** out at work recently.
uneasy	[ˌʌn'iːzi] *a.* 心神不安的 (causing physical or mental discomfort) 【例】They were watching the match in ***uneasy*** silence. 【用】be uneasy about/at sth. 对…感到不安，对…忧虑
high-strung	['hai'strʌŋ] *a.* 高度紧张的 (having an extremely nervous or sensitive temperament) 【例】A ***high-strung*** person becomes angry or emotional very quickly.

尽管 (although, despite, in spite of, even though/ if, in the face of, for all, nevertheless, nonetheless, notwithstanding)

although	[ɔːl'ðəu] *conj.* 虽然，尽管 (regardless the fact that) 【例】***Although*** it was pretty cold, David went out without an overcoat.
despite	[di'spait] *prep.* 尽管，不管 (without being affected by something) 【例】Wilber still loves Della, ***despite*** the fact that she left him.
in spite of	尽管，不管 【例】***In spite of*** great efforts they failed to carry their plans through.
even though/ if	即使，尽管 【例】***Even though*** my little sister is annoying, I like her very much.
in the face of	不顾，尽管 【例】Finally Rory succeeded ***in the face of*** great difficulties.
for all	尽管，虽然 【例】***For all*** her wealth and fame, Maria is still unhappy.

nevertheless	[ˌnevəðə'les] *conj.* /*ad.* 尽管如此；然而 (in spite of this; however)
	【例】It's a difficult race. ***Nevertheless***, thousands of runners participate every year.
nonetheless	[ˌnʌnðə'les] *ad.* 尽管如此；但是 (despite what has just been said; however)
	【例】This ring is very expensive, ***nonetheless***, I decide to buy it.
notwithstanding	[ˌnɔtwiθ'stændiŋ] *prep.* /*ad.* 虽然，尽管如此 (despite something)
	【例】***Notwithstanding*** her parents were against the match, Emma married the poor guy.

经验丰富的 (experienced, veteran, seasoned, professional, practiced, worldly-wise)

experienced	[ik'spiəriənst] *a.* 富有经验的，熟练的 (skillful or wise through experience)
	【例】They hired a team packed with ***experienced*** and mature professionals.
veteran	['vetərən] *a.* 经验丰富的 (very experienced and skilled in a particular activity)
	【例】Newman was a ***veteran*** actor of stage and screen.
	【用】veteran car 老爷车
seasoned	['siːzənd] *a.* 有经验的，训练有素的 (experienced in a particular activity or job)
	【例】Tom was a ***seasoned*** traveler.
professional	[prəu'feʃənəl] *a.* 职业的，专业的 (having a particular profession as a permanent career)
	【例】This has been the worst time for injuries since I started as a ***professional*** footballer.
practiced	['præktist] *a.* 熟练的，老练的 (experienced, skilled)
	【例】Once you are ***practiced*** at this sort of relaxation you will feel quite refreshed afterwards.
	【用】be practiced in sth. 善于…；在…方面熟练
worldly-wise	['wəːldli'waiz] *a.* 善于处事的，老于世故的 (possessing a practical and often shrewd understanding of human affairs)

【例】Roger was a ***worldly-wise*** business man.

惊讶（surprise, astonish, amaze, startle, wonder, marvel）

surprise　［sə'praiz］ *v.* 使诧异，使惊奇（to cause to feel wonder, astonishment, or amazement）
【例】Steven decided to ***surprise*** Angie with flowers on Saint Valentine's Day.

astonish　［ə'stɔniʃ］ *v.* 使惊讶，使吃惊（to surprise someone very much）
【例】These tricks ***astonished*** many children.
【用】It astonishes sb. that 让…吃惊的是

amaze　［ə'meiz］ *v.* 使大为惊奇，惊愕（to surprise someone very much, especially by being very impressive）
【例】What ***amazes*** me is that Ted never get tired.
【用】sth. never ceases to amaze sb. 一直让…吃惊的是

startle　［'stɑːtl］ *v.* 使惊吓，使…吃惊（to make a person or animal feel suddenly frightened or surprised by doing something they do not expect）
【例】I'm sorry, if I've ***startled*** you.

wonder　［'wʌndə］ *v.* （对…）感到惊讶或诧异（to feel great surprise, admiration, etc.）
【例】We all ***wondered*** to hear Maggie's voice in the next room.
【用】wonder at sth. 对…感到惊奇

marvel　［'mɑːvəl］ *v.* 对…感到惊异（to show or feel surprise or admiration）
【例】We ***marveled*** that Kate walked away unhurt from the car accident.
【用】marvel at sth. 对…大为惊奇

竞争，赶超（compete, emulate, rival, match, vie, contend）

compete　［kəm'piːt］ *v.* 竞争，对抗（to strive consciously or unconsciously for an objective such as position, profit, or a prize）
【例】More than 2,300 candidates from 90 political parties are ***competing*** for 486 seats.

	【用】compete with/against sb. 与…竞争
emulate	['emjuleit] *v.* 竞争，赶超（to try to do as well as or better than somebody） 【例】The girl *emulated* her elder sister at the piano. 【用】emulate sb. at sth. 在…上同…竞争
rival	['raivəl] *v.* 竞争（to be in competition with somebody or something） 【例】The stores *rivaled* each other in window displays. 【用】rival sth./sb. for/in sth. 在…上同…竞争
match	[mætʃ] *v.* 使竞争（to make a person or team compete against a particular opponent） 【例】The United States *matched* with France in the finals. 【用】match sb. against/with sb. 使…与…竞争
vie	[vai] *v.* 竞争（to compete with other people for something that is difficult to get） 【例】The two were *vying* for the support of New York voters. 【用】vie with sb. for sth./to do sth. 为了…与…激烈竞争；vie for sth. 争夺…
contend	[kən'tend] *v.* 竞争（to compete against someone，for example for a victory or for power） 【例】The two main political groups *contended* for power. 【用】contend for sth. 为了…竞争

（使）聚焦，（使）集中（focus, center on, center, zero in on, pinpoint, fix, concentrate, spotlight）

focus	['fəukəs] *v.* （使）聚焦，（使）集中（to concentrate attention or effort） 【例】All eyes were *focused* on the speaker. 【用】focus on/upon 聚焦在…
center on	集中于 【例】Our thoughts all *centered on* the young girl about to be married.
center	['sentə] *v.* （把…）集中于（to give a central focus or basis） 【例】The talk *centered* around trade relations with China.

zero in on	将注意力集中于…；将焦点调到…
	【例】The police *zeroed in on* the suspicious man.
pinpoint	['pinpoint] *v.* 准确描述，精确地定位（to locate or aim with great precision or accuracy）
	【例】I could *pinpoint* his precise location on a map.
fix	[fiks] *v.* 使集中（to hold or direct steadily）
	【例】She *fixed* her eyes on the road ahead when she was driving.
	【用】fix sb. with one's eyes 用眼睛盯牢…
concentrate	['kɔnsəntreit] *v.* 集中，聚集（to bring or direct toward a common center or objective）
	【例】You'll be fired if you don't *concentrate* on your work.
	【用】concentrate on sth. 集中在…
spotlight	['spɔtlait] *v.* 集中注意力于（to direct attention to）
	【例】The budget crisis also *spotlighted* the weakening American economy.

居住（live, inhabit, occupy, reside, dwell）

live	[liv] *v.* 居住，住（to have your home in a particular place）
	【例】London is a nice place to *live*.
	【用】live at home 与父母同住
inhabit	[in'hæbit] *v.* 居住于，（动物）栖居于（to live in a particular place）
	【例】The islands are *inhabited* by 13,000 people.
occupy	['ɔkjupai] *v.* 居住（to live in or have possession of a house, etc.）
	【例】The Smith family has *occupied* this farm for over a hundred years.
reside	[ri'zaid] *v.* 居住，定居（to live in a particular place）
	【例】Ben *resided* in Salt Lake City.
	【用】reside in/at 居住于
dwell	[dwel] *v.* 居住（to live somewhere）
	【例】Many pigmies *dwelled* in the forest.

拒绝（refuse，reject，veto，deny，decline，spurn，turn down）

refuse
[ri'fju:z] *v.* 拒绝，不接受（to say you will not do something that someone has asked you to do）
【例】Michael *refused* to answer personal questions.
【用】refuse to do sth. 拒绝做…

reject
[ri'dʒekt] *v.* 拒绝，抵制（to refuse to accept，submit to，or believe）
【例】The court *rejected* the prisoner's appeal for a new trial.

veto
['vi:təu] *v.* 否决，禁止（not to agree to an offer，proposal，or request）
【例】The President *vetoed* the economic package passed by Congress.

deny
[di'nai] *v.* 拒绝给予，拒绝…的要求（to refuse to give somebody something or to prevent somebody from having something）
【例】Lily was very angry at being *denied* the opportunity to see her father.
【用】deny sth. to sb. 拒不给予…

decline
[di'klain] *v.* 拒绝，谢绝（to say politely that you will not accept something or do something）
【例】Ben *declined* an invitation to a dinner party.
【用】decline to do sth. 拒绝做…

spurn
[spə:n] *v.* 拒绝，摈弃（to refuse to accept something，do something，or deal with something）
【例】Mark would be *spurned* out of doors with a kick.

turn down
拒绝，不理会
【例】I thanked him for the offer but *turned* it *down*.

捐赠，赠送（donate，contribute，grant，confer，bestow，bequeath）

donate
[dəu'neit] *v.* 捐赠，赠送（to give something such as money or goods to an organization，especially to a school，political party，or charity）

【例】The government ***donated*** 100 million dollars to the flood-struck area.

【用】donate to sb. /sth. 捐赠给…

contribute 〔kən'tribjuːt〕v. 捐赠；做出贡献（to give money, goods, or effort to achieve something, especially when other people are also helping）

【例】They say they would like to ***contribute*** more to charity，but money is tight this year.

【用】contribute to sb. /sth. 捐赠给…

grant 〔ɡrɑːnt; ɡrænt〕v. 授予（to give something formally or legally）

【例】Permission was ***granted*** a few weeks ago.

【用】grant sth. to sb. 将…授予…

confer 〔kən'fəː〕v. 赠予，授予（to give something such as authority, a legal right，or an honor to someone）

【例】The university ***conferred*** an honorary degree on the professor.

【用】confer sth. on sb. 将…授予…

bestow 〔bi'stəu〕v. 赠与，授予（to give valuable property or an important right or honor to someone）

【例】The chairman of the sports committee ***bestowed*** the trophy upon the winner.

【用】bestow sth. on/upon sb. 将…授予…

bequeath 〔bi'kwiːð〕v. 遗赠（to give someone money or property after one dies by making a legal document called a will）

【例】The millionaire ***bequeathed*** all his money to the charity.

【用】bequeath sth. to sb. 将…遗赠给…

卷，盘绕（coil, wind, spiral, twist, loop, twirl, twine, convolute）

coil 〔kɔil〕v. 卷，盘绕（to wind something long and thin into a shape like a series of rings）

【例】Alfred turned off the water and began to ***coil*** the hose.

【用】coil oneself/sth. round sth. /up 将…卷成螺旋形

wind 〔wind〕v. 绕，缠绕（to encircle something around itself or something else）

【例】The horse jumped forwards and round Sheila，***winding*** the rope round her.

【用】wind up 卷起，卷拢；上紧发条

spiral

['spaiərəl] *v.* 盘旋上升（或下降）(to move in the shape of a spiral，or to make something do this)

【例】Vines *spiraled* upward toward the roof.

【用】spiral upward/downward 盘旋上升或下降

twist

[twist] *v.* 缠绕，扭曲 (to force something out of its original shape by bending it or turning it around)

【例】The steel lamp posts were *twisted* together by the explosion.

【用】twist off 扭断，拧断

loop

[lu:p] *v.* （使）成环，（使）成圈 (to form a circle or make something into a circle)

【例】He *looped* the rope round the wood.

【用】loop the loop 翻跟头飞行

twirl

[twə:l] *v.* （使某物）盘绕，缠绕 (to move in circles，or make something move in circles)

【例】Sarah lifted her hand and started *twirling* a strand of hair.

twine

[twain] *v.* （使某物）缠绕或卷绕某物 (to wind around something，or make something wind around something)

【例】These strands of molecules *twine* around each other to form cable-like structures.

【用】twine sth. around sth. 将…缠绕在

convolute

['kɔnvəlu:t] *v.* 盘绕，卷起 (to fold or cause to coil or fold in overlapping whorls)

【例】The plastic sheet *convolutes* when it is heated.

决定 (decide, choose, determine, settle, opt, commit oneself, rule, resolve)

decide

[di'said] *v.* 决定 (to make a choice about what you are going to do)

【例】It was *decided* at our meeting to limit the examination period to one week.

【用】decide on/upon sth. 选定，决定…

choose

[tʃu:z] *v.* 决定 (to decide to do something)

【例】Mike *chose* not to go home until 5 o'clock.

determine [di'tə:min] *v.* 决定 (to officially decide something)

【例】It is for the court to ***determine*** whether Shirley is guilty.

【用】determine on sth. 决定…

settle ['setl] *v.* 决定 (to decide something definitely)

【例】It was ***settled*** that Claud would leave before dark.

【用】settle down 定居

opt [ɔpt] *v.* 选择或决定 (to make a choice or decision from a range of possibilities)

【例】After recent setbacks in the market，most people are now ***opting*** for low-risk investments.

【用】opt for sth. 选择…；opt to do sth. 选择做…

commit oneself 做决定 (to make a definite decision)

【例】I would advise people to think very carefully about ***committing themselves*** to working on Sundays.

rule [ru:l] *v.* （做出）裁决（或裁定）(to make and announce a decision，usually about a legal matter)

【例】The procedure was ***ruled*** out as unparliamentary.

【用】rule out sth. 划去，取消…；rule against sth. 否决…

resolve [ri'zɔlv] *v.* 决心，决定 (to make a formal decision，usually after a discussion and a vote at a meeting)

【例】My father has ***resolved*** to give up smoking.

【用】resolve to do sth. 下定决心做…

开动，激励 (actuate, activate, impel, ignite, motivate, spur, rouse)

actuate ['æktjueit] *v.* 开动，激励 (to put into mechanical action or motion；to move to action)

【例】The desire for conquest ***actuated*** the explorers of the sixteenth century.

activate ['æktiveit] v. 激活，使活动（to make a piece of equipment or a process start working）

【例】Judy's work was not finished，but it attracted and *activated* others.

impel [im'pel] v. 驱使，推进（to urge to action or to drive forward）

【例】The man was *impelled* by the courage and competitiveness to take risks.

【用】impel sb. to sth. 驱使…做…

ignite [ig'nait] v. 激起，引发（to cause the passionate of；to start a particular feeling in someone）

【例】The recent fighting in the area could *ignite* regional passions far beyond the borders.

motivate ['məutiveit] v. 驱动，激励（to make someone feel determined to do something or enthusiastic about doing it）

【例】Students were *motivated* to learn more by the encouragement of a good teacher.

【用】motivate sb. to do sth. 激励…做…

spur [spə:] v. 刺激，激励（to encourage someone to do something；to cause something to happen）

【例】It is the money that *spurs* these fishermen to risk a long ocean journey in their flimsy boats.

【用】spur sb. /sth. on/to sth. 激励或刺激…

rouse [rauz] v. 鼓舞（to make someone become active，especially when they are tired，lazy，or unwilling to do something）

【例】Eddy did more to *rouse* the crowd than anybody else.

【用】rouse sb. /sth. from sth. 使…活跃起来

开始（start, commence, begin, set about, set to）

start [sta:t] v. 开始，着手（to begin to happen or take place）

【例】We took refuge under an cave when it *started* to rain.

【用】start doing/to do sth. 开始做…

commence [kə'mens] v. 开始，倡导（to begin, or to begin something）

【例】The movie will *commence* right after dinner.

【用】commence sth. /doing sth. 开始…

begin	[bi'gin] *v.* 开始 (to start doing something) 【例】She **began** shouting at them. 【用】begin to do/doing sth. 开始做…
set about	开始，着手 (to start doing something with vigour or determination) 【例】The new owner of that house **set about** renovating the sitting room and bathrooms.
set to	开始认真做 (to begin doing something vigorously) 【例】My cousin **set to** with bleach and scouring pads to render the vases spotless.

慷慨的 (lavish, generous, bountiful, unsparing)

lavish	['lævi∫] *a.* 过分的，慷慨的 (expending or bestowing profusely) 【例】The critics were **lavish** with their praise to this film. 【用】be lavish in/of/with sth. 对…大方，慷慨；lavish in doing sth. 在做…方面慷慨
generous	['dʒenərəs] *a.* 慷慨的，大方的 (giving people more of your time or money than is usual or expected) 【例】The star made a **generous** donation to the orphanage.
bountiful	['bauntiful] *a.* 慷慨的 (liberal in bestowing gifts or favors) 【例】The headmaster praised those **bountiful** donors.
unsparing	[ʌn'speəriŋ] *a.* 大方的，慷慨的 (not frugal) 【例】The woman give out the food and clothes with an **unsparing** hand. 【用】be unsparing in sth. 在…上大方的，慷慨的

可耻的 (shameful, disgraceful, dishonorable, humiliating, embarrassing, scandalous, infamous, ignominious, despicable)

shameful	['∫eimful] *a.* 可耻的，不道德的 (so bad that you feel ashamed of it) 【例】What you have done is **shameful**.

disgraceful [dis'greisful] *a.* 可耻的，丢脸的（extremely bad or shocking）

【例】Telling a lie is a *disgraceful* conduct.

dishonorable [dis'ɔnərəbl] *a.* 不名誉的；可耻的（characterized by or causing dishonor or discredit）

【例】The soldier was given a *dishonorable* discharge from the army.

humiliating [hju:'milieitiŋ] *a.* 丢脸的，耻辱的（making you feel very embarrassed and ashamed）

【例】This was a *humiliating* defeat.

embarrassing [im'bærəsiŋ] *a.* 令人为难的（making you feel nervous, ashamed, or stupid）

【例】That was an *embarrassing* situation for me.

scandalous ['skændələs] *a.* 出丑的，可耻的（causing scandal）

【例】Clare had a series of *scandalous* affairs that shocked the community.

infamous ['infəməs] *a.* 声名狼藉的；无耻的（well known for something bad）

【例】The king was *infamous* for his cruelty.

【用】be infamous for 因…而声名狼藉

ignominious [,ignəu'miniəs] *a.* 可耻的，不名誉的（very embarrassing, especially because of making you seem very unsuccessful or unimportant）

【例】At last the two countries concluded an *ignominious* treaty.

despicable ['despikəbl] *a.* 可鄙的，卑劣的（deserving of contempt or scorn）

【例】To steal money from a blind man is a *despicable* act.

【用】be despicable of sb. to do sth. …做…是卑鄙的

可靠的（reliable, credible, trusty, trustworthy, dependable）

reliable [ri'laiəbl] *a.* 可靠的，可信赖的（suitable or fit to be relied on）

【例】Jimmy is not a *reliable* friend.

credible	['kredəbl] *a.* 可信的，可靠的（able to be believed or trusted） 【例】I don't think the witness's story is *credible*.
trusty	['trʌsti] *a.* 可信赖的，可信任的（used for describing a thing or person you have had or known for a long time and can depend on） 【例】This is my *trusty* old bicycle.
trustworthy	['trʌst,wə:ði] *a.* 值得信赖的，可靠的（able to be trusted as being honest, safe, or reliable） 【例】I'm a *trustworthy* person that you can trust forever.
dependable	[di'pendəbl] *a.* 可信赖的，可靠的（capable of being depended on） 【例】This system is secure, *dependable* and manageable.

可能的（possible, probable, likely, potential, conceivable, imaginable）

possible	['pɔsəbl] *a.* 可能的（considered capable of happening, existing, being done, or being true, but not very likely） 【例】Run as fast as *possible*.
probable	['prɔbəbl] *a.* 可能的（likely to happen or be true） 【例】It is possible but not *probable* that Nick will pass the examination.
likely	['laikli] *a.* 可能的，有希望的（possessing the qualities or characteristics that make something probable） 【例】It is *likely* that it's going to rain.
potential	[pəu'tenʃəl] *a.* 潜在的，可能的（possible or likely in the future） 【例】We are aware of the *potential* problems and have taken every precaution.
conceivable	[kən'si:vəbl] *a.* 可能的（possible, or possible to imagine） 【例】It is just *conceivable* that a single survivor might be found.
imaginable	[i'mædʒinəbl] *a.* 可想像得到的，可能的（conceivable in the imagination） 【例】This is the only solution *imaginable*.

渴望 (long, yearn, hunger, desire, crave, thirst, hanker, wish for, pine)

long
[lɔŋ; lɔːn] *v.* 渴望 (to want something very much)
【例】Tom *longed* for a bicycle.
【用】long for sth. 渴望得到…; long to do sth. 渴望做…

yearn
[jəːn] *v.* 盼望，渴望 (to want something a lot, especially something that you know you may not be able to have)
【例】The wife *yearned* for her husband's return.
【用】yearn for sb. /sth. 渴望…，盼望…

hunger
['hʌŋgə] *v.* 渴望，渴望得到 (to have an eager desire)
【例】All the players *hungered* for the championship.
【用】hunger for/after/ sth. /sb. 渴望得到…

desire
[di'zaiə] *v.* 向往，渴望 (to hope for)
【例】Money and success are things most of us *desire*.
【用】desire to do sth. 渴望做…

crave
[kreiv] *v.* 渴望得到 (to want something very much and in a way that is very hard to control)
【例】He *craves* for the recognition of the society.
【用】crave for sth. 渴望得到…

thirst
[θəːst] *v.* 渴望，渴求 (to have a strong desire for)
【例】Mary *thirsted* for words of love from him.
【用】thirst for sth. 渴求…

hanker
['hæŋkə] *v.* 渴望，追求 (to have a strong feeling of wanting something)
【例】Tom *hankered* to revisit his childhood home.
【用】hanker after/for sth. 渴求…; hanker to do sth. 渴求做…

wish for
希望，盼望
【例】They do not *wish for* pity.

pine
[pain] *v.* 渴望或想念某人 (某事物) (to desire intensely and persistently especially for something unattainable)
【例】She *pined* for some excitement in her life.
【用】pine for sb. /sth. 渴望或想念…

空的，闲置的 (blank, vacant, bare, hollow, void)

blank [blæŋk] *a.* 空白的，空着的 (without writing or printing; empty)

【例】Take a *blank* sheet of paper and write your name at the top.

【用】go blank（脑子）一片空白

vacant ['veikənt] *a.* 空着的，未占用的 (not filled or occupied)

【例】The room on the third floor is *vacant* at present.

【用】a vacant expression/look 面无表情

bare [beə] *a.* 空的，几乎空的 (empty or almost empty)

【例】Jim walked into the bedroom and found it *bare* of furniture.

【用】bare of 空的，几乎空了的

hollow ['hɔləu] *a.* 空的，中空的 (empty inside)

【例】These chocolate candies are all *hollow*.

【用】ring hollow（话语、文章等）空洞缺乏诚意；beat sb. hollow 给…以致命打击

void [vɔid] *a.* 空的，空闲的 (containing nothing; not occupied or inhabited)

【例】Suddenly the street was *void* of people.

【用】void of 缺少…；null and void 无效的

（使）恐惧，（使）震惊 (horrify, dismay, shock, frighten, terrify, appall, scare)

horrify ['hɔrifai] *v.* （使）恐惧，（使）震惊 (to cause to feel horror)

【例】Everyone was *horrified* by the news.

dismay [dis'mei] *v.* （使）惊慌，（使）沮丧 (to cause to lose courage or resolution (as because of alarm or fear))

【例】We were *dismayed* by the violence of his reaction.

shock [ʃɔk] *v.* （使）震动，（使）震惊 (to strike with surprise, terror, horror, or disgust)

【例】I was *shocked* when I heard about the news of air crash.

frighten ['fraitən] *v.* （使）惊恐，吓唬 (to make afraid)

【例】The thunder *frightened* my younger brother.

【用】frighten sb. to death/frighten the life out of sb. 吓得要死

terrify ['terifai] *v.* 使恐怖，使惊吓（to fill with terror）

【例】The ghost story *terrified* the young children.

appall [ə'pɔːl] *v.* 使惊骇，使恐怖（to shock or offend someone very much）

【例】The public were *appalled* when they heard the president had been shot.

scare [skeə] *v.* 使害怕，受惊吓（to make someone feel frightened or worried）

【例】The firecracker blew up and *scared* the birds away.

【用】scare sb. out of doing sth. 吓得…不敢做；scare sb. into / doing sth. 吓得…做

枯萎（shrivel, wither, dehydrate, desiccate, wilt, wizen, dry up）

shrivel ['ʃrivəl] *v.* （使）蔫，枯萎（becoming smaller and thinner than usual and not looking fresh and healthy）

【例】Leaves of the tree *shrivel* in the hot sun.

【用】shrivel sth. up 使…枯萎

wither ['wiðə] *v.* 枯萎，凋零（to become weaker or smaller and then disappear）

【例】Crops *wither* after being cut.

【用】wither away 枯萎；wither sth. up 使…枯萎

dehydrate [ˌdiː'haidreit] *v.* 脱水（to lose so much water from your body that you feel weak or sick）

【例】After finishing his ten-thousand miles, the man was *dehydrated*.

desiccate ['desikeit] *v.* （使）完全干涸；脱水（to dry out thoroughly）

【例】Mom decided to buy some *desiccated* fruit.

wilt [wilt] *v.* （使）凋谢，枯萎（to droop or lose freshness）

【例】In the droughty season, most of our plants *wilt*.

wizen ['wizən] *v.* 使干枯，枯萎（to wither, shrivel, or dry up）

【例】There would be a day when his face would be wrinkled and *wizened*.

dry up 干涸，枯竭

【例】If the foreign aid *dries up*, the situation will be desperate.

夸奖 (flatter, compliment, praise, laud, extol)

flatter

［'flætə］ v. 夸奖 (to lavishly or insincerely praise someone)

【例】Ken *flattered* her about her cooking.

【用】flatter oneself 自吹自擂

compliment

［'kɔmplimənt］ v. 赞美，恭维 (to say something nice to or about somebody)

【例】John *complimented* Jean on her beautiful new dress.

【用】compliment sb. on sth. 因…表扬…

praise

［preiz］ v. 赞扬，表扬 (to express strong approval or admiration for somebody or something)

【例】The boy *praised* his friend as being one of the finest human beings he had ever met.

【用】praise sb. for (doing) sth. 表扬…做了…

laud

［lɔːd］ v. 赞美，称赞 (to praise somebody or something)

【例】The small child was *lauded* for his achievement in piano.

extol

［ik'stəul］ v. 赞颂，赞美 (to praise something in a very enthusiastic way)

【例】The man was *extolled* as a hero.

【用】extol sb. as sth. 把…称颂为…

快的，迅速的 (rapid, prompt, fleet, expeditious)

rapid

［'ræpid］ a. 迅速的，快的 (happening, moving, or acting quickly)

【例】We are seeing a *rapid* growth in the use of the Internet.

【用】make rapid strides 取得巨大进步

prompt

［prɔmpt］ a. 急速的，迅速的 (immediate or quick)

【例】Thank you for your *prompt* attention to this matter.

【用】be prompt to do/in doing sth. 迅速地做…

fleet

［fliːt］ a. 快速的，敏捷的 (fast, light and quick in moving)

【例】Nicholas is *fleet* of foot.

expeditious

［ˌekspi'diʃəs］ a. 迅速的，敏捷的 (quick and effective)

【例】We'll give you an *expeditious* repose.

宽广的 (broad, extensive, spacious, ample, roomy)

broad [brɔːd] *a.* 宽广的 (extending far and wide)

【例】There was a **broad** shady path to the downtown.

extensive [ik'stensiv] *a.* 广阔的 (spreading over a large area)

【例】An **extensive** desert covers much of northern Africa.

spacious ['speiʃəs] *a.* 宽广的，广阔的 (having or providing much space)

【例】The interior of the house is **spacious** and bright.

ample ['æmpl] *a.* 宽敞的，宽广的 (generous or more than adequate in size，scope，or capacity)

【例】Our company rented an office complex with **ample** parking.

roomy ['ruːmi] *a.* 有很多空间的，宽敞的 (large and providing you with a lot of space)

【例】Our new house has a **roomy** kitchen.

困扰 (beset, plague, harass, torment, badger, hassle, vex)

beset [bi'set] *v.* 困扰 (to cause someone difficulty or danger over a period of time)

【例】The customer service department was **beset** by angry customers.

【用】beset by doubts 为疑问所困扰

plague [pleig] *v.* 烦扰，使苦恼 (to cause a lot of problems for someone or something for a long period of time)

【例】Brain was **plagued** with doubts and fears.

【用】plague sb. /sth. with sth. 以…（一再询问或要求）烦扰…

harass ['hærəs] *v.* 侵扰，烦扰 (to attack an enemy army repeatedly；to annoy or upset someone repeatedly)

【例】Pirates **harassed** the villages along the coast.

【用】sexually harass sb. 性骚扰

torment [tɔː'ment] *v.* 折磨，烦扰 (to make someone suffer severe physical or mental pain；to annoy someone)

【例】At times the memories returned to **torment** her.

badger	['bædʒə] *v.* 烦扰，纠缠（to try to make someone do something by asking them many times）
	【例】Friends kept phoning and writing, ***badgering*** me to go back.
	【用】badger sb. with/for sth. 为了…纠缠…
hassle	['hæsl] *v.* 打扰，麻烦（to annoy someone or to cause problems for them）
	【例】If you are tired of being ***hassled*** by unreasonable parents, leave home and go your own way.
vex	[veks] *v.* 恼火，使烦恼（to make someone annoyed, confused or worried）
	【例】It ***vexed*** me to think of others gossiping behind me.
	【用】a vexed question 引起争论的问题

浪费的（lavish, extravagant, prodigal）

lavish	['læviʃ] *a.* 奢侈的，浪费的（characterized by or produced with extravagance and profusion）
	【例】The waiter led us into a ***lavish*** living room that offers a sweeping view of the Bay.
extravagant	[ik'strævəgənt] *a.* 奢侈的，铺张的（spending or costing a lot of money, especially more than reasonable）
	【例】Tom seems to have had no ***extravagant*** habit.
prodigal	['prɔdigəl] *a.* 浪费的，铺张的（wasting a lot of money or supplies）
	【例】The new couple was ***prodigal*** in their expenditures.
	【用】prodigal of sth. 对…是不吝啬的，慷慨的

乐观的 (optimistic, hopeful, forward-looking, sanguine, upbeat, expectant, sunny, bullish, confident)

optimistic [ˌɔptiˈmistik] *a.* 乐观(主义)的 (hopeful about the future and tends to expect that good things will happen)

【例】We are not *optimistic* about the future of the company.

hopeful [ˈhəupful] *a.* 怀有希望的 (believing that something will happen the way you want it to be)

【例】We resumed negotiations but we're not very *hopeful*.

【用】be hopeful of/about sth. 对…怀有希望

forward-looking *a.* 向前看的 (looking at the future in a positive way)

【例】We should make a *forward-looking* policy.

sanguine [ˈsæŋgwin] *a.* 乐观的 (confident and hopeful about what might happen)

【例】Tom was less *sanguine* about the situation.

【用】be sanguine about sth. 对…乐观，对…充满希望

upbeat [ˈʌpbiːt] *a.* 活泼的；乐观的 (happy and positive because you are confident you will get what you want)

【例】The players seemed *upbeat* about their chances of winning.

expectant [ikˈspektənt] *a.* 期望的，怀有希望的 (feeling excited about something you think is soon going to happen)

【例】The *expectant* fans waited for the star to pass.

sunny [ˈsʌni] *a.* 乐观的，快活的 (happy)

【例】It was always good to see Annie's *sunny* smile.

bullish [ˈbuliʃ] *a.* 乐观的 (expecting a successful future)

【例】The team was in a *bullish* mood before the game started.

confident [ˈkɔnfidənt] *a.* 确信的，肯定的 (marked by assurance, as of success)

【例】We were *confident* of victory.

【用】be confident of sth. 对…有把握，对…有信心

类似的 (similar, comparable, kindred, equivalent, akin, homologous, analogous)

similar [ˈsimilə] *a.* 相似的，类似的 (having characteristics in common)

【例】My girlfriend and I have *similar* taste in music.

【用】be similar to sb. /sth. 与…相似的，类似的

comparable [ˈkɔmpərəbl] *a.* 可比较的，类似的（capable of or suitable for comparison）

【例】There is no basketball player *comparable* to Jordan.

【用】be comparable with/to 与…相似

kindred [ˈkindrid] *a.* 同类的（of a similar nature or character）

【例】Those who enjoyed this movie had *kindred* emotions.

【用】a kindred spirit 意气相投的人

equivalent [iˈkwivələnt] *a.* 相同的，相当的（equal in force, amount, or value）

【例】There was a decrease of 10% in property investment compared with the *equivalent* period in the last year.

【用】be equivalent to sth. 与…是相等的，等价的，等值的

akin [əˈkin] *a.* 近似的（essentially similar, related or compatible）

【例】Pity is often *akin* to love.

【用】be akin to sth. 与…相近的；与…有密切关系的

homologous [hɔˈmɔləgəs] *a.* 相应的，类似的（having the same relative position, value, or structure）

【例】The two analyses concluded a *homologous* results.

analogous [əˈnæləgəs] *a.* 类似的（similar to another situation, process）

【例】This proposal was *analogous* with the one we discussed at the last meeting.

【用】be analogous to sth. 类似于…，与…类似

理论的（theoretical, hypothetical, speculative, academic, conjectural, notional, untried, unproven, untested）

theoretical [ˌθiəˈretikəl] *a.* 理论（上）的（relating to or having the character of theory）

【例】Applied ethics is grounded upon *theoretical* ethics.

hypothetical [ˌhaipəuˈθetikəl] *a.* 假定的，假设的（based on situations or events that seem possible rather than on actual ones）

【例】Scientists put forward a *hypothetical* proposition.

speculative [ˈspekjulətiv] *a.* 推理的（based on guesses or on a little information, not on facts）

【例】David was a great inventor and builder，but he had little interest in the *speculative* side of science.

academic [ˌækəˈdemik] *a.* 理论的（based on learning from books and study instead of on practical skills and experience）
【例】Edwin realized that Mary's protest must have been more or less *academic*.

conjectural [kənˈdʒektʃərəl] *a.* 推测的，猜测的（involving or based on conjecture）
【例】What he said was merely *conjectural*，not proved.

notional [ˈnəuʃənəl] *a.* 概念的，理论的（theoretical，speculative）
【例】Do you know what the *notional* value of state estate means?

untried [ˌʌnˈtraid] *a.* 未经试验的（not tested or proved by experience or trial）
【例】We won't adopt your plan for its feasibility is *untried*.

unproven [ˌʌnˈpruːvən] *a.* 未经证明的（not proved to be a fact or true）
【例】The willingness of Americans to throw money at *unproven* but exciting new endeavors is nothing new.

untested [ˌʌnˈtestid] *a.* 未经证明的（not tested to be a fact or true）
【例】All of us were *untested* for what lay ahead.

理性的（rational, sane, reasonable, sensible, levelheaded, sober, lucid, logical）

rational [ˈræʃənəl] *a.* 理性的，合理的（based on sensible practical reasons instead of emotions）
【例】A *rational* woman wouldn't weep just because her husband had forgotten her birthday.

sane [sein] *a.* 理智的，明智的（thinking and speaking in a reasonable way and behaving normally）
【例】It wasn't the act of a *sane* person.

reasonable [ˈriːzənəbl] *a.* 合理的，有道理的（governed by or being in accordance with reason or sound thinking）
【例】Everybody is rational though not all are *reasonable* in judgment.

sensible	['sensəbl] *a*. 理智的，明智的 (reasonable and practical)

sensible ['sensəbl] *a*. 理智的，明智的 (reasonable and practical)
【例】The **sensible** thing is to leave them alone.

levelheaded ['levəl'hedid] *a*. 头脑冷静的 (behaving in a calm and sensible way)
【例】Simon is **levelheaded** and practical.

sober ['səubə] *a*. 清醒的，自制的 (marked by self restraint)
【例】We are now far more **sober** and realistic.
【用】as sober as a judge 非常清醒的；极认真郑重的

lucid ['lju:sid] *a*. 清醒的，理智的 (capable of thinking clearly)
【例】Blare is **lucid** about political affairs.

logical ['lɔdʒikəl] *a*. 合乎逻辑的，合理的 (connecting ideas or reasons in a sensible way)
【例】Your conclusion is not **logical**.

例证，以…为例 (exemplify, typify, represent, illustrate, demonstrate, symbolize, stand for, personify)

exemplify [ig'zemplifai] *v*. 例证，以…为例 (to be a typical example of something)
【例】The teacher **exemplified** how to use the word.

typify ['tipifai] *v*. 代表，作为…的典型 (to be an excellent or typical example of something)
【例】The high quality **typifies** all his work.
【用】be typified by sth. 成为…的代表

represent [ˌrepri'zent] *v*. 作为…的代表(或代理) (to speak or act officially for another person, group, or organization)
【例】The general secretary may **represent** the president at some official ceremonies.

illustrate ['iləstreit] *v*. 说明，举例说明 (to show what something is like, or show that something is true)
【例】The story **illustrated** her true generosity very clearly.
【用】illustrate a point 说明一点

demonstrate ['demənstreit] *v*. 论证，证明 (to clearly show the existence or truth of something by giving proof or evidence)

【例】Our teacher **demonstrated** the laws of physics with laboratory equipment.

【用】demonstrate that 证明…

symbolize	['simbəlaiz] *v.* 象征 (to be a symbol of something)
	【例】The bald eagle **symbolizes** the United States.
stand for	代表，象征
	【例】AIDS **stands for** Acquired Immune Deficiency Syndrome.
personify	[pə'sɔnifai] *v.* 代表 (to be a very clear example of a particular quality)
	【例】This character **personifies** evil.

凉爽的，寒冷的 (cool, freezing, chilly, chill, icy, glacial, frigid)

cool	[ku:l] *a.* 凉爽的 (rather cold, often in a pleasant way)
	【例】Store the food in a **cool** and dry place.
freezing	['fri:ziŋ] *a.* 严寒的 (very cold)
	【例】My feet are **freezing** cold!
chilly	['tʃili] *a.* 寒冷的，冷得难受的 (cold enough to be unpleasant)
	【例】It's warm in the daytime but **chilly** at night.
chill	[tʃil] *a.* 寒冷的 (unpleasantly cold in the air, in the body, in water, etc.)
	【例】The **chill** homeless huddled around the campfire.
icy	['aisi] *a.* 寒冷的，冻冰的 (very cold; as cold as ice)
	【例】The little kid fell into the **icy** cold water.
glacial	['gleisjəl] *a.* 寒冷的，冰冷的 (extremely cold)
	【例】A **glacial** wind blew from the South.
frigid	['fridʒid] *a.* 寒冷的，严寒的 (very cold in temperature)
	【例】With the furnace out of order, the classroom was **frigid**.

旅行，行程 (journey, trip, wayfaring, tour, excursion, voyage, safari, junket, hike)

journey	['dʒə:ni] *n.* 旅行，行程 (an occasion when you travel from one place to another)

【例】Tom's making a long *journey*.

trip　[trip] *n.* 旅行，旅游（an occasion when you go somewhere and come back again）

【例】The idea of taking a *trip* with Jim makes me sick.

wayfaring　['wei,feəriŋ] *n.* 徒步旅行（traveling, especially on foot）

【例】They met a lot of risks in their *wayfaring*.

tour　[tuə] *n.* 旅行，旅游（a trip in which you visit several places for pleasure）

【例】Matthew and his wife have gone on a *tour* to the U. S.

excursion　[ik'skə:ʃən] *n.* 远足，短途旅游（a short visit to an interesting place arranged by a tourist organization）

【例】Our *excursion* to Boston seemed like a dream.

voyage　['vɔiidʒ] *n.* 旅行（a long trip, especially by boat or into space）

【例】Tom made a *voyage* across the Asian continent.

safari　[sə'fɑːri] *n.* （徒步）旅行（队）（a trip, especially to Africa, in order to watch, take pictures of, or hunt wild animals）

【例】My friend is prepared for a photographic *safari* to Africa.

【用】safari park 野生动物园

junket　['dʒʌŋkit] *n.* 公费旅游（a trip or meeting that people say is for business but is really for pleasure）

【例】A group of men on a *junket* stood at the platform, waiting for the train.

hike　[haik] *n.* 徒步旅行（a long walk in the countryside）

【例】People started the *hike* again after five minutes' rest.

裸露的 (uncovered, naked, nude, bare, exposed)

uncovered　[,ʌn'kʌvəd] *a.* 无遮盖的；赤裸的（not supplied with a covering）

【例】The man's *uncovered* legs were bleeding.

naked　['neikid] *a.* 裸露的；无遮蔽的（not wearing any clothes; not covered）

【例】The *naked* body was found on the river bank.

【用】half-naked 半裸的；strip naked 脱光衣服；naked to the waist 上半身裸露的；stark/buck naked 全裸的

nude	[nju:d] *a.* 裸体的 (not wearing clothes) 【例】Many famous artists have painted **nude** models.
bare	[beə] *a.* 赤裸的；无遮盖的 (not covered by any clothes; having no covering or decoration) 【例】She wore a low-necked dress and her arms were **bare**.
exposed	[ik'spəuzd] *a.* 无掩蔽的，暴露的 (not covered or hidden and therefore able to be seen) 【例】Their house was in a very **exposed** position at the top of the hill.

漫步 (ramble, roam, wander, drift, stroll, meander, saunter, traipse)

ramble	['ræmbl] *v.* 漫步 (to walk about casually or for pleasure) 【例】They **rambled** through the woods.
roam	[rəum] *v.* 漫游，闲逛 (to move or travel with no particular purpose) 【例】The lovers **roamed** across the fields in complete forgetfulness of the time.
wander	['wɔndə] *v.* 闲逛，漫步 (travel without purpose) 【例】When he got bored, he **wandered** around the fair. 【用】wander about/around 徘徊，闲逛
drift	[drift] *v.* 漂泊，游荡 (to move somewhere slowly as though you do not know where you are going) 【例】I walked in the street and **drifted** among the crowd.
stroll	[strəul] *v.* 闲逛，漫步 (to walk without hurrying, often for pleasure) 【例】After dinner, I **strolled** around the city.

| meander | [miˈændə] *v.* （指人）漫步，闲逛 (to move slowly without a particular direction or purpose in mind) |

【例】Vagabonds **meander** through life.

| saunter | [ˈsɔːntə] *v.* 闲逛，漫步 (to walk in a slow and relaxed way) |

【例】The old lady **saunters** through the woods every morning.

| traipse | [treips] *v.* 漫步，闲荡 (to walk or travel about without apparent plan or a purpose) |

【例】That vagrant **traipsed** around southern England for 18 weeks.

（使）迷惑，（使）为难 (puzzle, confuse, bewilder, befuddle, confound, perplex, mystify, baffle, disorient)

| puzzle | [ˈpʌzl] *v.* （使）迷惑，（使）为难 (to make someone worry and think hard，by being difficult to understand) |

【例】The boy was **puzzled** by his neighbour's odd looks.
【用】puzzle over sth. 对…苦苦思索

| confuse | [kənˈfjuːz] *v.* 打乱，（使）迷惑 (to make someone unable to think clearly) |

【例】They **confused** their teacher by having the same names.
【用】confuse sth. with sth. 混淆…与…

| bewilder | [biˈwildə] *v.* 使迷惑；使为难 (to make someone feel confused) |

【例】The silence from Alex had hurt and **bewildered** her.

| befuddle | [biˈfʌdl] *v.* 使迷惑 (to make someone very confused and unable to think clearly) |

【例】The writer likes to **befuddle** his readers with at least one unfamiliar word per article.

| confound | [kənˈfaund] *v.* 使迷惑 (to throw a person into confusion or surprise) |

【例】The patient's unusual symptoms **confounded** the doctor.
【用】confound sth. with sth. 使（思想等）混乱

| perplex | [pəˈpleks] *v.* 使（某人）困惑 (to make unable to grasp something clearly or to think logically about something) |

【例】Rosie was **perplexed** by Tom's refusal to tell where he was going.

mystify	['mistifai] *v.* 使（某人）困惑不解；使迷惑（to make someone confused through lack of understanding） 【例】The magician's tricks *mystified* the audience.
baffle	['bæfl] *v.* 使困惑，难倒（to defeat by confusing or puzzling） 【例】The odd noises and flashes of light in the empty house completely *baffled* Eric.
disorient	[dis'ɔːrient] *v.* 使迷失方位；使迷惑（to make someone confused about where they are; to make someone unable to think clearly） 【例】The strange streets *disoriented* him.

迷人的 (attractive, charming, enchanting, alluring, engaging, glamorous, catchy, winning)

attractive	[ə'træktiv] *a.* 有吸引力的，有魅力的（having the power to attract） 【例】Her new hair style was very *attractive*.
charming	['tʃɑːmiŋ] *a.* 有魅力的，迷人的（extremely pleasing or delightful） 【例】Amy gave him her most *charming* smile.
enchanting	[in'tʃɑːntiŋ] *a.* 迷人的（very interesting and attractive） 【例】Ann was an absolutely *enchanting* child.
alluring	[ə'ljuəriŋ] *a.* 吸引人的，迷人的（attractive in an exciting way） 【例】Belinda used to be an *alluring* actress.
engaging	[in'geidʒiŋ] *a.* 迷人的，有魅力的（attractive and pleasant in a way that makes people like you） 【例】Our math teacher was an *engaging* person.
glamorous	['glæmərəs] *a.* 富有魅力的，迷人的（attractive and interesting in an exciting and unusual way） 【例】It's a very *glamorous* vacation spot.
catchy	['kætʃi] *a.* 有魅力的，迷人的（attractive or appealing） 【例】The new television series got a *catchy* title.
winning	['winiŋ] *a.* 迷人的（attractive） 【例】I love Cindy's *winning* smile.

迷住 (obsess, preoccupy, haunt, possess, occupy)

obsess　[əb'ses] *v.* 迷住 (to preoccupy the mind of someone excessively)
【例】Martin was *obsessed* by the desire for revenge now.

preoccupy　[priː'ɔkjupai] *v.* 迷住 (to engage or engross the interest or attention beforehand or preferentially)
【例】The group of students *preoccupied* themselves with a game of Bingo.

haunt　[hɔːnt] *v.* (思想，回忆等)萦绕在心头，缠绕 (to come to mind continually)
【例】Images of the war still *haunted* Jenny.

possess　[pə'zes] *v.* 缠住，迷住 (to cause to be influenced or controlled，as by an idea or emotion)
【例】The thought of getting rich *possessed* Jill all the time.

occupy　['ɔkjupai] *v.* 把精神集中于 (to fill or preoccupy the mind or thoughts)
【例】Many anxieties *occupied* the manager's mind.
【用】occupy oneself with sth. /in doing sth. 忙碌于…

迷住，迷惑 (charm, captivate, fascinate, enchant, enthrall, bewitch)

charm　[tʃɑːm] *v.* 吸引，迷住 (to please, soothe, or delight by compelling attraction)
【例】Zoe's graciousness *charmed* everyone at the party.
【用】charm sth. from/out of sb. 使用迷人手段从…得到…

captivate　['kæptiveit] *v.* 迷住，迷惑 (to attract or interest someone very much)
【例】The child *captivated* every one with his sunny smile.

fascinate　['fæsineit] *v.* 迷住 (to attract and interest someone very strongly)
【例】The *fascinating* smile of the beautiful girl made me faint.

enchant　[in'tʃɑːnt] *v.* (使)陶醉，(使)入迷 (to interest and attract someone very strongly)
【例】She was *enchanted* with the music.

enthrall	[in'θrɔ:l] *v.* 迷惑，迷住（to make you so interested or excited that you give it all your attention） 【例】The magic show *enthralled* the audience.
bewitch	[bi'witʃ] *v.* 迷住（to captivate completely; enchant） 【例】Merry's sweet smile had *bewitched* Bob，and he could refuse her nothing.

秘密的 (secret, covert, confidential, private, stealthy, clandestine)

secret	['si:krit] *a.* 秘密的，机密的（deliberately not told to other people or kept hidden from other people） 【例】This is a *secret* deal between you and me. 【用】keep sth. secret from sb. 对…保密
covert	['kəuvə:t] *a.* 秘密的，隐秘的（not openly practiced, avowed, engaged in, accumulated, or shown） 【例】What they have done is a *covert* threat to our future development.
confidential	[ˌkɔnfi'denʃəl] *a.* 秘密的，机密的（done or communicated in confidence） 【例】Only the manager has the access to these *confidential* letters.
private	['praivit] *a.* 私人的；秘密的（used only by a particular person or group, or available only to them） 【例】The two leaders held a *private* meeting. 【用】private eye 私人侦探
stealthy	['stelθi] *a.* 鬼鬼祟祟的；秘密的（marked by or acting with quiet, caution intended to avoid notice） 【例】The scout made a *stealthy* approach to the enemy position.
clandestine	[klæn'destin] *a.* 秘密的，暗中从事的（secret and often illegal） 【例】Because of the disapproval from parents, the young lovers had to make a *clandestine* date in the park.

描述 (describe, depict, characterize, picture, represent)

describe	[di'skraib] *v.* 描写，描述（to give details about what someone or something is like）

【例】I don't think that's quite the word to *describe* my feelings.

【用】describe sb. /sth. as sth. 将…描述为…；describe sb. /sth. to/for sb. 向…描述…

depict [di'pikt] *v.* 描绘，描述（to describe someone or something using words or pictures）

【例】The novel *depicts* the hero as a cynical opportunist.

【用】depict sb. as sth. 将…描述为…

characterize ['kærəktəraiz] *v.* 描绘（人或物的特性），描述（to describe someone or something as a particular type of person or thing）

【例】Shakespeare *characterizes* Richard Ⅲ as an evil king.

【用】characterize sb. /sth. as sth. 将…（的特点）描述成…

picture ['piktʃə] *v.* （生动地）描绘，描述（to describe vividly in words or make a verbal picture of）

【例】It was hard to *picture* him as a responsible husband and father.

【用】picture sb. as sth. 将…描绘成…

represent [,repri'zent] *v.* 描述，描绘（to describe someone or something in a particular way, especially when this influences other people's opinions）

【例】The movie *represented* Kennedy's assassination as a government conspiracy.

【用】represent sb. as sth. 将…描绘成…

明白 (understand, grasp, apprehend, comprehend, make out)

understand [,ʌndə'stænd] *v.* 理解，懂（to know what someone or something means）

【例】If you don't *understand*, just raise your hand.

【用】make oneself understood 让别人明白，清楚地表达

grasp [ɡrɑːsp；ɡræsp] *v.* 理解，领会（to understand something）

【例】Mabel found it difficult to *grasp* the meaning of the whole passage.

【用】grasp the meaning of sth. 理解或领会…的意思

apprehend [,æpri'hend] *v.* 领会，理解（to understand something）

【例】The expert *apprehended* it at a glance.

comprehend	[ˌkɔmpri'hend] v. 理解，领会（to understand something） 【例】It's impossible for you to **comprehend** the difficulties of my situation.
make out	理解，了解 【例】I cannot **make** Clare **out**.

明显的 (noticeable, perceivable, conspicuous, observable, discernible, palpable, obvious, visible, apparent, distinct, evident, perceptible, plain, seeable)

noticeable	['nəutisəbl] a. 明显的（easy to see, hear, or feel） 【例】There has been a **noticeable** improvement in her health. 【用】noticeable changes 明显的变化
perceivable	[pə'si:vəbl] a. 可察觉的，可知觉的（capable of being perceived especially by sight or hearing） 【例】That condition was not **perceivable** by the senses.
conspicuous	[kən'spikjuəs] a. 显著的（very noticeable or easy to see, especially because of being unusual or different） 【例】Polly might have felt less **conspicuous** if there had been other women. 【用】be conspicuous for sth. 因…惹人注目
observable	[əb'zə:vəbl] a. 看得见的，显著的（capable to be seen or noticed） 【例】There was no **observable** change in three days here.
discernible	[di'sə:nəbl] a. 可辨别的（can be seen, noticed, or understood） 【例】A small boat was clearly **discernible** in the middle of the lake.
palpable	['pælpəbl] a. 可触知的，明显的（easily felt or noticed） 【例】There are **palpable** differences between the service offered by the two hotels.
obvious	['ɔbviəs] a. 显而易见的（easily seen, recognized or understood; clear） 【例】The most **obvious** explanation is not always the correct one.

visible ['vizəbl] *a.* 可见的，看得见的（capable of being seen）

【例】The meadows are hardly *visible* from the house.

【用】be visible to sb. /sth. 对…是可见的

apparent [ə'pærənt] *a.* 显然的，清晰可见的（clear or manifest to the understanding）

【例】It was soon *apparent* to the crowd that our team was winning the match.

distinct [dis'tiŋkt] *a.* 清楚的，明显的（distinguishable to the eye or mind as discrete）

【例】There was a *distinct* note of annoyance in Mary's reply.

evident ['evidənt] *a.* 明显的，清楚的（clear to the vision or understanding）

【例】From the quick success of the business，it was *evident* that he had run it wisely.

【用】be evident to sth. …是很明显的

perceptible [pə'septəbl] *a.* 可察觉的（capable of being perceived especially by the senses）

【例】Tom still walks with a *perceptible* limp.

【用】be perceptible to sb. 对…是可感知的

plain [plein] *a.* 清晰的，明白的（free of impediments to view）

【例】The message was short，but the meaning was *plain* enough.

【用】in plain English 说话简洁明了；make oneself plain 清楚表达

seeable ['si:əbl] *a.* 看得见的，可见的（being able to be seen）

【例】The light was so weak that it wouldn't be *seeable* ten meters away.

明智的（judicious, wise, sage, sagacious, thoughtful, astute）

judicious [dʒu:'diʃəs] *a.* 明智的（showing intelligence and good judgment）

【例】Jon's choice was usually *judicious*.

wise [waiz] *a.* 英明的，明智的（able to make good choices and decisions because one has a lot of experience）

【例】What a *wise* man we have for an Emperor!

【用】be wise after the event 事后聪明

sage	[seidʒ] *a.* 贤明的；明智的（wise and showing good judgment） 【例】The teacher gave me a *sage* advice about my study.
sagacious	[sə'geiʃəs] *a.* 聪明的（wise and able to make good practical decisions） 【例】I coincided in opinion against the old feudal system with the *sagacious* man.
thoughtful	['θɔːtful] *a.* 沉思的，思考的（thinking seriously about something） 【例】Mort was *thoughtful* for a moment before giving his answer.
astute	[ə'stjuːt] *a.* 精明的（good at judging situations and people quickly and able to use this knowledge for personal benefit） 【例】The boss's quite *astute* but I am trying to kill him.

凝视，注视（gaze, stare, peer, ogle, eye, scrutinize, watch, survey, scan, glare）

gaze	[geiz] *v.* 凝视，注视（to fix the eyes in a steady intent look often with eagerness or studious attention） 【例】Father used to *gaze* at the famous painting. 【用】gaze on/upon sth. 看…
stare	[steə] *v.* 盯，凝视（to look fixedly often with wide-open eyes） 【例】Don't *stare* at me like that. 【用】stare at sth. 凝视…
peer	[piə] *v.* 仔细看，费力地看（to look very carefully, especially because something is difficult to see） 【例】Sandy *peered* at the neighbors from behind the curtain. 【用】peer at sth. 凝视…；peer through sth. 费力地看…

ogle　　　['əugl] *v.* 注视（to glance with amorous invitation or challenge）

【例】Paula was not used to everyone *ogling* at her while she undressed backstage.

【用】ogle at sb. 色迷迷地看…

eye　　　[ai] *v.* 看，注视（to look at someone or something carefully）

【例】The man *eyed* every change in the stock market.

scrutinize　　　['skru:tinaiz] *v.* 详细检查，细察（to examine closely and minutely）

【例】Her purpose was to *scrutinize* Claude's features to see if he was an honest man.

watch　　　[wɔtʃ] *v.* 注视，观看（to look at）

【例】He *watched* the barman prepare the beer he had ordered.

【用】watch out（for）密切注意，提防，留神

survey　　　[sə'vei] *v.* 审视，观察（to look at or examine something）

【例】Two women were *surveying* the other people on the platform.

scan　　　[skæn] *v.* 细看，审视（to examine by point-by-point observation or checking）

【例】Tracy was nervous and kept *scanning* the crowd for Paul.

glare　　　[gleə] *v.* 怒目而视（to look at someone or something in an angry way）

【例】The teacher *glared* at the noisy student.

【用】glare at sb. 对…怒目而视

虐待（abuse, mistreat, maltreat, ill-treat, torture）

abuse　　　[ə'bju:z] / [ə'bju:s] *v.* / *n.* 虐待（to treat someone in a cruel or violent way）

【例】Prisoners reported being regularly *abused* by their guards.

mistreat　　　[,mis'tri:t] *v.* 虐待（某人）（to treat someone in an unfair or cruel way）

【例】The animals used in the movie are in no way *mistreated*.

maltreat　　　[,mæl'tri:t] *v.*（暴力）虐待（to be violent or cruel to a person or animal）

【例】The man was accused of *maltreating* his wife.

ill-treat ［ˌilˈtriːt］ v. 虐待（to treat someone in a cruel or unkind way）

【例】The little girl felt the life was tough because she was *ill-treated* by her step-mother.

torture ［ˈtɔːtʃə］ v. 对…施以苦刑，折磨（to hurt a person or animal deliberately in a cruel way）

【例】Three members of the group had been *tortured* to death.

攀登，爬（climb, ascend, scale, mount, clamber, shinny, scramble）

climb ［klaim］ v. 攀登，爬（to go upward or raise oneself especially by grasping or clutching with the hands）

【例】A car slowly *climbed* the hill.

【用】climb down 爬下；撤回

ascend ［əˈsend］ v. 攀登（to climb a mountain, stairs, etc.）

【例】The car rapidly *ascended* the steep grade.

【用】ascend to 升至…；追溯到…

scale ［skeil］ v. 攀登，爬越（to climb to or over the top of a high steep object such as a mountain or a wall）

【例】The prisoner *scaled* the wall and escaped.

mount ［maunt］ v. 登上（to go upstairs or to climb up somewhere）

【例】The man *mounted* the look-out point for a view of the bay.

【用】mount up 增长，上升

clamber ［ˈklæmbə］ v. 爬上，攀登（to climb something with difficulty, using one's hands and feet）

【例】They *clambered* up the stone wall.

【用】clamber up sth. 爬上…

shinny ［ˈʃini］ v. 攀爬（to move oneself up or down something vertical with hands and feet together）

【例】It is very dangerous to **shinny** up that high wall.

【用】shinny up sth. 爬上…

scramble　['skræmbl] *v.* 攀登，爬 (to move or climb hastily on hands and knees)

【例】Tourists were **scrambling** over the rocks looking for the perfect camera angle.

蹒跚 (limp, hobble, stagger, hitch, totter)

limp　[limp] *v.* 蹒跚 (to walk with difficulty because of an injured leg or foot)

【例】The player **limped** off the football field.

【用】limp along 蹒跚

hobble　['hɔbl] *v.* 蹒跚 (to walk slowly and with difficulty because of sore or injured feet)

【例】I hurt my foot and had to **hobble**.

【用】hobble across/along/down 蹒跚

stagger　['stægə] *v.* 蹒跚，摇晃 (to walk in an uncontrolled way, as if under a great weight)

【例】The wounded soldier **staggered** along.

【用】stagger along 摇摇晃晃地走

hitch　[hitʃ] *v.* 蹒跚 (to move with halts and jerks)

【例】An old man **hitched** along on his cane.

【用】hitch a ride〈口〉要求（免费）搭车

totter　['tɔtə] *v.* 步履蹒跚 (to stand or move in a way that is not steady)

【例】The patient was able, after five days, to **totter** feebly out upon the veranda.

庞大的，巨大的 (huge, gigantic, colossal, immense, enormous, gargantuan, prodigious, whopping, tremendous, jumbo, stupendous)

huge　[hju:dʒ] *a.* 庞大的，巨大的 (very large or extensive)

【例】The **huge** monster was brought to the earth by a spaceship.

gigantic [dʒaiˈgæntik] *a.* 巨大的，庞大的（exceeding the usual or expected（as in size, force, or prominence））

【例】The new airplane looked like a *gigantic* bird.

colossal [kəˈlɔsəl] *a.* 巨大的，庞大的（extremely great or large）

【例】The Titanic was a *colossal* ship.

immense [iˈmens] *a.* 巨大的，广大的（marked by greatness especially in size or degree; especially transcending ordinary means of measurement）

【例】Kevin made an *immense* amount of money in his business.

enormous [iˈnɔːməs] *a.* 巨大的，极大的（marked by extraordinarily great size, number, or degree; especially exceeding usual bounds or accepted notions）

【例】No small company like this could afford such *enormous* expenses.

gargantuan [gɑːˈgæntjuən] *a.* 巨大的，庞大的（extremely big）

【例】All of Washington is under the shadow of this *gargantuan* alien craft.

prodigious [prəuˈdidʒəs] *a.* （在体积、数量或程度上）大得令人惊叹的；巨大的（extraordinary in bulk, quantity, or degree）

【例】I have a *prodigious* amount of work to do before I leave.

whopping [ˈwɔpiŋ] *a.* 巨大的，庞大的（extremely large）

【例】Mary has a *whopping* pile of laundry to do this weekend.

tremendous [triˈmendəs] *a.* 惊人的；巨大的（notable by reason of extreme size, power, greatness, or excellence or unusually large）

【例】Setting off firecrackers would make a *tremendous* noise and cause serious air pollution.

jumbo [ˈdʒʌmbəu] *a.* 特大的，巨大的（larger than other things of the same type）

【例】The waitress brought us a platter containing five *jumbo* lobsters.

【用】jumbo jet 大型喷气式客机

stupendous [stjuːˈpendəs] *a.* 巨大的，大得惊人的（of amazing size or greatness）

【例】The mayor has done a *stupendous* job of fighting crimes.

胖的 (fat, obese, corpulent, plump, rotund, stout, chubby, paunchy)

fat　[fæt] *a.* 多脂肪的，肥胖的 (containing too much fat, large in size)
【例】Kate can eat whatever she likes and never gets *fat*.

obese　[əu'biːs] *a.* 肥胖的 (too fat, in a way that is dangerous for one's health)
【例】Growing *obese* is dangerous for your health.

corpulent　['kɔːpjulənt] *a.* 肥胖的，肥大的 (excessively fat)
【例】Our teacher got a rather *corpulent* face.

plump　[plʌmp] *a.* 丰满的，胖乎乎的 (slightly fat, in a pleasant way)
【例】Bob's mother was *plump*.

rotund　[rəu'tʌnd] *a.* (人)圆胖的 (round and fat)
【例】Monica saw a stout, *rotund* little man.

stout　[staut] *a.* 发胖的，胖而大的 (rather fat or of heavy build)
【例】My father was a *stout* man.

chubby　['tʃʌbi] *a.* 丰满的 (slightly fat, in the way a healthy baby or young child is)
【例】The baby has a cute *chubby* face.

paunchy　['pɔːntʃi] *a.* 大腹便便的 (having a potbelly)
【例】Three *paunchy* middle-aged men stopped her and asked where the station was.

喷射 (jet, stream, spew, spray, spring)

jet　[dʒet] *v.* 喷射 (to emit a stream)
【例】The water *jetted* out from the pipe.
【用】jet sth. out 喷出…；jet sth. from/out of sth. 使…从…里喷出

stream　[striːm] *v.* 流(出)，涌(出) (to produce a liquid or gas in a continuous flow)
【例】Tears *streamed* down his face when he heard the bad news.

spew　[spjuː] *v.* 喷出 (to flow out or make something flow out with a lot of force)

【例】Under the bridge，pipes *spew* sewage into the river.

【用】spew out 喷出

spray   ［sprei］ *v.* 向…喷射，喷（to be forced out of a container through an opening into the air）

【例】Butler says he doesn't want you to *spray* beer in his face.

【用】spray on/over sb./sth. 向…喷射雾状的液体

spring   ［spriŋ］ *v.* 涌现（to issue with speed and force or as a stream）

【例】The sweat *sprang* up on the player's forehead.

【用】spring a leak 破裂漏水

疲惫的（tired, exhausted, fatigued, weary, jaded, wear out）

tired   ［'taiəd］ *a.* 疲劳的，累的（needing to rest or sleep）

【例】I'm very *tired* after work.

【用】be tired of sb./sth./doing sth. 对…感到疲倦或厌烦

exhausted   ［ig'zɔːstid］ *a.* 疲惫的，精疲力竭的（extremely tired and without enough energy to do anything else）

【例】They are totally *exhausted* and virtually asleep.

fatigued   ［fə'tiːgid］ *a.* 疲惫的，疲乏的（feeling extremely tired, either physically or mentally）

【例】The whole scout troop felt *fatigued* after climbing the mountain.

weary   ［'wiəri］ *a.* 疲劳的，疲倦的（very tired, especially because of hard work or activity）

【例】Ted collapsed onto his bed，too *weary* to get changed.

【用】be weary of sth. 对…感到厌倦

jaded   ［'dʒeidid］ *a.* 疲惫不堪的（tired and lacking zest）

【例】These guys looked *jaded* after an all-night party.

wear out   疲惫不堪的，筋疲力尽的

【例】Alex was *worn out* after the swimming marathon.

平静的（calm, composed, dispassionate, sober, collected）

calm   ［kɑːm］ *a.* 冷静的，平静的（not affected by strong emotions such as excitement，anger，or fear）

【例】She tried to stay *calm* and collected，but couldn't.

【用】stay/keep/remain calm 保持冷静

composed　［kəm'pəuzd］*a.* 镇静的，平静的（having one's feelings and expression under control）

【例】She talked in a *composed* voice to the reporter about her terrible ordeal.

dispassionate　［dis'pæʃənət］*a.* 冷静的（able to make fair judgments or decisions）

【例】I was too angry to make a *dispassionate* judgement.

【用】be dispassionate about sth. 对…很冷静或无动于衷

sober　['səubə］*a.* 未醉的，清醒的（not drunk；sensible）

【例】I will continue this conversation with you tomorrow，when you are *sober*.

collected　［kə'lektid］*a.* 镇定的，镇静的（able to control nervous or confused feelings）

【例】The soldier always stays cool and *collected* in a crisis.

【用】remain/stay collected 保持镇定

评价，估计（evaluate, appraise, assess, estimate, assay, gauge, rate

evaluate　［i'væljueit］*v.* 评价，估计（to think carefully about sth. before making a judgment about its value, importance, or quality）

【例】The market situation was difficult to *evaluate*.

appraise　［ə'preiz］*v.* 评价，评定（to form an opinion about how successful, effective, etc. somebody or something is）

【例】The diamond was *appraised* at ten thousand dollars.

assess　［ə'ses］*v.* 评定，估价（to carefully consider a situation, person, or problem in order to make a judgment）

【例】They are *assessing* Bill's house.

【用】assess sth. at sth. 评定为…（某数额）

estimate　['estimeit］*v.* 估计，估量（to say what you think an amount or value will be）

【例】We *estimated* that it would take three months to finish the work.

【用】estimate sth. at sth. 估计为…

assay	[ə'sei] *v.* 评价，估价 (to evaluate)
	【例】Professors held a conference to **assay** Luxun's literary efforts.
gauge	[geidʒ] *v.* 评估 (to make a judgment or guess about a situation, action, or person)
	【例】One's mood can be **gauged** by his reaction to the most trivial incidents.
rate	[reit] *v.* 对…估价，评估 (to consider that somebody or something has a particular quality or has achieved a particular standard or level)
	【例】My car was **rated** at only 1,000 dollars.
	【用】rate sb. /sth. as sth. 评估为…

评论 (comment, remark, observe, criticize, touch on, expound)

comment	['kɔment] *v.* 评论 (to make a written or spoken remark, especially giving an opinion)
	【例】Everyone **commented** on Ginny's new hat.
	【用】comment on sth. 对…发表评论
remark	[ri'mɑːk] *v.* 谈论，评论 (to express one's opinion about something)
	【例】Mother **remarked** that my hands would be better for a wash.
	【用】remark on sth. 对…评论
observe	[əb'zəːv] *v.* 评说，评论 (to make a written or spoken remark about someone or something)
	【例】I **observed** nothing on this subject.
	【用】observe on sth. 对…发表评论
criticize	['kritisaiz] *v.* 批评，非难 (to say what you think is wrong or bad about something)
	【例】The regime has been harshly **criticized** for serious human rights violations.
	【用】criticize sb. /sth. for sth. 因…责备…
touch on	谈到，论及
	【例】Their long talk **touched on** a multitude of topics.
expound	[ik'spaund] *v.* 详加说明或解释 (to explain something or express one's opinion about it in detail)

【例】Ford continued to *expound* his views on economics and politics.

【用】expound on/upon sth. 详述…

破坏，毁灭 (destroy, demolish, wreck, devastate, wipe out, eradicate, crush, raze, obliterate)

destroy	[di'strɔi] *v.* 破坏，毁灭 (to damage something so severely that it no longer exists or can never return to its normal state) 【例】The whole city was *destroyed* by the big fire. 【用】destroy oneself 自杀
demolish	[di'mɔliʃ] *v.* 破坏，拆除 (to deliberately destroy a building) 【例】The old factory will be *demolished* at the end of the year.
wreck	[rek] *v.* 破坏 (to severely damage a vehicle or building) 【例】The two cars were *wrecked* in the collision.
devastate	['devəsteit] *v.* 毁坏，破坏 (to seriously damage or completely destroy something) 【例】A few days before, a fire had *devastated* large parts of Windsor Castle.
wipe out	消灭 (to destroy or get rid of something completely) 【例】We want to *wipe out* world hunger by the year 2010.
eradicate	[i'rædikeit] *v.* 根除，消灭 (to get rid of something completely, especially something bad) 【例】The government made great effort to *eradicate* superstition. 【用】eradicate sth. from sth. 从…消灭…
crush	[krʌʃ] *v.* 压碎，碾碎 (to hit or press something so hard that one damages it severely or destroys it, especially by making its shape flatter) 【例】Scott's vehicle was *crushed* by an army tank. 【用】crush down 压倒，碾碎
raze	[reiz] *v.* 彻底破坏或摧毁 (to completely destroy a building or town) 【例】The air strike *razed* the city to the ground. 【用】raze out 削去

| obliterate | [ə'blitəreit] *v.* 彻底破坏或毁灭（某事物）(to destroy something completely)
【例】Their nuclear warheads are enough to ***obliterate*** the whole world several times over. |

普遍存在的 (everywhere, ubiquitous, omnipresent, widespread, all-over, pervasive, universal, worldwide)

everywhere	['evriweə] *a.* 到处，各处 (in every place or part) 【例】Dust is ***everywhere*** in this world.
ubiquitous	[ju:'bikwitəs] *a.* 无处不在的，普遍存在的 (existing or being everywhere at the same time) 【例】We were plagued throughout our travel by the ***ubiquitous*** mosquitoes.
omnipresent	[ˌɔmni'prezənt] *a.* 无处不在的 (present in all places at all times) 【例】During those years everybody was filled with the ***omnipresent*** fear of war.
widespread	['waid'spred] *a.* 分布（或散布）广的，普遍的 (widely extended or spread out) 【例】Paul's proposals have attracted ***widespread*** support.
all-over	['ɔ:l,əuvə] *a.* 遍布表面的 (covering the surface of something completely) 【例】I'd like a piece of wallpaper with an ***all-over*** pattern.
pervasive	[pə:'veisiv] *a.* 遍及的，弥漫的 (pervading or tending to pervade) 【例】The influence of the army was ***pervasive*** in national life.
universal	[ˌju:ni'və:səl] *a.* 普遍的 (involving all the members of a group or society) 【例】The insurance industry has produced its own proposals for ***universal*** health care.
worldwide	['wə:ldwaid] *a.* 全世界的 (extended throughout or involving the entire world) 【例】Hardware-damaging virus is a ***worldwide*** problem.

欺骗，蒙蔽（deceive, mislead, delude, trick, defraud, beguile）

deceive
［di'si:v］ v. 欺骗，蒙蔽（to trick someone by behaving in a dishonest way）
【例】The seller ***deceived*** his employer by manipulating the accounts of the business.
【用】deceive sb. into doing sth. 蒙蔽…做…

mislead
［ˌmis'li:d］ v. （使）误入歧途；（使）误解（to lead in a wrong direction or into a mistaken action or belief often by deliberate deceit）
【例】She was ***misled*** by the sign into going to the wrong way.
【用】mislead sb. into doing sth. 骗…做…

delude
［di'lu:d］ v. 欺骗，哄骗（to make someone believe something that is not true）
【例】Arthur had ***deluded*** himself into believing that it would all come right in the end.
【用】delude oneself 自欺

trick
［trik］ v. 欺诈，哄骗（to cheat or to practice trickery or deception）
【例】Stephen is going to be pretty angry when he finds out how you ***tricked*** him.
【用】trick sb. into doing sth. 哄骗…做…

defraud
［di'frɔ:d］ v. 欺骗，骗取（to get money from a person or organization in a dishonest way）
【例】They conspired to ***defraud*** the federal government of millions of dollars in income taxes.
【用】defraud sb. of sth. 从…骗取…

beguile　　　　[bi'gail] *v.* 欺骗（to persuade or trick someone into doing something，especially by saying nice things to them）

【例】I was *beguiled* by Don's flattery into trusting him.

欺骗，愚弄 (fool, kid, cheat, dupe)

fool　　　　[fu:l] *v.* 欺骗，愚弄（to trick someone by making them believe something that is not true）

【例】The father taught the boy how to *fool* a trout with a little bit of floating fur and feather.

【用】fool sb. into doing sth. 愚弄…做…

kid　　　　[kid] *v.* 戏弄（to say something that is not true，especially as a joke）

【例】Are you *kidding* me? 你在开玩笑吗？

【用】just/only kidding 开玩笑

cheat　　　　[tʃi:t] *v.* 欺骗，骗取（to deprive of something valuable by the use of deceit or fraud）

【例】The department store *cheated* customers by overcharging them for purchases.

【用】cheat sb. (out) of sth. 欺骗…的…

dupe　　　　[dju:p] *v.* 欺骗，愚弄（to trick someone into believing something that is not true or into doing something that is stupid or illegal）

【例】The agency *duped* her into signing up for ＄200 worth of lessons.

【用】dupe sb. into doing sth. 愚弄…做…

奇怪的 (queer, odd, weird, bizarre, abnormal, singular, funny, quaint)

queer　　　　[kwiə] *a.* 奇怪的，异常的（strange，especially in an unpleasant way）

【例】Have you heard some *queer* noises outside the window?

【用】a queer fish 古怪的人

odd [ɔd] *a.* 奇怪的，古怪的（unusual or unexpected in a way that attracts your interest or attention）

【例】It was *odd* that Paula had never left the village.

【用】an odd fish 古怪的人

weird [wiəd] *a.* 古怪的，离奇的（strange and unusual, sometimes in a way that upsets you）

【例】It made me feel *weird* to go back to Liverpool.

bizarre [bi'zɑː] *a.* 奇形怪状的，怪诞的（strange and difficult to explain）

【例】The game was also notable for the *bizarre* behavior of the team's manager.

abnormal [æb'nɔːməl] *a.* 反常的，变态的（not usual or typical）

【例】The little child has an *abnormal* fear of strangers.

singular ['siŋgjulə] *a.* 奇怪的，奇特的（noticeable because of being strange or unusual）

【例】All the children listened to his *singular* adventures with eager attention.

funny ['fʌni] *a.* 稀奇的，古怪的（strange or unusual）

【例】It's *funny* how love can come and go.

quaint [kweint] *a.* 离奇有趣的（interesting or attractive with a slightly strange and old-fashioned quality）

【例】I found that lady's hat very *quaint*.

起源，发生（originate, initiate, inaugurate）

originate [ə'ridʒəneit] *v.* 起源（to begin to exist or appear for the first time）

【例】The bullfight *originated* in Spain.

【用】originate in/from/with 起源于，产生于

initiate [i'niʃieit] *v.* 开始，发起（to make something start）

【例】They wanted to *initiate* a discussion on economics.

inaugurate [i'nɔːgjureit] *v.* 开始，开创（to start or introduce something new and important）

【例】The Ministry of Foreign Affairs *inaugurated* a new immigration policy yesterday.

起皱 (rumple, wrinkle, crinkle, crumple, crease, ripple, furrow, dishevel, mess up, muss up)

rumple	[ˈrʌmpl] v. 弄皱，弄乱 (to wrinkle or form into folds or creases) 【例】Roger **rumpled** up the paper and tossed it in the garbage.
wrinkle	[ˈrɪŋkl] v. (使)起皱纹 (to form, or cause something to form, small lines or folds) 【例】The medicine made Tim **wrinkle** up his nose in disgust.
crinkle	[ˈkrɪŋkl] v. (使)变皱 (to make a lot of small messy folds) 【例】The end of the map burns and **crinkles**. 【用】crinkle sth. (up) 使…起皱
crumple	[ˈkrʌmpl] v. 弄皱，压皱 (to crush something such as paper or cloth so that it forms messy folds) 【例】I quickly **crumpled** up the letter and shoved it in my pocket. 【用】crumple sth. into sth. 把…压成…；crumple sth. up 把…压皱
crease	[kriːs] v. 弄皱，起皱 (to make lines on cloth or paper by folding or crushing it) 【例】Alice was careful not to **crease** her dress.
ripple	[ˈrɪpl] v. 起涟漪 (moving gently in small waves) 【例】A slight wind **rippled** the lake's surface.
furrow	[ˈfʌrəu] v. 弄皱 (to form grooves or deep wrinkles) 【例】Gavin strokes his chin and **furrows** his brow, sinking deep into thought.
dishevel	[diˈʃevəl] v. 使蓬乱，弄皱 (to loosen and let fall in disarray) 【例】Jon's robe is **disheveled**.
mess up	搞乱，弄脏 【例】Who **messed up** my clean bedroom?
muss up	凌乱，弄乱 【例】Tom **musses up** the boy's hair.

强调 (stress, emphasize, punctuate, accentuate, underscore, underline, accent)

stress　[stres] *v.* 强调，着重 (to emphasize something such as an idea, fact, or detail)

【例】China's leaders have *stressed* the need for increased cooperation between the Third World countries.

emphasize　['emfəsaiz] *v.* 强调，着重 (to give particular importance or attention to something)

【例】The speaker *emphasized* the difference between the interests of the individual and the interests of the community.

punctuate　['pʌŋktjueit] *v.* 强调，加强 (to stress or emphasize)

【例】Mike *punctuated* his remarks with gestures.

accentuate　[æk'sentjueit] *v.* 突出，强调 (to emphasize something or make it more noticeable)

【例】His shaven head *accentuates* his large round face.

underscore　[ˌʌndə'skɔː] *v.* 强调 (to emphasize something or show that it is important)

【例】The Labor Department figures *underscore* the shaky state of the economic recovery.

underline　[ˌʌndə'lain] *v.* 强调 (to show clearly that something is important or true)

【例】The decision to keep Billy in hospital for a second night *underlines* the seriousness of his injury.

accent　['æksənt] *v.* 强调，侧重 (to focus attention on something, to emphasize something)

【例】This program *accents* the development of leadership.

强迫，迫使 (force, coerce, compel, oblige, pressure, press, exact, constrain, push)

force　[fɔːs] *v.* 强迫，迫使 (to make someone do something that they do not want to do)

【例】I *forced* myself to practice daily.

【用】force sb. to do sth. 强迫…做…

coerce ［kəu'ə:s］ *v.* 强制，迫使（to make someone do something by using force or threats）

【例】The government sent troops to *coerce* the strikers into compliance.

【用】coerce sb. into sth. /doing sth. 强迫或威胁…做…

compel ［kəm'pel］ *v.* 强迫（to cause to do or occur by overwhelming pressure）

【例】Duty *compelled* the soldiers to volunteer for the mission.

【用】compel sb. to do sth. 强迫…做…

oblige ［ə'blaidʒ］ *v.* 迫使（to make someone do something because it is a law, a rule, or a duty）

【例】They were *obliged* to leave their homeland.

【用】be/feel obliged to do sth. 不得不做…

pressure ['preʃə] *v.* 对…施加压力（或影响）（try to make someone do something）

【例】The children are not *pressured* to empty their plates.

【用】pressure sb. into (doing) sth. 强迫…做…

press ［pres］ *v.* 催促，逼迫（to try in a determined way to make someone do something or tell you something）

【例】Our manager is *pressing* us to make a quick decision.

【用】press sb. into (doing) sth. 强迫…做…

exact ［ig'zækt］ *v.* 强求（to get something from someone by threatening or using your authority）

【例】My girlfriend *exacted* a promise from me.

【用】exact sth. from sb. 从…强索…

constrain ［kən'strein］ *v.* 强迫（to make someone do something that they do not want to do）

【例】They *constrained* us to instant action.

【用】feel constrained to do sth. 不得不做…

push ［puʃ］ *v.* 催逼，逼迫（to make someone in a determined way do something they do not want to do）

【例】There is no point in **pushing** them unless they are talented and enjoy it.

【用】push sb. to do sth. 逼迫…做…

强制性的 (mandatory, required, obligatory, requisite, compulsory, demanded)

mandatory　['mændətəri；'mændə,tɔːri] *a*. 强制性的 (ordered by a law or rule)

【例】It's **mandatory** to wear a seat belt in this country.

required　[ri'kwaiəd] *a*. 必需的；〈美〉必修的（大学课程）(demanded as necessary or essential)

【例】Chinese was taught as a separate and **required** course here.

【用】required reading 必读物

obligatory　[ɔ'bligətəri] *a*. 强制性的 (binding in law or conscience)

【例】It is **obligatory** for members to be insured.

requisite　['rekwizit] *a*. （成功）必要的 (necessary for a particular purpose)

【例】Decision is a **requisite** quality to a boss.

compulsory　[kəm'pʌlsəri] *a*. 强制性的 (mandatory or enforced)

【例】A school outfit is no longer **compulsory** now.

demanded　[di'mɑːndid] *a*. 要求的 (asking or calling for with authority)

【例】The **demanded** witness refused to make the confirmation.

强壮的 (strong, tough, muscular, athletic, sinewy, brawny)

strong　[strɔŋ；strɔːŋ] *a*. 强壮的，强有力的 (physically powerful and healthy)

【例】Are you **strong** enough to carry that heavy box?

tough　[tʌf] *a*. 强壮的 (capable of enduring strain, hardship, or severe labor)

【例】Christopher used to be a **tough** soldier.

muscular ['mʌskjulə] *a.* 强健的，强壮的（of or relating to physical strength）

【例】All that exercise has made me quite ***muscular***.

athletic [æθ'letik] *a.* 体格健壮的（physically strong，active，and good at sports）

【例】Dennis is a tall，***athletic*** young man.

sinewy ['sinjuːi] *a.* 强壮有力的，肌肉发达的（tough，having strong sinews）

【例】The acrobat has ***sinewy*** arms.

brawny ['brɔːni] *a.* （人）强壮的（physically strong，with big muscles）

【例】David was a blacksmith and he had ***brawny*** arms.

敲；碰撞 (knock，bump，bang，punch，pound，pummel，batter，thump，rap)

knock [nɔk] *v.* 敲；碰撞（to hit something，causing damage or harm）

【例】I ***knocked*** my head on the wall in the dark.

【用】knock the bottom out of sth. 使…垮台

bump [bʌmp] *v.* 碰撞（to hit against something solid once or many times）

【例】The car ***bumped*** into a tree.

【用】bump against/into 碰撞或敲击到…

bang [bæŋ] *v.* 猛撞；"砰"地敲（或推、扔）（to hit something hard，making a loud noise）

【例】There is someone ***banging*** outside.

punch [pʌntʃ] *v.* 重击，猛击（to hit someone or something with your fist，usually as hard as you can）

【例】The boxer ***punched*** Tom on the nose.

pound [paund] *v.* 强烈打击，（连续）猛击（to hit something several times with a lot of force）

【例】The troops was ***pounded*** with mortar fire.

【用】pound away at/against/on sth. 连续地猛击…

pummel ['pʌməl] *v.* （用拳）接连地打（to hit someone or something many times，especially with your fists）

【例】Robinson ***pummeled*** the bully soundly.

batter	['bætə] v. 连续猛击 (to hit something very hard several times)

【例】Bob will **batter** you to a pulp if you abuse his sister.

【用】batter on/at sth. 连续猛击…

thump	[θʌmp] v. 重击，捶击 (to hit against something heavily)

【例】They beat, kicked and **thumped** the poor boy.

rap	[ræp] v. （轻而快地）敲击，急敲 (to hit something hard and quickly)

【例】He **rapped** the table with his fist.

钦佩，赞赏 (admire, regard, esteem, respect, look up to, revere, worship, honor)

admire	[əd'maiə] v. 钦佩，赞赏 (to have a feeling of great respect for someone or something)

【例】I **admired** the way Sally had coped with life.

【用】admire sb. for sth. 因…钦佩…

regard	[ri'gɑːd] v. 尊敬，尊重 (to show respect or consideration for something)

【例】Sophia **regards** her teachers highly.

esteem	[i'stiːm] v. 尊重，尊敬 (to admire and respect someone)

【例】I **esteem** the man for his honesty.

respect	[ri'spekt] v. 尊敬；尊重 (to consider something worthy of high regard)

【例】I want him to **respect** me as a career woman.

【用】respect oneself 自重，自尊

look up to	赞赏或尊敬某人 (to admire and respect someone)

【例】Grace was a popular girl and a lot of younger boys **looked up to** her.

revere	[ri'viə] v. 尊敬，尊崇 (to have a lot of respect and admiration for someone or something)

【例】Today he's still **revered** as the father of the nation.

【用】revere sb./sth. for sth. 因…而尊敬…；revere sb./sth. as sth. …被尊为…

worship	['wə:ʃip] v. 崇拜，崇敬 (to love and admire someone or something very much)

【例】Most people enjoy going to church and **worshipping** God.

honor	['ɔnə] v. 尊敬，给以荣誉 (to show your respect or admiration for someone，especially by giving them a prize or title，or by praising them publicly)

【例】Last week two American surgeons were **honored** with the 2,000 Nobel Prize for Medicine and Physiology.

【用】honor sb. /sth. with sth. 向…致敬；给…以荣誉

勤奋的 (hardworking, diligent, industrious, assiduous)

hardworking	['hɑ:d,wə:kiŋ] a. 勤勉的 (working with effort and energy)

【例】Wendy was **hardworking** and reliable.

diligent	['dilidʒənt] a. 勤奋的，勤勉的 (characterized by steady, earnest，and energetic effort)

【例】Lily has been a **diligent** student of art.

【用】be diligent in sth. /doing sth. 认真做…

industrious	[in'dʌstriəs] a. 勤奋的，勤勉的 (always working very hard)

【例】A willing，**industrious** man always strives to succeed.

assiduous	[ə'sidjuəs] a. 勤勉的 (hard-working and thorough)

【例】The statistics were the result of five years' **assiduous** research.

【用】be assiduous in sth. 认真地做…

轻视 (scorn, disdain, despise, look down on/upon)

scorn	[skɔ:n] v. 轻蔑，瞧不起 (to treat someone or something as if they do not deserve your approval or respect)

【例】People always **scorn** me because I have a single parent.

disdain	[dis'dein] v. 鄙视，蔑视 (to think that someone or something is not important and does not deserve any respect)

【例】The poor man was rather strange and often **disdained** other people's offer of help.

despise	[di'spaiz] *v.* 鄙视，看不起（to hate someone or something and have no respect for them） 【例】How I *despised* myself for my cowardice! 【用】despise sb./sth. for sth. 因…而鄙视…
look down on/upon	看不起，轻视 【例】Alice *looked down on/upon* those who had never been to university.

情感，情绪（feeling, affection, emotion, passion, sentiment）

feeling	['fiːliŋ] *n.* 感觉，感情（a thing that is felt through the mind or the sense; emotion） 【例】Your words offended Wendy and hurt her *feelings*. 【用】bad/ill feeling 反感，不满；hurt one's feelings 伤害…的感情
affection	[ə'fekʃən] *n.* 喜爱，情感（a feeling of liking and caring about someone or something） 【例】Anna's *affections* tend to be variable. 【用】affection for 对…的热爱
emotion	[i'məuʃən] *n.* 感情，激情，情绪（a feeling that you experience, for example, love, fear, or anger） 【例】Jealousy is an uncomfortable and destructive *emotion*.
passion	['pæʃən] *n.* 激情，热情（a powerful emotion such as love or anger） 【例】Jason argued with his classmates with great *passion*. 【用】passion for 对…强烈的爱
sentiment	['sentimənt] *n.* 情感，情绪（feelings of sympathy, sadness, or love that may seem inappropriate） 【例】There is no room for *sentiment* in negotiation. 【用】popular sentiment 大众心理

情况（condition, circumstance, state, case, posture, status）

condition	[kən'diʃən] *n.* 情形，状况（the situation or environment in which something happens or exists）

【例】The criminal complained bitterly about prison **conditions**.

【用】in poor condition 破旧不堪

circumstance ['sə:kəmstəns] *n.* 境况，情况 (the facts or conditions that affect a situation)

【例】They will investigate the **circumstances** surrounding the child's death.

【用】under/in... circumstances 在…的环境或情况里；in/under no circumstances 无论怎样都不

state [steit] *n.* 状态，情况 (the condition of something at a particular time)

【例】The city is drifting into a **state** of chaos after the flood.

【用】a state of 一种…的状态

case [keis] *n.* 情况，事实 (a situation or set of conditions, especially one involving a particular person or thing)

【例】This was the **case** in the past，but now lifestyle is changing rapidly.

【用】if that's the case 如果那是真的

posture ['pɔstʃə] *n.* 状态，情况 (the situation of something)

【例】The scandal was an awkward **posture** for the entire family.

status ['steitəs] *n.* 情形，状况 (a position of affairs，especially in political or commercial contexts)

【例】They are working on a report about the **status** of the negotiation.

请求 (beg, pray, request, entreat, ask for, plead, appeal, implore)

beg [beg] *v.* 请求，恳求 (to ask for help, an opportunity, etc.)

【例】Lily had written a letter **begging** her husband to come back.

【用】beg sb. (not) to do sth. 恳求…做 (不做)…；beg (sb.) for sth. (向…) 祈求…

pray [prei] *v.* 祈祷，请求 (to speak to God or a Saint, for example，to give thanks or ask for help)

【例】The little girl **prayed** that her mother would soon recover.

【用】pray for sth. 祈祷…

request	[ri'kwest] *v.* 请求，要求（to ask for something，or ask someone to do something，in a polite way） 【例】The factory ***requested*** a large amount of fuel for its needs. 【用】request sb. to do sth. 要求…做…
entreat	[in'tri:t] *v.* 恳求，乞求（to ask someone earnestly or anxiously to do something） 【例】The criminal ***entreated*** the jury for mercy.
ask for	请求（to speak or write to someone for letting them give you something） 【例】He's always reluctant to ***ask for*** anyone's help.
plead	[pli:d] *v.* 恳求，请求（to ask for something in an urgent or emotional way） 【例】She ***pleaded*** with the manager to give her a chance. 【用】plead for sth. 恳求…；plead with sb. to do sth. 恳求…做…
appeal	[ə'pi:l] *v.* 呼吁，恳求（to make an urgent request for people to give you something that you need） 【例】The besieged nation ***appealed*** to the neighbor for aid. 【用】appeal（to sb.）for sth.（向…）请求…；appeal to sb. to do sth. 请求…做…
implore	[im'plɔ:] *v.* 哀求，恳求，乞求（to ask someone to do something in a very emotional way） 【例】"Don't leave me!" the old man ***implored***. 【用】implore sb. to do sth. 请求…做…

穷困的 (poor, penniless, down-and-out, destitute, impoverished, bankrupt)

poor	[puə] *a.* 贫困的，穷的（having little money and few possessions） 【例】Most countries in Africa are extremely ***poor***. 【用】the poor 穷人
penniless	['penilis] *a.* 赤贫的，身无分文的（having no money） 【例】Caroline's parents arrived in the country as ***penniless*** immigrants.
down-and-out	*a.* 穷困潦倒的（very poor，with nowhere to live and no job） 【例】The sonless old woman was ***down-and-out***, and she had to beg for a living.

destitute	['destitju:t] *a.* 贫乏的，穷困的（lacking possessions and resources; especially suffering extreme poverty） 【例】When Gavin died, his family was left ***destitute***.
impoverished	[im'pɔvəriʃt] *a.* 穷困的，赤贫的（reduced to poverty; poverty-stricken） 【例】Jeff's parents lived on a remote and ***impoverished*** island.
bankrupt	['bæŋkrʌpt] *a.* 破产的（officially admitting that a person or business has no money and cannot pay what they owe） 【例】Many of the companies that they had invested in went ***bankrupt***. 【用】go bankrupt 破产

取缔，禁止（ban, restrict, boycott, forbid, bar, exclude）

ban	[bæn] *v.* 取缔，禁止（to say officially that people must not sell or use something; to say officially that someone is not allowed to do something） 【例】The film became an enormous success while the book had been ***banned*** on the ground of obscenity. 【用】ban sb. from doing sth. 禁止…做…
restrict	[ri'strikt] *v.* 限制，约束（to keep something within strict limits; to physically limit or control the movement） 【例】There is talk of raising the admission requirements to ***restrict*** the number of students on campus. 【用】restrict sb./sth. to sth. 限制或约束…
boycott	['bɔikɔt] *v.* 抵制（贸易）（not to take part in an event or not buy or use something as a protest） 【例】They are ***boycotting*** foreign goods.
forbid	[fə'bid] *v.* 不许，禁止（to state that something is not allowed, according to a rule, law, or custom） 【例】Prisoners were ***forbidden*** to talk to each other. 【用】forbidden fruit 禁果；forbidden ground 禁区；forbid sb. to do/doing 禁止…做…

bar　　　　　［bɑː］ *v.* 阻止，禁止（to officially say that something must not happen，or that someone must not do something or go somewhere）

【例】Father *bars* smoking on the dinner table.

【用】bar sb. out 闩上门使…无法进入；bar doing sth. 禁止做…

exclude　　　［iks'kluːd］ *v.* 把 … 排 斥 在 外（to deliberately prevent someone or something from being involved in an activity or from entering a place）

【例】The army should be *excluded* from political life.

【用】exclude sb. /sth. from sth. 把…排除在外；禁止…进入

取消（cancel，call off，revoke，countermand，abort）

cancel　　　　［'kænsəl］ *v.* 取消（to say something will not be done or take place）

【例】Vera *cancelled* her trip to the south as she felt ill.

【用】cancel out 取消，抵消

call off　　　取消（某活动）；停止做某事

【例】Why was the meeting *called off*?

revoke　　　［ri'vəuk］ *v.* 撤销，取消（to officially say that something is no longer legal，for example a law or document）

【例】The government formally *revoked* the state.

countermand　［ˌkauntə'mɑːnd］ *v.* 撤回（命令）（to cancel a command）

【例】The commander *countermanded* the air strikes.

abort　　　　［ə'bɔːt］ *v.* 中止（计划）（to stop something before it is finished）

【例】When the decision to *abort* the mission was made，there was a great confusion.

去除（remove，eliminate，exterminate）

remove　　　［ri'muːv］ *v.* 除去，消除（to get rid of a problem，difficulty，or something that annoys you）

【例】The bill is intended to **remove** obstacles that may discourage foreign investors.

【用】remove sb. /sth. from sth. 将…从…除去

eliminate ［i'limineit］ *v.* 消除，清除（to get rid of something that is not wanted or needed）

【例】Many infectious diseases have been **eliminated** many years ago.

【用】eliminate sth. from sth. 将…从…地方清除

exterminate ［ik'stə:mineit］ *v.* 灭绝，消除（to get rid of completely, usually by killing off）

【例】We had to **exterminate** rats to prevent the spread of plague.

确实的（certain, positive, absolute, definite, decided）

certain ['sə:tən] *a.* 确实的，无疑的（having no doubts that something is true）

【例】You can be pretty **certain** she will love the present I prepared for her.

【用】be certain (that) 能够确定…；be certain of/about 对…表示确定

positive ['pɔzətiv] *a.* 确实的，明确的（with no possibility of doubt）

【例】I am **positive** I have seen him.

【用】be positive (that) 很肯定…；be positive of/about 对…表示确定

absolute ['æbsəlju:t] *a.* 绝对的，完全的（with no doubt）

【例】Her story is an **absolute** lie.

definite ['definit] *a.* 肯定的，无疑的（not vague or doubtful）

【例】The secretary was **definite** about the caller's message.

【用】be definite (that) 对…很肯定；be definite about 对…表示肯定

decided [di'saidid] *a.* 明显的，明确的（impossible to doubt and easy to see）

【例】We cannot deny the **decided** improvement on the security system.

热心的 (warm, enthusiastic, ardent, cordial, fervent)

warm　[wɔːm] *a.* 热情的，热心的 (kind and friendly in a way that makes other people feel comfortable)
【例】A *warm* smile appeared on mother's face.

enthusiastic　[inˌθjuːziˈæstik] *a.* 热心的，热情的 (very interested in something or excited by it)
【例】Business leaders gave an *enthusiastic* welcome to the proposal.
【用】be enthusiastic about sth. 对…充满热情

ardent　[ˈɑːdənt] *a.* 热心的 (feeling or showing a particular emotion very strongly, especially in support of someone or something)
【例】They remain *ardent* supporters of the Democratic Party.

cordial　[ˈkɔːdjəl] *a.* 热情而真诚的 (warm and sincere; friendly)
【例】Relations between the two countries remained *cordial*.

fervent　[ˈfəːvənt] *a.* 热心的，热烈的 (very enthusiastic and sincere, especially about something you believe in or support)
【例】I have always been one of Michael Jackson's most *fervent* admirers.

忍受 (withstand, bear, endure, tolerate, weather, put up with)

withstand　[wiðˈstænd] *v.* 经受住，忍受住 (to stand up against)
【例】Explorers have to *withstand* hardships.

bear　[beə] *v.* 忍受，忍耐 (to accept or allow oneself to be subjected to; especially without giving away)

【例】You must face the trouble and *bear* it.

【用】bear with 忍受，忍耐

endure　[in'djuə] *v.* 忍受，忍耐 (to undergo hardship especially without giving in)

【例】Jill *endured* solitude and torture for months at a time.

tolerate　['tɔləreit] *v.* 容忍，忍受 (to put up with; endure)

【例】We *tolerate* all opinions.

weather　['weðə] *v.* 经受住 (to bear up against and come safely through)

【例】The company succeeded in *weathering* a financial crisis.

put up with　忍受，容忍

【例】They had to *put up with* behavior from their sons which they would not have tolerated from anyone else.

认出，识别 (recognize, distinguish, discern, spot, identify, pick out)

recognize　['rekəgnaiz] *v.* 认出，识别 (identify someone or something for having encountered them before)

【例】I *recognized* your father from the description you had given.

【用】recognize sb. /sth. by sth. 通过…认出…

distinguish　[dis'tiŋgwiʃ] *v.* 辨别，区分 (to recognize the differences between things)

【例】He learned to *distinguish* a great variety of birds，fishes and insects.

【用】distinguish between 在…（两者间）区分；distinguish sth. from sth. 将…与…区分开

discern　[di'sə:n] *v.* 识别，认出 (to notice something after thinking about it carefully)

【例】That kid is too young to *discern* right and wrong.

spot　[spɔt] *v.* 发现，辨认出 (see，notice，or recognize someone or something that is difficult to detect)

【例】The robber was *spotted* by the victim.

identify　[ai'dentifai] *v.* 认出，识别 (to establish or indicate who or what is)

【例】He fainted after *identifying* the dead woman as his wife.

【用】identify sb. as sth. 认出···是···

pick out 辨认出，分辨出（to recognize someone or something from a group）

【例】You can *pick out* the liar by the nervous voice when they are speaking.

任意的（random, haphazard, casual, accidental, unplanned, arbitrary, fortuitous, aimless）

random ['rændəm] *a.* 任意的，随机的（chosen or happening without any particular method, pattern, or purpose）

【例】The man fired a few *random* shots.

haphazard [ˌhæp'hæzəd] *a.* 偶然的，任意的（done in a way that does not seem to be carefully planned or organized）

【例】Angus works in a very *haphazard* way.

casual ['kæʒuəl] *a.* 随便的（relaxed and informal）

【例】Our long friendship began with a *casual* meeting at a party.

【用】casual wear 便装

accidental [ˌæksi'dentl] *a.* 意外的，偶然（发生）的（happening without being planned or intended）

【例】Their *accidental* meeting led to a renewal of their acquaintance.

unplanned [ˌʌn'plænd] *a.* 意外的，计划外的（not intended or expected）

【例】I think they must be crazy to carry out an *unplanned* adventure.

arbitrary ['ɑːbitrəri] *a.* 任意的（not based on any particular plan or done for any particular reason）

【例】It was an *arbitrary* choice that we stopped at the first motel we passed.

fortuitous [fɔː'tjuːitəs] *a.* 偶然发生的，意外的（happening by chance, especially in a way that is lucky or convenient）

【例】Their success was the result of a *fortuitous* combination of circumstances.

aimless ['eimlis] *a.* 无目的的（without any particular purpose or plan）

【例】Peters had been adrift and *aimless*.

熔合，合并 (fuse, smelt, commingle, weld, alloy)

fuse	［fju:z］ *v.* 熔合，合并 (to blend thoroughly by or as if by melting together) 【例】Conception occurs when a single sperm *fuses* with an egg.
smelt	［smelt］ *v.* 熔解，熔炼 (to melt (as ore) often with an accompanying chemical change usually to separate the metal) 【例】In this factory, high grade tin is *smelted* from ores.
commingle	［kɔ'miŋgl］ *v.* 搀和，混合 (to mix thoroughly into a harmonious whole) 【例】Fact is inextricably *commingled* with fiction.
weld	［weld］ *v.* 焊接 (to unite (metallic parts) by heating and allowing the metals to flow together or by hammering or compressing with) 【例】It's possible to *weld* stainless steel to ordinary steel.
alloy	［æ'lɔi］ *v.* 将···铸成合金；融合 (to mix so as to form a homogeneous mixture or solid solution of two or more metals; to combine or mix) 【例】It's an idealism that is *alloyed* with political skill.

柔软的 (flexible, lithe, limber, pliant, supple, bendable, lithesome, lissome)

flexible	［'fleksəbl］ *a.* 易弯曲的，柔韧的 (able to bend or move easily) 【例】She fits the *flexible* tube around her head like a headlamp.
lithe	［laið］ *a.* 柔软的，易弯曲的 (easily bent or flexed) 【例】She is young and *lithe* as a cat. 【用】as lithe as 像···一样柔软
limber	［'limbə］ *a.* 易弯曲的 (bending or flexing readily) 【例】He felt the effect of electricity upon the skin like "a number of fine, *limber* hairs".
pliant	［'plaiənt］ *a.* 易弯的；柔软的 (soft and changing shape when pressed) 【例】We caught the *pliant* body of a sapling on the rock.

supple	['sʌpl] *a.* 柔软的；易弯曲的 (soft to bend easily)
	【例】She's got long, *supple* legs that make men go mad.
bendable	['bendəbl] *a.* 柔软的，弯曲的 (able to bend)
	【例】By mixing fiber in concrete scientists create a *bendable* material.
lithesome	['laiðsəm] *a.* 柔软的 (easily bent or flexed)
	【例】Martin was as *lithesome* and strong as an athlete.
lissome	['lisəm] *a.* 柔软的 (easily flexed)
	【例】Her dress, yellow like burnished gold, was very *lissome* and soft.

散播 (broadcast, spread, disseminate, scatter)

broadcast	['brɔːdkɑːst; 'brɔːdkæst] *v.* 散播 (to tell people something, especially something that you wanted to be a secret)
	【例】Donald soon *broadcasted* the news to all his friends.
spread	[spred] *v.* 散布 (to become distributed or widely dispersed)
	【例】The disease *spreads* very rapidly.
	【用】spread out (人群等) 散开
disseminate	[di'semineit] *v.* 散布，传播 (to make something such as information or knowledge available to a lot of people)
	【例】The man spent his life *disseminating* the Gospel.
scatter	['skætə] *v.* 散布，散开 (to move quickly in different directions)
	【例】The searchers *scattered* all over the countryside looking for the missing girl.

【用】scatter about 撒；使散布在各处

杀 (murder, slay, slaughter, assassinate, gun down, strangle, decapitate, butcher)

murder ['mə:də] *v.* 谋杀，凶杀 (to commit the crime of killing someone deliberately)
【例】Helen was *murdered* on her own doorstep.

slay [slei] *v.* 杀，残杀 (to kill someone in a violent way)
【例】Alex was *slain* in a battle in 673.

slaughter ['slɔ:tə] *v.* 屠杀，杀戮 (to kill many people in a violent way)
【例】Thousands of people were *slaughtered* during the conflict.

assassinate [ə'sæsineit] *v.* 暗杀 (to kill a famous or important person, especially for political reasons or for payment)
【例】Justin was hanged for conspiring to *assassinate* the king.

gun down 枪杀
【例】The bank robber was *gunned down* by the police.

strangle ['stræŋgl] *v.* 扼死，勒死 (to kill a person or an animal by squeezing their throat so that they cannot breathe)
【例】Alfred *strangled* his wife with a telephone cord.

decapitate [di'kæpiteit] *v.* 杀头 (to cut off someone's head)
【例】The king ordered his captive to be *decapitated*.

butcher ['butʃə] *v.* 残杀，滥杀 (to kill someone, often many people, in a cruel and violent way)
【例】Many innocent children and women were *butchered* by the rebels.

删除，删略 (delete, strike out, omit, erase)

delete [di'li:t] *v.* 删除，删略 (to cross out something or to remove information stored in a computer)
【例】Simon *deleted* all his personal files from the computer.

【用】delete sth. from sth. 从…删除…

strike out
划掉，删去
【例】*Strike out* the witness' last remark.

omit
［əu'mit］*v.* 省去（to fail to include or mention；leave out）
【例】You *omitted* a word in the title of the article.
【用】omit to do sth. 未做…

erase
［i'reiz］*v.* 擦掉（to remove writing, drawing, or marks made by a pencil or pen by rubbing it off with an eraser）
【例】The pupil was told to *erase* the marks on the blackboard.
【用】erase sth. from sth. 从…抹去…

闪光 (flash, blink, flicker, flare, shine, glow, glint, shimmer)

flash
［flæʃ］*v.* 闪光（to shine brightly for a very short time, or to shine on and off very quickly）
【例】The lightning *flashed*.
【用】flash across/by/on/past 闪过

blink
［bliŋk］*v.* 闪亮，闪烁（to go on and off continuously）
【例】Stars *blink* in the sky.

flicker
［'flikə］*v.*（指灯光或火焰）闪烁（to burn unsteadily or fitfully）
【例】A television *flickered* in the corner.

flare
［fleə］*v.*（火焰）闪耀（to suddenly burn or shine brightly）
【例】Camp fires *flared* like beacons in the dark.
【用】flare up 闪耀

shine
［ʃain］*v.* 发光，发亮（to produce a bright light）
【例】It is a mild morning and the sun is *shining*.
【用】shine through 展现

glow
［gləu］*v.* 发光（to shine with a soft light）
【例】The night lantern *glowed* softly in the darkness.

glint
［glint］*v.* 闪烁，发微光（to shine with quick flashes of light）
【例】Her eyes *glinted* when she saw the money.

shimmer	['ʃimə] v. 闪烁，微微发亮 (to reflect a gentle light that seems to shake slightly)
	【例】The lake *shimmered* in the moonlight.

身体的 (physical, corporeal, fleshly, material)

physical	['fizikəl] a. 身体的 (relating to body)
	【例】Bill's bodily pains were induced by *physical* exhaustion.
corporeal	[kɔː'pɔːriəl] a. 身体的；物体的 (relating to the physical world, and not to spiritual or emotional states)
	【例】Spanking is *corporeal* punishment.
fleshly	['fleʃli] a. 肉体的，肉欲的 (of or relating to the body)
	【例】John gets old, his *fleshly* strength vanishes.
material	[mə'tiəriəl] a. 肉体的，身体的 (of or concerned with the physical as distinct from the intellectual or spiritual)
	【例】One cannot think too much of *material* comforts.

神秘的 (mysterious, inexplicable, enigmatic, inscrutable, cryptic, unfathomable, mystical, arcane)

mysterious	[mi'stiəriəs] a. 神秘的 (of, relating to, or being a mystery)
	【例】The police are investigating the *mysterious* disappearance of a young man.
inexplicable	[,inik'splikəbl] a. 无法解释的 (impossible to explain)
	【例】For some *inexplicable* reason, Rose chose that moment to break the news.
enigmatic	[,enig'mætik] a. 神秘的，高深莫测的 (difficult to understand)
	【例】Little is known about this solitary and *enigmatic* writer.
inscrutable	[in'skruːtəbl] a. 高深莫测的，不可理解的 (difficult to understand)
	【例】Anna's face remained *inscrutable*, no one could figure out what she was thinking.
cryptic	['kriptik] a. 神秘的 (expressing something in an indirect way so that it is difficult to understand)

【例】There is a *cryptic* smile on the old man's face.

【用】a cryptic message 神秘的信息

unfathomable [ˌʌnˈfæðəməbl] *a*. 深不可测的（impossible to explain or understand）

【例】My *unfathomable* love shows itself in my passion.

mystical [ˈmistikl] *a*. 神秘的（of or relating to mystic rites or practices）

【例】The rites and ceremonies of this religion are very *mystical*.

arcane [ɑːˈkein] *a*. 神秘的（not explained and difficult to understand）

【例】These *arcane* customs are attractive to the tourists.

渗出 (bleed, ooze, exude, flow, seep, percolate)

bleed [bliːd] *v*. 渗出，流出（to exude a fluid such as sap）

【例】I scraped my knee and it's *bleeding*.

【用】bleed sb. white 榨取…所有的钱

ooze [uːz] *v*. 渗出；泄漏（to flow or leak out slowly）

【例】The cut on his arm was *oozing* blood.

【用】ooze from/out of sth. 从…慢慢流出，从…中渗出；ooze out 渗出，流出

exude [igˈzjuːd] *v*. 使慢慢流出，渗出（to discharge or emit a liquid or gas gradually）

【例】Annie's hands were *exuding* sweat.

【用】exude from/through sth. 从…缓缓流出，从…渗出

flow [fləu] *v*. 流动，涌流（to move or run smoothly with unbroken continuity）

【例】Hot water *flows* through the pipes.

seep [siːp] *v*. 漏出，（指液体）渗出（to flow into or out of something through small holes）

【例】The rain had *seeped* through Jack's clothes.

【用】seep in 渗入

percolate [ˈpəːkəleit] *v*. 渗透（to drain or seep through a porous material or filter）

【例】Rainwater *percolates* slowly through the soil.

湿的，潮湿的 (humid, moist, damp, wet, vaporous, clammy, dank, misty)

humid ['hjuːmid] *a.* 湿的，潮湿的（hot and wet in a way that makes you feel uncomfortable）

【例】During the rainy season, it gets very hot and **humid** here.

moist [mɔist] *a.* 潮湿的，湿润的（slightly wet）

【例】The boy's words made Shirley's eyes **moist** with tears.

damp [dæmp] *a.* 潮湿的（slightly or moderately wet）

【例】Mother wiped the table with a **damp** rag after lunch.

wet [wet] *a.* 湿的，潮的（not yet dry or solid; or covered with water or another liquid）

【例】Don't sit on the bench. The paint is still **wet**.

【用】like a wet rag 又累又湿又脏的

vaporous ['veipərəs] *a.* 多蒸汽的，似蒸汽的（consisting or characteristic of vapor）

【例】The air in the bathroom was **vaporous** and steamy.

clammy ['klæmi] *a.* 冷而粘湿的（cold and wet in an unpleasant way）

【例】The sick patient had **clammy** hands.

【用】clammy weather 潮湿的天气

dank [dæŋk] *a.* 阴湿的，阴冷的（unpleasantly moist or wet）

【例】The villagers went into the **dank** and chilly cave to take shelter for the bombardment.

misty ['misti] *a.* 充满雾气的（obscured by mist or consisting of or marked by mist）

【例】The flight is delayed for the **misty** weather.

时期，时代 (period, age, epoch, era)

period ['piəriəd] *n.* （一段）时间，时期，时代（an amount of time during which something happens）

【例】Those years was the happiest **period** in my life.

【用】a short period of time 短暂的一段时间

age [eidʒ] *n.* 时代（a period of history with special events or characteristics）

【例】Nowadays, we are in a materialistic **age**.

— 256 —

epoch   [ˈiːpɔk; ˈepək] *n.* 时期，时代（a long period of time in the history, especially one marked by notable events or characteristic）
【例】Newton's theory marked a new *epoch* in physics.
【用】make a new epoch in 开创了…的新纪元

era   [ˈiərə] *n.* 纪元，年代，时代（a period in history starting from a particular time or event; a period in history marked by an important event or development）
【例】The *era* of space travel has started.
【用】the era of …的时代

实际的，真实的（actual, authentic, bona fide, genuine, veritable）

actual   [ˈæktʃuəl] *a.* 实际的，真实的（existing in fact; real）
【例】What David told us was not a lie but an *actual* happening.

authentic   [ɔːˈθentik] *a.* 真正的，真实的（real, not false or copied; accurate or based in fact）
【例】This is an *authentic* painting by Vinci.
【用】an authentic signature 亲笔签名

bona fide   [ˌbəunəˈfaidi] *a.* 〈拉〉真正的，真诚的（neither specious nor counterfeit; sincere）
【例】He was a *bona fide* buyer.
【用】a bona fide agreement 真诚的协议

genuine   [ˈdʒenjuin] *a.* 真正的（real, rather than pretended or false）
【例】This ring was made of *genuine* silver unmixed with base metal.
【用】the genuine article 货真价实的物品

veritable   [ˈveritəbl] *a.* 确实的（being in fact the thing named; not false, unreal, or imaginary）
【例】The salesman is a *veritable* fox.

使缠绕（twine, braid, entwine, interlace, intertwine, knit, weave, wreathe）

twine   [twain] *v.* 使缠绕（to twist together）
【例】Climbing plants had *twined* around the branches of the dead tree.

【用】twine sth. around sth. 将…缠绕…

braid ［breid］v. 编织（to twist fibers around each other to make a rope or braid）

【例】Mary's hair is **braided** across her head in a Nordic fashion.

entwine ［in'twain］v. 使…缠绕（to twine together or around）

【例】Mary **entwines** her fingers around her boyfriend's.

【用】entwine sth.（with/round sth.）将…缠绕（在另一物上）

interlace ［,intə'leis］v.（使）交织，（使）交错（to unite by or as if by lacing together）

【例】Tom's hands were **interlaced** behind his head.

【用】interlace sth. with sth. 使…和…相交织

intertwine ［,intə'twain］v. 缠，绕（to unite by twining one with another）

【例】The vines are **intertwined** to make a wreath.

knit ［nit］v. 编织（to form by interlacing yarn or thread in a series of connected loops with needles）

【例】Mary reads and **knits** to pass the time.

【用】knit one's brow（s）皱眉

weave ［wi:v］v. 编织（to form (cloth) by interlacing strands）

【例】The women shut themselves behind closed doors to **weave** their cloth.

【用】weave sth. into sth. 把…织成…；weave sth.（out of /from sth.）用…编成…

wreathe ［ri:ð］v. 环绕盘旋（to move or extend in circles or spirals）

【例】Blue smoke **wreathed** upward into the dark sky.

【用】wreathe sth. in/with sth. 用…环绕…；wreathe oneself/ sth. round sb. /sth. 将自己、手臂等环绕…

使缓和，减轻（comfort, alleviate, mitigate, relieve, unburden, salve, assuage）

comfort ［'kʌmfət］v. 使缓和，减轻（to ease physically）

【例】Charles **comforted** his aching feet in a tub of hot water.

alleviate ［ə'li:vieit］v. 减轻，缓解（to make something less painful, severe, or serious）

【例】Heat often **alleviates** pain.

mitigate	['mitigeit] *v.* 使缓和，减轻 (to reduce the harmful effects of something) 【例】The government made plans to ***mitigate*** the disruptive effects of slum living.
relieve	[ri'li:v] *v.* 缓解，减轻 (to make pain or another bad physical feeling less unpleasant) 【例】Aspirin will usually ***relieve*** a headache. 【用】relieve... of... 解除，消除
unburden	[ˌʌn'bə:dn] *v.* 卸下负担 (to free or ease from a burden) 【例】Diana was ***unburdening*** herself to her closest friends. 【用】unburden oneself to sb. 向…吐露心事
salve	[sælv] *v.* 减轻痛苦，缓和 (to do or say something that makes people feel less guilty or embarrassed) 【例】I ***salved*** my conscience by apologizing. 【用】salve one's conscience 减轻良心的不安
assuage	[ə'sweidʒ] *v.* 缓和，减轻 (to make an unpleasant or painful feeling less severe) 【例】Dustin did all he could to ***assuage*** her fears.

使能够，授予权力 (enable, empower, capacitate, endow, authorize, invest)

enable	[i'neibl] *v.* 使能够，授予权力 (to give somebody the ability or opportunity to do something) 【例】The large wings ***enable*** the bird to fly high and fast. 【用】enable sb. /sth. to do sth. 使…能够做…
empower	[im'pauə] *v.* 授权给某人采取行动 (to give a person or an organization the legal authority to do something) 【例】The new law ***empowered*** the police to search private houses.
capacitate	[kə'pæsiteit] *v.* 使能够，赋予能力 (to render fit or make qualified) 【例】The new teaching method will ***capacitate*** students lagging behind to catch up quickly.
endow	[in'dau] *v.* 赋予，捐赠 (to provide with something freely or naturally; to give a large amount of money to somebody)

【例】 Nature *endowed* her with a beautiful singing voice.

【用】 endow sb. /sth. with 捐赠…给…

authorize ['ɔ:θəraiz] *v.* 授权，批准（to give official permission for something to happen）

【例】 The parliament was willing to *authorize* the president to use force if necessary.

【用】 authorize sb. to do sth. 授权…做…

invest [in'vest] *v.* 授予，赋予（to give a person or an organization power, or authority; to give something or someone a particular quality）

【例】 The constitution had *invested* him with certain powers and he was determined to deploy them.

【用】 invest sb. /sth. with sth. 将…给予…

使疲倦的，乏味的（wearisome, tiresome, exhausting, laborious, arduous, tedious, boring, monotonous, humdrum）

wearisome ['wiərisəm] *a.* 使疲倦的，乏味的（causing physical or mental tiresomeness）

【例】 These high wild hills and rough uneven ways made the hikers *wearisome*.

tiresome ['taiəsəm] *a.* 令人疲劳的（wearisome，tedious）

【例】 Checking all the address labels was a *tiresome* task.

exhausting [ig'zɔ:stiŋ] *a.* 令人疲惫不堪的（extremely tiring）

【例】 It was an *exhausting* schedule she had set for herself.

laborious [lə'bɔ:riəs] *a.* 费力的，艰难的（devoted to labor）

【例】 The negotiations were rather *laborious* and futile.

arduous ['ɑ:djuəs] *a.* 费力的，艰巨的（marked by great labor or effort）

【例】 The task was more *arduous* than Tom had calculated.

tedious ['ti:diəs] *a.* 乏味的，单调的（tiresome because of length or dullness）

【例】 Life is as *tedious* as a twice told story.

boring ['bɔ:riŋ] *a.* 无趣的，乏味的（uninteresting and tiresome; dull）

【例】The *boring* conversation made me sleepy.

monotonous [məˈnɔtənəs] *a.* 单调的，无聊的（tediously uniform or unvarying）

【例】The food may get a bit *monotonous*, but there'll be enough of it.

humdrum [ˈhʌmdrʌm] *a.* 单调的，乏味的（monotonous, dull）

【例】The new government seemed rather *humdrum*.

使丧失能力（paralyze, immobilize, incapacitate, disable, cripple, numb, anesthetize）

paralyze [ˈpærəlaiz] *v.* （使）瘫痪，麻痹（to make someone lose the ability to move their body or a part of it）

【例】Bill's married sister had been *paralyzed* in a road accident.

【用】be paralyzed with（fear, horror）因（恐惧、恐怖）而不知所措

immobilize [iˈməubilaiz] *v.* 使不能正常运作，使不动（to make someone unable to move）

【例】Severe weather *immobilized* the rescue team.

incapacitate [ˌinkəˈpæsiteit] *v.* 使不能，（使）失去能力（to make someone or something unable to live or work normally）

【例】A serious fall *incapacitated* the 68-year-old congressman.

【用】incapacitate sb. for sth. / from doing sth. 使…不能做…

disable [disˈeibl] *v.* （使）丧失能力（to harm someone so that part of their body or brain no longer works normally）

【例】An accident *disabled* him from playing football.

cripple [ˈkripl] *v.* 使…成为残废（to make someone physically disabled, especially unable to walk）

【例】Mr. Easton was seriously *crippled* in an accident and had to leave his job.

numb [nʌm] *v.* 使麻木，使失去知觉（to make a part of body lose its ability to feel）

【例】The horror of my experience has *numbed* my senses.

anesthetize [æˈniːsθətaiz; əˈnesθətaiz] *v.* 麻痹，使麻痹（to give someone an anesthetic so that they do not feel pain during a medical operation）

【例】The patient must be **anesthetized** before the operation.

使适应（adapt, adjust, accommodate, orient, acclimate, habituate）

adapt ［əˈdæpt］ *v.* 使适应（to change something to make it more appropriate for a new use or situation）
【例】Can you **adapt** your way of working to the new job?

adjust ［əˈdʒʌst］ *v.* 改变…以适应（to change so as to match or fit）
【例】Astronauts in flight must **adjust** to weightlessness.
【用】adjust to 使适合，使适应

accommodate ［əˈkɔmədeit］ *v.* 使适应，顺应（to change attitude and behavior in order to deal with a new situation）
【例】A westerner visiting the Far East must **accommodate** himself to habits of life that may seem very strange to him.
【用】accommodate sb. /sth. to sth. 使…适应…

orient ［ˈɔːrient］ *v.* 使熟悉情况（to acquaint with the existing situation or environment）
【例】You will need the time to **orient** yourself to the new food.
【用】orient oneself to sth. 使自己熟悉…

acclimate ［əˈklaimit；ˈæklə‚meit］ *v.* 使服水土，使适应新环境（to get used to a new temperature, altitude, climate, environment, or situation）
【例】It took me a long time to **acclimate** myself to living in the countryside.
【用】become/get acclimated to sth. 使适应…；acclimate oneself to sth. 使自己适应…

habituate ［həˈbitjueit］ *v.* 使习惯（to make someone experience something regularly so that they become familiar with it）
【例】He **habituated** himself to getting up early.
【用】habituate oneself to sth. 使自己习惯于…

使痛苦（pain, smart, irritate, harm, excruciate, afflict）

pain ［pein］ *v.* 使痛苦（to suffer or distress）
【例】It **pains** me to think of you struggling all alone.

smart [smɑːt] *v.* 剧痛，刺痛（to hurt with a sudden sharp pain）
【例】The incision on my leg *smarts*.

irritate ['iriteit] *v.* 使（身体某部分）不适，使疼痛（to hurt a part of body, making it painful, red or swollen）
【例】The smoke *irritated* my eyes.

harm [hɑːm] *v.* 伤害，损害（to injure, damage, or have a bad effect on someone or something）
【例】The hijackers seemed anxious not to *harm* anyone.

excruciate [ik'skruːʃieit] *v.* 擦伤（to inflict severe pain on）
【例】Bill's legs were *excruciated* by the prickles.

afflict [ə'flikt] *v.* 使苦恼，折磨（to inflict grievous physical or mental suffering on）
【例】Grandparents were *afflicted* with arthritis.
【用】be afflicted with 受…的苦，疼痛

使用 (use, employ, apply, exploit, utilize, make use of, avail oneself of, take advantage of, trade on)

use [juːz] *v.* 用，使用，利用（employ something for purpose, bring something into service）
【例】May I *use* your cell phone?
【用】be used for sth. /doing sth. 被用于做…；use sth. to do sth. 用…做…；use sth. as sth. 将…用做…

employ [im'plɔi] *v.* 用，使用（to use something for a particular purpose）
【例】Two methods can be *employed* to solve this problem.
【用】employ sb. /sth. in/on sth. 使用或利用…；employ sth. as sth. 把…用作…

apply [ə'plai] *v.* 应用，运用（to make practical use of something）
【例】A new technique will be *applied* to the treatment of AIDS.
【用】apply sth. to sth. 将…运用于…

exploit [ik'splɔit] *v.* 使用，开发利用（to use a situation to get benefit from it, even if it is wrong or unfair to do this）
【例】In some factories, child labors are *exploited*.

utilize ['juːtilaiz] *v.* 利用 (to use something)

【例】Sometimes, this room is ***utilized*** for training purposes.

【用】be utilized for sth. /doing sth. 被用于做…; utilize sth. as sth. 将…用做…

make use of 使用，利用

【例】You should ***make*** full ***use of*** every opportunity to practise your spoken English.

avail oneself of 利用，使用

【例】***Avail yourself of*** every chance to get more time to read.

take advantage of 利用

【例】You'd better ***take*** full ***advantage of*** the hotel's facilities.

trade on (为达到利己目的而)利用 (to make use of something for one's own advantage)

【例】You shouldn't ***trade on*** your friend's generosity.

事故，事件 (accident, casualty, mishap, occurrence, incident)

accident ['æksidənt] *n.* 事故 (a sudden event, usually caused by someone making a mistake)

【例】Ten men were killed in a serious mining ***accident*** yesterday.

【用】without accident 安然无恙地

casualty ['kæʒuəlti] *n.* 伤亡事故 (an accident, especially one involving serious injury or loss of life)

【例】There were no reports of ***casualties*** from the attack.

【用】heavy casualties 伤亡惨重

mishap [mis'hæp] *n.* 不幸事故 (an unfortunate accident)

【例】Hundreds of children ended up in the hospital after some preventable ***mishap***.

【用】without mishap 完好无损地

occurrence [ə'kəːrəns; ə'kʌrəns] *n.* 事件 (something that happens, especially something unexpected and unpleasant)

【例】Actually, computer errors are a common ***occurrence***.

incident ['insidənt] *n.* 事件，事变 (something that happens, especially a violent, criminal, or dangerous event)

【例】Police are looking for witnesses to the *incident*.

【用】without incident 无事件发生

适当的 (suitable, fitting, apt, proper, appropriate, becoming)

suitable	['sjuːtəbl] *a.* 适 当 的，合 适 的（right for a particular purpose，person，or situation） 【例】This movie is not *suitable* for young children. 【用】be suitable for sb. /sth. 适合于…；be suitable to do sth. 适合做…
fitting	['fitiŋ] *a.* 适 合 的，恰 当 的（appropriate for a particular situation） 【例】The dinner was a *fitting* end to Carter's 25 years with the company.
apt	[æpt] *a.* 适当的（to the point；well suited） 【例】It seemed *apt* that the winning goal was scored by the captain.
proper	['prɔpə] *a.* 合适的，恰当的（appropriate for the purpose or situation） 【例】You have to have the *proper* tools for the job. 【用】be proper for sth. 适合于…
appropriate	[ə'prəupriit] *a.* 适 当 的（suitable or right for a particular situation or purpose） 【例】This isn't the *appropriate* time to discuss the problem. 【用】appropriate for/to sth. 合适或适合于…
becoming	[bi'kʌmiŋ] *a.* 合 适 的，相 称 的（appropriate or correct for someone or the situation） 【例】Your *becoming* hair-style made you more attractive.

收集；聚集 (collect, accumulate, heap, pile up, gather, aggregate, stack up, amass, assemble)

collect	[kə'lekt] *v.* 收 集；聚 集（to get things and keep them together for a particular reason） 【例】Barry *collects* stamps as a hobby.

accumulate [əˈkjuːmjuleit] *v.* 积聚，堆积（to get more and more of something over a period of time）

【例】Dust soon **accumulates** if the room is not swept.

heap [hiːp] *v.* （使）成堆，堆起（to make a big messy pile of things）

【例】They were **heaping** wood up for a bonfire.

【用】heap sth. up 堆积…

pile up 堆积，积累

【例】Newspapers and magazines were **piled up** on the floor.

gather [ˈgæðə] *v.* 聚集，收集（to bring together）

【例】Football fans **gathered** around the TV in the corner of the bar.

【用】gather round sb. /sth. 聚在…周围

aggregate [ˈægrigeit] *v.* 聚集，合计（to put things together in a group；to add amounts together）

【例】All the salaries in the department **aggregate** well over four hundred thousand a month.

【用】aggregate sb. to sth. 吸收…加入（多为政党）

stack up 堆积

【例】Plates of delicious food **stacked up** on the counters.

amass [əˈmæs] *v.* 积聚（to collect a lot of things such as money or information over a period of time）

【例】They had **amassed** a fortune worth about $ 51 billion.

【用】amass a fortune 积累财富

assemble [əˈsembl] *v.* 聚集，集合（to bring a group of things or people together in one place for a particular purpose）

【例】How long would it take to **assemble** a team for a project like this?

【用】assemble evidence 收集证据

瘦的，皮包骨头的（skinny, lean, bony, slender, spare, spindly）

skinny [ˈskini] *a.* 瘦的，皮包骨头的（very thin, in a way that is not attractive）

【例】Lily is **skinny** and a little freckled and her eyes are green.

lean	[li:n] *a.* 瘦的 （thin and looking physically fit; healthy or with little fat）
	【例】The farmer tried to fatten his ***lean*** pig for market.
bony	['bəuňi] *a.* 似骨的; 瘦的 （be so thin that the shape of the bones can be seen）
	【例】Tom took off his T-shirt, revealing his ***bony*** chest.
slender	['slendə] *a.* 修长的，苗条的 （tall or long and thin in an attractive way）
	【例】Linda was ***slender*** as a wicker.
spare	[speə] *a.* 瘦削的 （thin）
	【例】Mary was tall and ***spare***.
spindly	['spindli] *a.* 细长的，纤弱的 （long and thin and looks as if it would break easily）
	【例】There are a few ***spindly*** plants in the flower pot.

熟练的 (skillful, expert, adept, proficient, masterly)

skillful	['skilful] *a.* 熟练的，娴熟的 （very good at doing something that involves special ability or training）
	【例】Only the most ***skillful*** pilots are employed by airlines.
	【用】be skillful at doing sth. 做…非常娴熟
expert	['ekspə:t] *a.* 熟练的，精湛的 （having, involving, or displaying special skill or knowledge derived from training or experience）
	【例】The riders were all ***expert*** horsemen.
	【用】be expert in/on/at sth. /doing sth. 做…很熟练
adept	['ædept] *a.* 熟练的; 精通的 （skillful at doing something）
	【例】The flatfish is remarkably ***adept*** at hiding itself on the ocean floor.
	【用】be adept at doing sth. 精于做…
proficient	[prəu'fiʃənt] *a.* 熟练的; 精通的 （very skillful at something that you have learned）

【例】Grace was *proficient* in mathematics.

【用】be proficient in sth. 做…很熟练

masterly   ['mɑːstəli; 'mæstəli] *a.* 熟练的，精湛的（having or showing the knowledge or skill of a master）

【例】Most people appreciated their *masterly* handling of the difficult situation.

衰退（decay, deteriorate, degenerate, wane）

decay   [di'kei] *v.* 衰退（to become gradually worse in quality, or weaker in power or influence）

【例】At that time, the Roman Empire had already *decayed*.

deteriorate   [di'tiəriəreit] *v.* 变坏，恶化（to become worse; to become impaired in quality, functioning, or condition）

【例】Grant's health steadily *deteriorated*.

【用】deteriorate into sth. 蜕变成…（不好的事物）

degenerate   [di'dʒenəreit] *v.* 衰退（to become worse in quality）

【例】Inactivity can make your joints stiff, and the bones may begin to *degenerate*.

【用】degenerate into sth. 堕落为…

wane   [wein] *v.* 衰落（to fall gradually from power, prosperity, or influence）

【例】His enthusiasm for music was *waning* fast.

【用】wane to the close 接近尾声，即将结束

睡觉（doze, slumber, nap, drowse, go to bed, fall asleep, lie in, turn in）

doze   [dəuz] *v.* 小睡，打盹（to sleep for a short time, especially during the day）

【例】Dad *dozed* off in front of the television.

【用】doze off 打盹

slumber   ['slʌmbə] *v.* 睡眠，安睡（to sleep lightly）

【例】Be quiet! Our baby is *slumbering* peacefully.

nap	[næp] *v.* 小睡，打盹儿（to sleep for a short period of time, usually during the day） 【例】It's common to *nap* for a while after lunch for many people. 【用】catch sb. napping 发现…精神不集中
drowse	[drauz] *v.* 昏睡（to be in a light sleep or to feel that you are going to sleep） 【例】It's a pleasure to *drowse* away a hot afternoon. 【用】drowse sth. away 半醒半睡地度过（时间）
go to bed	睡觉 【例】I was just *going to bed* when the phone rang.
fall asleep	入睡 【例】After a whole day's work, James *fell asleep* as soon as his head touched the pillow.
lie in	睡懒觉 【例】I used to *lie in* on weekends.
turn in	上床睡觉（to go to bed at night） 【例】Mom told me to *turn in* before 10:00 p.m.

死亡（die, expire, decease, depart, perish, breathe one's last, pass away）

die	[dai] *v.* 死，死亡（to stop being alive） 【例】Helen's grandfather *died* of cancer. 【用】die of 死于（疾病）；die from 死于（疾病以外的原因）
expire	[ik'spaiə] *v.* 断气，去世（to breathe one's last breath; die） 【例】The old man *expired* the moment he made his testament.
decease	[di'si:s] *v.* 死亡（to die） 【例】Both Carla's parents *deceased* last year.
depart	[di'pɑ:t] *v.* 死亡（to die） 【例】Bernard *departed* this life in the winter of 1973.
perish	['periʃ] *v.* 丧生，死亡（to die, usually because of an illness or something that happens suddenly） 【例】All their horses *perished* in the fire.

breathe one's last　〈委婉〉断气（to die）

【例】The cancer patient ***breathed his last*** on the operating table.

pass away　去世（to die）

【例】Edward ***passed away*** in his sleep at the age of eighty-four.

搜索（search, grub, poke, forage, hunt）

search　［səːtʃ］ *v.* 搜索，探查（to look into or over carefully or thoroughly in an effort to find or discover something）

【例】All men in the village were out to ***search*** for the missing girl.

【用】search out 找出，搜出

grub　［grʌb］ *v.* 搜索（to search about）

【例】The old professor ***grubbed*** about in the library for material.

poke　［pəuk］ *v.* 刺探（to pry or meddle）

【例】Somebody likes ***poking*** into another's business.

【用】poke about/around 搜索，探问

forage　［ˈfɔridʒ］ *v.* 寻找（食物），搜寻（to search in a wide area for something，especially food）

【例】Ray ***foraged*** for food in the cupboard.

hunt　［hʌnt］ *v.* 搜寻，寻找（to try to find someone or something）

【例】Police were ***hunting*** down the escaped convict.

【用】hunt for sth. 寻找…

缩短，删节（abridge, contract, shorten, condense, abbreviate, curtail）

abridge　［əˈbridʒ］ *v.* 缩短，删节（to shorten without losing of sense）

【例】Ralph ***abridged*** the novel for its inclusion in a magazine.

contract　［kənˈtrækt］ *v.* 收缩（to reduce to smaller size by or as if by squeezing or forcing together）

【例】New research shows that an excess of meat and salt can ***contract*** muscles.

【用】contract sth. to sth. 将…缩减成…

shorten [ˈʃɔːtən] v. 缩短，使…变短（to become shorter，or make something shorter）

【例】Because of the bad weather，Norman *shortened* his stay in Canada.

condense [kənˈdens] v.（使）压缩，精简（to make anything shorter or smaller）

【例】Our month-long training course had been *condensed* into two weeks.

【用】condense sth. into sth. 把…精简成…

abbreviate [əˈbriːvieit] v. 缩短，缩写（to make briefer，especially to reduce to a shorter form intended to stand for the whole）

【例】The December is *abbreviated* to Dec.

【用】abbreviate sth. to sth. 将…缩写为…

curtail [kəˈteil] v. 缩短，削减（to reduce or limit something，especially something good）

【例】The government had to *curtail* public spending.

【用】curtail one's holidays 缩短假期

缩小（reduce，decrease，diminish，lessen）

reduce [riˈdjuːs；riˈduːs] v. 减少，缩小（to make something smaller or less in size，amount，importance）

【例】The workforce will be *reduced* by around 30 percent at the end of this year.

【用】reduce sth. by 将…减少（多少）；reduce sth. from A to B 将…从 A（的程度）减少到 B（的程度）；reduce sth. in size/number etc. 缩小…的大小；减少…的数量等

decrease [diˈkriːs] v. 减小，减少（to become less）

【例】Prices are expected to *decrease* by less than 10 percent this year.

【用】decrease in 在某一方面有所下降

diminish [diˈminiʃ] v. 变小，减少（to make less or cause to appear less）

【例】Her enthusiasm in music was by now fast *diminishing*.

— 271 —

| lessen | ['lesən] v. 变少，减少 (to become smaller in amount, level, importance)
【例】Traffic had **lessened** and the Mercedes began to pick up speed. |

逃脱，逃走 (escape, run away, break out, abscond, elope, flee, decamp)

escape	[i'skeip] v. 逃脱，逃走 (to get away from a place where you are in danger) 【例】They **escaped** from the burning house. 【用】escape from 从…逃离
run away	逃脱，离开 【例】The boy broke up the window and **ran away**.
break out	逃脱，逃走 【例】All prisoners **broke out** of the jail.
abscond	[əb'skɔnd] v. 潜逃，逃亡 (to leave quickly and secretly and hide oneself, often to avoid arrest or prosecution) 【例】The club's treasurer had **absconded** with the funds. 【用】abscond with sth. 携…潜逃
elope	[i'ləup] v. 私奔 (to go away secretly to get married) 【例】The girl **eloped** with her boyfriend.
flee	[fli:] v. 逃离，逃跑 (to escape from a dangerous situation or place very quickly) 【例】The rest of the defeated troops **fled** from the battle field. 【用】flee from 逃离…
decamp	[di'kæmp] v. 逃走，逃往 (to depart secretly or suddenly)

【例】The lodger has ***decamped*** without paying his bill.

【用】decamp with sth. 携…逃走

提高（improve, enhance, uplift, amend, better）

improve
[im'pru:v] *v.* 改进，改善（to make something better）

【例】The course will ***improve*** the students' grasp of chemistry.

enhance
[in'hɑ:ns; in'hæns] *v.* 提高，增强（to improve something, or make it more attractive or more valuable）

【例】The company tried to ***enhance*** the influence of its product.

uplift
[ʌp'lift] *v.* 提高，抬高，鼓舞（尤指在精神、道德或情绪方面）（to make someone feel happier or more hopeful）

【例】The mysteries of Islam ***uplifted*** them.

amend
[ə'mend] *v.* 改进（to change a document, law, agreement, etc. for the better）

【例】The Marriage Law was ***amended*** recently.

better
['betə] *v.* 提高（to improve something）

【例】This is definitely an important step towards ***bettering*** the relations between the two corporations.

提名（nominate, select, propose, name）

nominate
['nɔmineit] *v.* 提名，推荐（to officially suggest that someone should be given a job or position）

【例】Alfred had already been ***nominated*** as a candidate.

【用】nominate sb. for/as sth. 提名…为…

select
[si'lekt] *v.* 选拔（to choose somebody especially as the best or most suitable person）

【例】We're going to ***select*** two students to represent the school.

【用】select sb. as sth. 选拔…为…

propose
[prə'pəuz] *v.* 推荐，提名（to put forward somebody for an office, etc.）

【例】Many people ***propose*** Mary as a candidate for the manager.

【用】propose sb. for/as sth. 推荐…为…

name [neim] *v.* 提名（to choose someone for a particular job, position, or prize）
【例】Brian was **named** player of the year at the awards ceremony.
【用】name sb. for/as sth. 提名…为…

天生的（natural, native, born, inherent, inborn, inbred, innate）

natural ['nætʃərəl] *a.* 天生的，天赋的（not acquired; inherent）
【例】You can learn and improve but you need **natural** talent.

native ['neitiv] *a.* 天生的，与生俱来的（belonging to a person's basic personality or character, not acquired by education, etc.）
【例】That boy has a great deal of **native** ability.

born [bɔːn] *a.* 天生的（having a specific natural quality or ability）
【例】Natalie was a **born** dancer.

inherent [in'hiərənt] *a.* 内在的，生来就有的（existing as a natural or permanent feature or quality of somebody or something）
【例】Girls have an **inherent** love of beauty.
【用】inherent in sth. 生来就有的

inborn ['inbɔːn] *a.* 天生的，天赋的（possessed by an organism at birth）
【例】Beethoven has an **inborn** talent for music.

inbred ['in'bred] *a.* 生来的，先天的（rooted and ingrained in one's nature as deeply as if implanted by heredity）
【例】Every body has an **inbred** love of freedom.

innate [ˌi'neit] *a.* 天生的，固有的（of quality or felling, etc. in one's nature, possessed from birth）
【例】Correct ideas are not **innate** in the mind, but come from social practice.

天真的（naive, innocent, ingenuous, childlike, unworldly）

naive [nɑː'iːv] *a.* 天真的（marked by unaffected simplicity）
【例】This **naive** simple creature is very eager to believe appearances.

innocent ['inəsənt] *a.* 天真的（not very experienced concerning life and tend to trust people too much）

【例】Lucy was not as *innocent* as what she seemed like.

ingenuous [in'dʒenjuəs] *a.* 单纯的（easy to believe everything that people tell them）

【例】Alice's joy expressed itself upon her *ingenuous* face.

childlike ['tʃaildlaik] *a.* 天真烂漫的（similar to the way a child looks, behaves, or thinks, and usually pleasant for that reason）

【例】Bill's face holds a *childlike* wonder.

unworldly [ˌʌn'wəːldli] *a.* 天真的（trusting other people too much and being therefore easily tricked）

【例】Tom was an *unworldly* young scientist.

挑选（choose, pick, elect, single out, opt for）

choose [tʃuːz] *v.* 挑选（to decide which you want from a number of people or things）

【例】Will you help me *choose* a new hat?

【用】choose from sth. 从…挑选

pick [pik] *v.* 挑选，选择（to choose someone or something from a group, especially thoughtfully and carefully）

【例】I don't know which of the three dresses to *pick*—I like them all.

【用】pick sb. /sth. out 挑选出…

elect [i'lekt] *v.* 选择（to pick out）

【例】The doctrine of predestination teaches that God *elects* those who are to be saved.

【用】elect sb. as sth. 选…担任（职位等）

single out 挑选（to choose one person from a group for special attention）

【例】They all did wrong, so why *singled* him *out* for punishment?

opt for 选择，挑选

【例】Ida has *opted* now *for* an American lifestyle.

通知（inform, notify, advertise, advise, apprise, instruct, give notice）

inform [in'fɔːm] *v.* 通知，报告（to officially tell someone something or give them information about something）

【例】Parents were ***informed*** that the school would be closed for one day next week.

【用】inform sb. of/about sth. 通知或报告…

notify	['nəutifai] *v.* 通知，报告 (to give formal notice to)

【例】We've ***notified*** our clients of the changes affecting their policies.

【用】notify sb. of sth. 通知…

advertise	['ædvətaiz] *v.* 通告，宣传 (to make something generally or publicly known)

【例】It might be better not to ***advertise*** your presence.

advise	[əd'vaiz] *v.* 通知，告知 (to tell someone facts or information that they need to know)

【例】We'll ***advise*** you of the dispatch of the goods by letter.

【用】advise sb. of sth. 通知…

apprise	[ə'praiz] 通知，告诉 (to tell someone about something)

【例】I haven't been ***apprised*** of the committee's decision.

【用】apprise sb. of sth. 通知…

instruct	[in'strʌkt] *v.* 通知 (to inform somebody of something, especially in law)

【例】We are ***instructed*** by our clients that you owe them 1,000 dollars.

give notice	通知

【例】Mark gave his manager two weeks' ***notice***.

推动，促进 (facilitate, expedite, quicken, further, speed up)

facilitate	[fə'siliteit] *v.* 推动，促进 (to make it possible or easier for something to happen)

【例】The new airport will ***facilitate*** the development of tourism.

expedite	['ekspidait] *v.* 加快，加速 (to make something happen quickly or easily)

【例】We tried to help you ***expedite*** your plans.

quicken	['kwikən] *v.* 加快，变快 (to happen or move more quickly)

【例】Ken ***quickened*** his pace toward home.

further	['fə:ðə] *v.* 促进，推进 (to help the progress of something so that it is more likely to be successful)

【例】The crisis conditions *furthered* the spreading of rumors.

speed up　加快速度

【例】The car *speeded up* as soon as it reached the freeway.

退潮；衰退 (ebb, recede, decline, retreat, fade, withdraw)

ebb　[eb] *v.* 退潮；衰退 (to recede from the flood; to fall from a higher to a lower level or from a better to a worse state)

【例】The financial resources of the company *ebbed* rapidly.

recede　[ri'si:d] *v.* 退，退去 (to move back from a high point or level)

【例】The flood *receded* three days ago.

【用】recede from sth. 自…后退或避开

decline　[di'klain] *v.* 下降；衰落 (to become less or worse)

【例】The number of staff has *declined* from 217,000 to 114,000.

【用】decline sharply/rapidly/dramatically 猛降；one's declining years 晚年

retreat　[ri'tri:t] *v.* 退却；退缩 (to draw back after being defected or when faced with danger or difficulty)

【例】The defeated army had to *retreat* hastily from the battle field to the mountains.

【用】retreat from 从…撤退

fade　[feid] *v.* 消退 (to become less gradually in loudness, strength, or visibility)

【例】The lights and music *faded* as we set sail from the harbor.

【用】fade away 逐渐消退

withdraw　[wið'drɔ:] *v.* 撤退；收回 (to take somebody or something back or away; to take back a promise or an offer, etc.)

【例】The prosecutor *withdrew* the accusation.

【用】withdraw funding 收回基金；withdraw from 从…撤退

退缩 (wince, cower, cringe, flinch, quail, recoil, shrink, draw back)

wince　[wins] *v.* 退缩，畏缩 (to shrink back involuntarily (as from pain))

【例】I *winced* when the dentist's drill touched my tooth.

cower	['kauə] *v.* 畏缩，退缩（to shrink away or crouch especially for shelter；to cringe in fear） 【例】The hostages *cowered* in their seats.
cringe	[krindʒ] *v.* 畏缩（to move back slightly from something that is unpleasant or frightening） 【例】Chris had *cringed* at the thought of using her family for publicity. 【用】cringe at/from sth. 因…退缩
flinch	[flintʃ] *v.* 退缩，畏缩（to withdraw or shrink from or as if from pain） 【例】Dick didn't *flinch* once when the doctor was cleaning the wound. 【用】flinch from sth. /doing sth. 不想或不做…（不愉快的事）
quail	[kweil] *v.* 畏惧，畏缩（to recoil in dread or terror） 【例】They felt their heart *quailing* under their multiplied hardships. 【用】quail at/before sb. /sth. 因…而畏缩
recoil	[ri'kɔil] *v.* 后退，退缩（to shrink back physically or emotionally） 【例】Mary had so great a dread of snakes that she *recoiled* in horror from the snake. 【用】recoil from sb. /sth. 因…而畏缩；recoil at sth. 因…而退缩
shrink	[ʃriŋk] *v.* 退缩，畏缩（to recoil instinctively） 【例】The shy girl *shrinks* from meeting strangers. 【用】shrink（away/back）from sth. /sb. 因…而退缩，畏缩；shrink from sth. /doing sth. 不愿做…
draw back	后退，后缩 【例】The crowd *drew back* to let the firemen through.

吞食 (consume, swallow up, devour, gobble up, wolf, gulp, gorge, bolt)

consume	[kən'sju:m；kən'su:m] *v.* 吃，喝（to eat or drink something） 【例】The hungry boy *consumed* everything on his plate.
swallow up	吞没，掩盖 【例】The thick fog *swallowed up* the whole city.

devour	［di'vauə］ v. 吞食（to eat something very fast because of hunger） 【例】Those hungry man ***devoured*** the braised steak. 【用】be devoured by sth. 心中充满了…（好奇、忧虑等）
gobble up	吞没；消耗掉 【例】The man ***gobbled up*** the few remaining tickets.
wolf	［wulf］ v. 狼吞虎咽（to eat something very quickly） 【例】Carl ***wolfed*** his food down with nothing left. 【用】wolf down 狼吞虎咽
gulp	［gʌlp］ v. 狼吞虎咽地吃，吞咽（to eat or drink quickly in a way that shows someone is very hungry） 【例】Tracy quickly ***gulped*** her meal. 【用】gulp down 吞咽
gorge	［gɔːdʒ］ v. 贪婪地吃，塞饱（to eat greedily；to eat or drink so much of something that you cannot eat or drink anymore） 【例】The fat woman ***gorged*** herself constantly with desserts. 【用】gorge oneself on /with sth. 猛吃…
bolt	［bəult］ v. 囫囵吞吃（to eat hastily or without chewing） 【例】The boy can ***bolt*** three hamburgers at a time. 【用】bolt down 吞吃

完成，实现（accomplish, achieve, effect, fulfill, complete, consummate, effectuate）

accomplish	［ə'kʌmpliʃ］ v. 完成，实现（to succeed in doing something, especially something that you have been trying to do for a period of time） 【例】We tried to arrange a peace talk but nothing ***accomplished***.

【用】an accomplished fact 既成事实

achieve [ə'tʃiːv] *v.* 实现，完成（to succeed in doing or having what you planned or intended, usually after a lot of efforts）

【例】This country *achieved* independence from France in 1957.

【用】achieve great success in 在…上取得巨大成功

effect [i'fekt] *v.* 招致，实现（to make something happen, carry out）

【例】Prospects for *effecting* real political change seemed to have taken a major step backwards.

【用】effect a change 引起变化

fulfill [ful'fil] *v.* 实现，完成（计划等）（to succeed in doing something that you wanted to do, or get something you hoped for）

【例】All the necessary conditions were *fulfilled*.

【用】fulfill oneself 充分发挥自己的能力

complete [kɔm'pliːt] *v.* 完成，结束（to finish doing something; to carry out doing something）

【例】Children don't *complete* their set of 20 baby teeth until they are two or three years old.

consummate [kən'sʌmit] *v.* 完成（to finish something, especially a business deal or agreement）

【例】There have been several close calls, but no one has been able to *consummate* a deal.

effectuate [i'fektjueit] *v.* 实行，完成（to make something that you have planned happen）

【例】Now we can begin to *effectuate* the cure.

危险的（dangerous, risky, hazardous, unsafe, threatening, parlous, perilous）

dangerous ['deindʒərəs] *a.* 危险的（likely to harm or kill someone or to damage or destroy something）

【例】Drinking water in some area in that country may be *dangerous*.

【用】it is dangerous (for sb.) to do sth. （对…来说）做…是危险的；be dangerous to sb./sth. 对…是有害的

risky ['riski] *a.* 冒险的；有风险的 (involving the possibility of danger, harm, or failure)

【例】It would be *risky* to invest all your parents' money in the project.

【用】be risky to do sth. 做…有风险

hazardous ['hæzədəs] *a.* 危险的，冒险的 (dangerous, especially to people's health or safety)

【例】Stock is definitely a *hazardous* investment.

unsafe [ˌʌn'seif] *a.* 不安全的 (not safe, dangerous)

【例】It's *unsafe* to be abroad at night in some parts of the city.

threatening ['θretəniŋ] *a.* 险恶的，危险的 (having a hostile or deliberately frightening quality or manner)

【例】She was a type I found *threatening*.

parlous ['pɑːləs] *a.* 危险的 (full of dangers or difficulties)

【例】They are planning a *parlous* journey on stormy seas.

perilous ['periləs] *a.* 充满危险的 (exposed to imminent risk of disaster or ruin)

【例】The economy of that country is in a *perilous* state.

威慑，阻止 (prevent, scare off, inhibit, check, hinder, stall)

prevent [pri'vent] *v.* 阻止 (to stop something from happening; to stop someone from doing something)

【例】Cecil said this would *prevent* companies from creating new jobs.

【用】prevent sb. (from) doing sth. 阻止…做…；prevent sth. (from) happening 防止…发生

scare off 吓跑

【例】The high price is *scaring off* potential buyers.

inhibit [in'hibit] *v.* 阻止，妨碍 (to prohibit somebody or something from doing something that should be natural or easy to do)

【例】The high lending rate is *inhibiting* industries from investments in new equipments.

【用】inhibit sb. from doing sth. 阻止…做…

| check | [tʃek] *v.* 制止（to stop oneself or someone else from doing something）|

【例】 The man ***checked*** himself and stood there motionlessly.

【用】 check sth. 制止…；check oneself 自己突然停止做

| hinder | ['hində] *v.* 阻碍，妨碍（to stop someone or something from making progress or developing）|

【例】 Landslides and bad weather are continuing to ***hinder*** the arrival of the relief supply to the area.

【用】 hinder sth. 妨碍…

| stall | [stɔːl] *v.* （使）停止（to bring to a standstill）|

【例】 Talks have ***stalled*** and both sides are preparing for war.

【用】 stall on/over 停止；拒绝

微不足道的（trivial, unimportant, insignificant, inconsequential, petty, trifling, piddling, worthless, paltry）

| trivial | ['triviəl] *a.* 琐屑的，微不足道的（of little worth or importance）|

【例】 Most people don't like to visit the doctor just for something ***trivial***.

| unimportant | [ˌʌnim'pɔːtənt] *a.* 不重要的，琐碎的（not important or relevant）|

【例】 It was an ***unimportant*** job and paid very little.

| insignificant | [ˌinsig'nifikənt] *a.* 无关紧要的，可忽略的（not significant; lacking in importance）|

【例】 In comparison with famine, a plane crash is almost ***insignificant***.

| inconsequential | [ˌinkɔnsi'kwenʃəl] *a.* 不重要的，微不足道的（of no significance）|

【例】 Seemingly ***inconsequential*** details can sometimes contain significant clues.

| petty | ['peti] *a.* 琐碎的，不重要的（having little or no importance or significance）|

【例】 The meeting degenerated into ***petty*** squabbling.

trifling	['traiflin] *a*. 不重要的，琐碎的（lacking in significance or solid worth） 【例】The cost of the requested equipment was *trifling*.
piddling	['pidlin] *a*. 琐碎的，微不足道（small or not important） 【例】The two men were arguing over *piddling* amounts of money.
worthless	['wə:θlis] *a*. 无价值的，没有用处的（lacking worth, useless） 【例】The guarantee could be *worthless* if the firm goes out of business.
paltry	['pɔːltri] *a*. 微不足道的；无价值的（trivial, not very good, important or valuable） 【例】The conversation with Tom seemed *paltry*.

为…辩护（justify, vindicate, defend, excuse）

justify	['dʒʌstifai] *v*. 为…辩护（to show a sufficient lawful reason for an act done） 【例】To *justify* his client, the lawyer collected a lot of evidence.
vindicate	['vindikeit] *v*. 为…辩护（to provide justification or support for） 【例】This star might *vindicate* his reputation by the lawyer.
defend	[di'fend] *v*. 为…辩护（to say things to support someone or something that is being criticized） 【例】Mary *defended* me against the criticism. 【用】defend sb. against sth./sb. 为…辩护
excuse	[ik'skjuːz] *v*. 为…辩解（to provide a reason or explanation for something bad that someone has done, in order to make it seem less bad） 【例】Tom arrived late and *excused* his tardiness in a bad manner. 【用】excuse for sth./doing sth. 为…辩解

惟一的（single, sole, unique, solitary）

single	['singl] *a*. 惟一的（only one） 【例】We ought to be able to complete the work in a *single* day.
sole	[səul] *a*. 单独的；惟一的（being the only one） 【例】Lucy was the *sole* survivor of the car crash.

unique [juːˈniːk] *a.* 惟一的，独一无二的（being the only one）

【例】Abraham's *unique* concern was his own comfort.

【用】be unique to sb. 只发生或出现在…上

solitary [ˈsɔlitəri] *a.* 惟一的，独一无二的（only one；single）

【例】Kate couldn't answer a *solitary* question correctly.

喂(养)，为…提供食物（feed, nourish, sustain, provide, serve, foster, cater, maintain）

feed [fiːd] *v.* 喂(养)，为…提供食物（to give food to a person or an animal）

【例】The mother *feeds* her baby with a spoon.

【用】feed sb./sth. on sth. 喂…吃…；feed sth. to sb./sth. 喂…给…吃

nourish [ˈnʌriʃ；ˈnəːriʃ] *v.* 养育，喂养（to give a person, animal, or plant the food and care they need）

【例】We only use milk to *nourish* our small baby.

sustain [səˈstein] *v.* 保持，维持（生命等）（to provide the conditions in which something can happen or exist）

【例】The cash subsidies from the government *sustained* them during the off-season.

provide [prəˈvaid] *v.* 供给，提供（to give somebody something that they want or need）

【例】Father worked day and night to *provide* food and shelter for the family.

【用】provide sth. for sb./provide sb. with sth. 提供…给…

serve [səːv] *v.* 提供（to provide food and drink for somebody to eat at a meal）

【例】These apples can *serve* ten people.

【用】serve sth. to sb. 提供…给…

foster [ˈfɔstə] *v.* 培养，孕育（bring up）

【例】The cash crisis was *fostered* by declining property values.

cater [ˈkeitə] *v.* 提供饮食及服务（to provide food and service）

【例】Duncan worked in a company that *caters* banquets and weddings.

【用】cater for 为…提供饮食

maintain
[men'tein] *v.* 维持，赡养（to make something stay the same; or provide someone with the money and other things that they need in order to live）
【例】We had enough food to *maintain* life on this ship.
【用】maintain stability 保持稳定

温柔的 (gentle, mild, easygoing, equable, placid)

gentle
['dʒentl] *a.* 温柔的，温和的（of a person who is kind and calm）
【例】Joan is such a *gentle*, loving girl.

mild
[maild] *a.* 温和的，温柔的（of a person who is kind and does not often become angry）
【例】Leo gave me the impression of being a *mild* man.

easygoing
['i:zi,gəuiŋ] *a.* 随和的，温和的（relaxed, calm, and not getting easily upset about things）
【例】Our manager's an *easygoing* person—he seldom gets angry.

equable
['ekwəbl] *a.* 性情温和的（not easily upset or annoyed, even-tempered）
【例】It's lucky that Cherry's mother-in-law is so *equable*.

placid
['plæsid] *a.* 温和的，平和的（not easily irritated; free from disturbance）
【例】The stranger gave me a *placid* smile.

污染 (contaminate, pollute, poison, blemish, blot)

contaminate
[kən'tæmineit] *v.* （使…受）污染（to make something dirty, polluted, or poisonous by adding a chemical, waste, or infection）
【例】The waste from nearby factories *contaminated* the water source for the city.
【用】contaminate sb. /sth. with sth. 用…污染…

pollute
[pə'lju:t] *v.* 弄脏，污染（to make physically impure or unclean）
【例】The exhausts from vehicles *polluted* our atmosphere.
【用】pollute sth. with sth. 用…污染…

poison	['pɔizən] *v.* 污染 (to pollute)

【例】Industrial wastes are ***poisoning*** the atmosphere.

blemish	['blemiʃ] *v.* 弄脏；玷污 (to spoil by a flaw)

【例】Neal's performance was ***blemished*** by several wrong notes.

blot	[blɔt] *v.* 弄脏 (to spot, stain, or spatter with a discoloring substance)

【例】My book was ***blotted*** by ink spots.

【用】blot one's copy-book 有损…(以往的)好形象

物质的 (physical, tangible, solid, concrete, substantial)

physical	['fizikəl] *a.* 物质的 (of or concerning material things)

【例】All living things are influenced by their ***physical*** environment.

【用】physical world 物质世界

tangible	['tændʒəbl] *a.* 可触摸的，有形的 (possible to touch)

【例】Air is not ***tangible***.

solid	['sɔlid] *a.* 固体的，实心的 (of definite shape and volume)

【例】There was a ***solid*** block of wood.

concrete	['kɔnkri:t] *a.* 具体的，实体的 (existing in material form, that can be touched, felt, etc.)

【例】Physics deals with the forces acting on ***concrete*** objects.

substantial	[səb'stænʃəl] *a.* 实际存在的，真实的 (having physical existence, not merely seen or heard or imagined)

【例】It was not a ghost, but something ***substantial***.

希望，期待 (hope, wish, expect, anticipate, look for, look forward to)

hope	[həup] *v.* 希望，期望 (to want and expect something to happen or be true)

【例】Doctors *hope* that someday they can eradicate disease.

【用】hope for the best 希望获得好结果

wish ［wiʃ］*v.* 希望（to want something to happen although it is unlikely）

【例】Duncan *wished* his wife would oppose him no more.

【用】as you wish 随你的便；wish sb. /sth. well/ill 希望…走运/倒霉

expect ［iks'pekt］*v.* 期待，期盼（to be waiting for someone or something to arrive）

【例】The old lady was *expecting* the parcel from her daughter.

【用】expect sth. from sb. /sth. 期盼（某人会到来或某事会发生）

anticipate ［æn'tisipeit］*v.* 期待，预期（to look forward to as certain, especially with pleasure）

【例】We *anticipate* great pleasure from our visit to Beijing.

look for 期待

【例】I'm *looking for* an improvement in my study this term.

look forward to 期望，期待

【例】You can *look forward to* your future in the company with security.

熄灭（extinguish, put out, quench, blow out, go out）

extinguish ［ik'stiŋgwiʃ］*v.* 熄灭，扑灭（to make a fire or cigarette stop burning）

【例】Finally, firefighters *extinguished* the blazing building quickly.

put out 熄灭，关灭

【例】Remember to *put out* the lamp when you go to bed.

quench ［kwentʃ］*v.* 熄灭，扑灭火焰（to put out fire, especially with water）

【例】Firemen tried their best to *quench* the flames.

blow out 吹熄

【例】Mom *blew out* the candle and walked out.

go out 熄灭

【例】The fire has *gone out* after burning for several hours.

显示；展出 (exhibit, show, display, present, demonstrate, showcase, parade)

exhibit
[igˈzibit] *v.* 显示；展出 (to put something interesting in a museum or other public place so that people can go and look at it)
【例】The gallery is *exhibiting* a new painter's works now.

show
[ʃəu] *v.* 显示；展出 (to give information; to put something in an exhibit or competition)
【例】The famous painter *showed* Alice's most recent paintings.
【用】show sth. to sth. 把…展示给…

display
[disˈplei] *v.* 展览；显示 (to put something in a particular place so that people can see it easily)
【例】Department stores *display* their goods in the windows.
【用】display sth. to sb. /sth. 把…展示给…

present
[priˈzent] *v.* 呈现 (to show somebody or something in a particular way)
【例】Mary's lawyer tried to *present* her in the most favourable light.
【用】present at/in 展示

demonstrate
[ˈdemənstreit] *v.* 显示，表露 (to show clearly that something is true or that it exists)
【例】The girl *demonstrated* her skills as a gymnast.
【用】demonstrate against sth. 表示反对…

showcase
[ˈʃəukeis] *v.* 展示 (to show somebody or something in a way that attracts attention and emphasizes their good qualities)
【例】The boy wanted to *showcase* his ability in the speaking contest.

parade
[pəˈreid] *v.* 展示 (to publicly show something that you are proud of)
【例】The boy was unwelcome because he always *paraded* his knowledge in class.
【用】parade through/past/around 展示，游行

显现，浮现 (emerge，appear，arise，surface，crop up，come out)

emerge　[i'mə:dʒ] *v.* 显现，浮现 (to come out of something or out from behind something)
　　【例】The sun finally *emerged* from the heavy clouds.
　　【用】emerge from 出现；emerge into 涌入

appear　[ə'piə] *v.* 出现，显露 (to be or come in sight，to show up)
　　【例】Gradually a smile *appeared* on Sarah's face.
　　【用】appear to do sth. 似乎…；it appears that 看起来…

arise　[ə'raiz] *v.* 产生，出现 (to become evident，to come into being)
　　【例】Hopes for a new spirit of freedom were *arising*.
　　【用】arise from/out of 出现

surface　['sə:fis] *v.* 浮现，显露 (to become known or obvious after being hidden)
　　【例】The old problem will *surface* again.

crop up　突然出现或发生 (to appear or happen suddenly or unexpectedly)
　　【例】Problems will *crop up* and hit you before you are ready.

come out　问世 ((of a book or a movie) to become available to buy or see)
　　【例】This book will *come out* this week.

限制，限定 (limit，bound，confine，restrain，hem in，curb，circumscribe)

limit　['limit] *v.* 限制，限定 (to reduce or control someone's freedom to do what they want)
　　【例】His wife *limits* him to smoke three cigarettes a day.
　　【用】set/impose a limit 设限

bound　[baund] *v.* 成为…的界线，给…划界 (to constitute the boundary or limit of)
　　【例】This park was *bounded* by busy streets.

confine　[kən'fain] *v.* 限制，禁闭 (to keep within limits)
　　【例】The teacher asked the students to *confine* their discussions to the topic at hand.
　　【用】confine sb./sth. in/to sth. 将…限制在…中

restrain	[ˌriːˈstrein] v. 限制 (to physically control the movements of a person or an animal)

【例】The doctor tries to **restrain** and calm the patient.

【用】restrain sb. /sth. from sth. /doing sth. 限制…做…

hem in	限制，约束 (to enclose someone or something and prevent them from moving or leaving)

【例】The enemies are **hemmed in** by our troops.

curb	[kəːb] v. 控制 (to control or limit something that is harmful)

【例】Increased interest rates should **curb** inflation.

circumscribe	[ˈsəːkəmskraib] v. 限制 (to limit something such as power, rights, or opportunities)

【例】Our life was extremely **circumscribed**, with long hours of study and little play.

相当地 (pretty, quite, considerably, fairly, moderately, reasonably, to a degree)

pretty	[ˈpriti] ad. 相当地，很 (very, to a fair degree)

【例】He looks **pretty** tired.

【用】pretty much/well/near 几乎

quite	[kwait] ad. 相当地，颇 (to some extent; rather)

【例】The boy wrote **quite** a long composition.

【用】quite a few 相当多；quite some time 相当长的时间

considerably	[kənˈsidərəbli] ad. 相当地 (large in extent or degree)

【例】We have a **considerably** larger house than the previous one.

fairly	[ˈfeəli] ad. 相当地，尚可 (rather)

【例】The sofa is **fairly** soft.

moderately	[ˈmɔdərətli] ad. 适度地，相当地 (to some degree but not to a great degree)

【例】Tim did **moderately** well in the exam.

reasonably	[ˈriːzənəbli] ad. 适度地，相当地 (to a fairly high degree, level, or standard)

【例】I'm **reasonably** sure this is the best solution.

to a degree　非常，相当地

【例】The film is boring *to a degree*.

相反的 (opposite, inverse, contrary, contradictory, antithetical, reverse)

opposite　['ɔpəzit] *a.* 对立的，相反的 (completely different)

【例】The car smashed into a truck coming from the *opposite* direction.

【用】be opposite to sth./sb. 与…相对的，与…相反的

inverse　['invə:s] *a.* 倒转的，反转的 (changing in the opposite way to something else)

【例】Marry went south and Mike set out in an *inverse* direction.

contrary　['kɔntrəri] *a.* 相反的，对抗的 (completely different or opposed to something else)

【例】The introduction of such a tax would be *contrary* to our policy.

contradictory　[ˌkɔntrə'diktəri] *a.* 相矛盾的，相反的 (mutually opposed or inconsistent)

【例】It seems that your schemes are *contradictory* to common sense.

antithetical　[ˌænti'θetikəl] *a.* 相反的，对立的 (being in diametrical opposition)

【例】Long speeches are *antithetical* to the nature of cinema.

reverse　[ri'və:s] *a.* 反向的，相反的 (turned backward in position, direction, or order)

【例】Now arrange the numbers in *reverse* order.

相信；认为 (believe, hold, maintain, presume, trust, suppose, assume, surmise)

believe　[bi'li:v] *v.* 相信；认为 (to have a firm conviction as to the goodness, efficacy, or ability of something; to hold an opinion)

【例】Experts *believe* that the coming drought will be extensive.

【用】believe it or not 信不信由你

hold　[həuld] *v.* 主张 (to have in the mind or express as a judgment, opinion, or belief)

【例】This doctrine *holds* that people are inherently good.

【用】hold to sth. 坚信、不放弃… (原则、观点等)

maintain [men'tein] *v.* 坚持，主张 (to continue to say that something is true)

【例】Ted has *maintained* that the money was donated for international purpose.

presume [pri'zju:m; pri'zu:m] *v.* 假定，认为 (to think something is true because it is likely, although you cannot be certain)

【例】The missing person is *presumed* dead.

trust [trʌst] *v.* 信任，信赖 (to be confident that someone is honest, fair, and reliable)

【例】Politicians just can't be *trusted*.

【用】trust in sb. /sth. 信任…

suppose [sə'pəuz] *v.* 假想，推测 (to believe that something is probably true, based on the information that you have)

【例】The policy is perfectly clear and I see no reason to *suppose* that it isn't working.

assume [ə'sju:m; ə'su:m] *v.* 假定，假设 to accept (sth.) as true before there is proof

【例】If the package is wrapped well, we *assume* the contents are also wonderful.

【用】assume sb. /sth. to be/do sth. 假定…是…/ 假定…做…

surmise [sə:'maiz] *v.* 推测，预测 (to guess something is true, when you do not have enough information to prove that it is true)

【例】There's so little to go on that we can only *surmise* what happened.

相一致，符合 (fit, accord, harmonize, match, conform, agree)

fit [fit] *v.* 相一致，符合 (to be the truth or the same as what somebody describes or asks for)

【例】Your observations *fit* the theory nicely.

【用】fit with sth. 与…符合

accord [ə'kɔ:d] *v.* 相符合，相一致 (to agree with or be the same as something else)

【例】My manager's opinion *accorded* with mine.

【用】accord with sth. 与…一致，符合

harmonize ['hɑːmənaiz] *v.* （使）和谐，（使）协调（to produce a pleasing combination）

【例】The colours of the furniture *harmonize* well with the decoration.

【用】harmonize with sth. 与…和谐

match [mætʃ] *v.* 和…相配，和…相称（to adapt or suit so that a balanced result is achieved）

【例】The government has adopted a new foreign policy that *matches* today's realities.

【用】match up 相配

conform [kən'fɔːm] *v.* 一致，符合（to correspond in form or character）

【例】The new building *conforms* with the old-blending-with-new character of the city.

【用】conform to/with sth. 与…一致

agree [ə'griː] *v.* 相符，一致（to be the same or suggest the same thing）

【例】The conclusion *agreed* with the evidence.

【用】agree with sth. 与…一致

想法，主意（idea, thought, scheme, theory, insight, belief, notion）

idea [ai'diə] *n.* 想法，主意（a thought that you have about how to do something or how to deal with something）

【例】Drinking coffee is not her *idea*.

【用】get the idea that 形成…的印象

thought [θɔːt] *n.* 想法，见解（a word, idea, or image that comes into your mind）

【例】After much *thought*，Carl decided to buy a second-hand computer.

【用】at first thought 乍一想

scheme [skiːm] *n.* 计划，方案（a plan for achieving something, especially something illegal or dishonest）

【例】He thought of a **scheme** to get some money.

【用】the scheme of things 事物的安排

theory
['θiəri] *n.* 意见，看法（an idea that you believe is true although you have no proof）

【例】Vera is full of fascinating **theories** about men and women.

【用】in theory 理论上，按理论

insight
['insait] *n.* 洞察力，洞悉（the power or act of seeing into a situation）

【例】I never questioned my grandpa's **insight**.

【用】have an insight into sth. 了解，洞悉…

belief
[bi'li:f] *n.* 信念，信仰（a strong feeling that something is true or real）

【例】My mother holds the **belief** deeply that everything will come out fine in the end.

notion
['nəuʃən] *n.* 想法，看法（an idea or understanding of something）

【例】Mike's naive **notions** about politics surprised his friends.

【用】have no notion of 完全不明白

削（peel, skin, husk, strip, scale, decorticate, shuck, shell）

peel
[pi:l] *v.* 削，剥（to strip or cut away the skin, rind or bark from）

【例】Would you **peel** me an orange?

【用】peel off 剥掉，脱去

skin
[skin] *v.* 剥皮（to remove an outer covering; peel off）

【例】The hunter **skinned** and gutted the rabbit.

【用】skin sb. alive（威胁用语）严惩…

husk
[hʌsk] *v.* 除去…的外壳；削皮（to remove the dry outer cover of some types of grain）

【例】Tony **husked** several walnuts and began eating.

strip
[strip] *v.* 剥去，除去（to remove clothing or covering from）

【例】The wind had **stripped** the leaves from the trees.

【用】strip sth. (off) 从…去除…；strip sb. of sth. 剥夺某人的…

scale
[skeil] *v.* 刮鱼鳞（to remove layers from fish）

【例】Mother **scaled** the fish with a knife.

【用】scale off 呈片状剥落

decorticate [di:'kɔːtikeit] *v.* 剥皮，剥皮（to remove the bark, husk, or outer layer from）
【例】Trees will wilt if you *decorticate* their barks.

shuck [ʃʌk] *v.* 剥壳，去皮（to remove the shell or outer part of something）
【例】On a good day, each employee will *shuck* 3,500 oysters.

shell [ʃel] *v.* 剥…的壳（to remove the outer part that covers nuts, peas, or other foods）
【例】Mary *shelled* and ate a few nuts.

消失（evaporate, dissipate, vanish, disappear, disperse）

evaporate [i'væpəreit] *v.* 消失（to disappear suddenly）
【例】Our fears at last *evaporated*.

dissipate ['disipeit] *v.* （使）驱散；耗尽（to gradually disappear by becoming less strong）
【例】Carl opened the window to *dissipate* the heat.

vanish ['væniʃ] *v.* 突然消失，消逝（to disappear in a sudden and mysterious way）
【例】Joe *vanished* and was never seen again.
【用】vanish from 从…消失；vanish from sight 不见

disappear [ˌdisə'piə] *v.* 不见，消失（to pass out of sight）
【例】The airliner *disappeared* from the radar.
【用】disappear from 从…消失

disperse [dis'pəːs] *v.* 分散，散开（to separate and go in different directions）
【例】The police *dispersed* the crowd.

小心的（careful, alert, vigilant; attentive, cautious, circumspect, wary, watchful, on one's guard）

careful ['keəful] *a.* 小心的，仔细的（filling with care or solicitude）
【例】Please be very *careful* with those plates!

【用】be careful about/of/with sth. 小心、当心…；be careful about/in doing sth. 小心、当心做…

alert ［ə'lə:t］*a.* 警惕的（watchful and prompt to meet danger or emergency）

【例】Parents must be ***alert*** to the symptoms of the disease.

【用】be alert to sth. 对…有所警觉

vigilant ［'vidʒilənt］*a.* 机警的，警惕的（alertly watchful especially to avoid danger）

【例】We should be eternally ***vigilant*** against our enemy's movements.

attentive ［ə'tentiv］*a.* 注意的（mindful，observant）

【例】Jack is ***attentive*** to what he is doing.

【用】be attentive to sb. /sth. 对…留心

cautious ［'kɔ:ʃəs］*a.* 十分小心的，谨慎的（marked by or given to caution）

【例】The students are ***cautious*** enough not to make any grammatical mistakes.

【用】be cautious about/of sb. /sth. 提防…

circumspect ［'sə:kəmspekt］*a.* 慎重的（careful to consider all circumstances and possible consequences）

【例】In order to adhere to the religious principle，his father lived the most ***circumspect*** life.

wary ［'weəri］*a.* 谨慎的；机警的（marked by keen caution, cunning, and watchfulness especially in detecting and escaping danger）

【例】A ***wary*** old politician never says too much.

【用】be wary of sb. /sth. 警惕…

watchful ［'wɔtʃful］*a.* 注意的，警惕的（carefully observant or attentive）

【例】Mom always tells me to be ***watchful*** for cars when I cross the street.

on one's guard 警惕，提防

【例】Be ***on your guard*** against thieves.

效仿，模仿（imitate，emulate，ape，mimic）

imitate ［'imiteit］*v.* 模仿，仿制（to copy something or to copy someone's actions，words，or behavior）

【例】The young writer tried to *imitate* Hemingway.

emulate　　['emjuleit] *v.* 效仿，模仿（to try to be like someone or something else, usually because you admire them）

【例】Sons are traditionally expected to *emulate* their fathers.

ape　　[eip] *v.* 模仿（to copy someone, especially the way they behave or speak）

【例】They howled with laughter at the way he *aped* the receptionist's dumb-broad voice.

mimic　　['mimik] *v.* 模仿（to copy someone's voice, behavior, or appearance, especially in order to make people laugh or to make someone feel annoyed）

【例】The actor *mimicked* some well-known people to amuse the audience.

心不在焉的 (absentminded, abstracted, distrait)

absentminded　　[,æbsənt'maindid] *a.* （思想集中在别处而）心不在焉的（absent in mind）

【例】Lydia made some *absentminded*, irrelevant answers, as if she had not heard the teacher's questions.

abstracted　　[,æb'stræktid] *a.* 心不在焉的，出神的（inattentive to one's surroundings）

【例】Do not do your work with an *abstracted* mind.

distrait　　[di:s'treit] *a.* 心不在焉的（not able to concentrate on something because you are worried about something else）

【例】Why do you always answer my questions in a *distrait* manner?

行得通的 (feasible, doable, attainable, viable)

feasible　　['fi:zəbl] *a.* 可做的，可实行的（possible or likely to succeed）

【例】Your plan sounds *feasible*.

doable　　['du:əbl] *a.* 可做的，可行的（able to be done）

【例】This program is tough but *doable*.

attainable	[ə'teinəbl] *a.* 可获得的，可实现的（possible to achieve，reach，or get） 【例】Your dream was not ***attainable***.
viable	['vaiəbl] *a.* 切实可行的，可实施的（able to be done，or worth doing） 【例】What we need is a ***viable*** plan.

虚弱的（weak, powerless, feeble, fragile, impotent）

weak	[wi:k] *a.* 虚弱的，无力的（lacking strength or energy） 【例】The spirit is willing，but the flesh is ***weak***. 【用】weak at the knees（因激动、恐惧等）一时两腿发软而站立不住
powerless	['pauəlis] *a.* 无力量的（devoid of strength or resources） 【例】Sheila was ***powerless*** to stop him. 【用】be powerless to do sth. 无力做…
feeble	['fi:bl] *a.* 虚弱的，衰弱的（markedly lacking in strength） 【例】The old lady is too ***feeble*** to do her own shopping.
fragile	['frædʒail] *a.* 虚弱的，弱的（not very strong or healthy） 【例】She has been in ***fragile*** health all winter.
impotent	['impətənt] *a.* 无力的，虚弱的（lacking in power，strength，or vigor） 【例】The smaller nations feel politically ***impotent*** on the world stage.

虚伪的（insincere, dishonest, deceptive, fake）

insincere	[,insin'siə] *a.* 虚假的（not expressing feelings or opinions honestly） 【例】Mike's sentimentalism at his wife's funeral was ***insincere***.
dishonest	[dis'ɔnist] *a.* 不诚实的（characterized by lack of truth，honesty，or trustworthiness） 【例】The teacher became furious about the student's ***dishonest*** answer.

deceptive	[di'septiv] *a.* 虚伪的，欺骗性的 (trying to trick someone by telling them something that is not true) 【例】The jury did not believe the witness's ***deceptive*** answers.
fake	[feik] *a.* 假的 (made to look like something else, especially something expensive) 【例】Only an expert can distinguish between a ***fake*** and a real diamond.

许多的 (numerous, copious, plentiful, considerable, myriad, innumerable, numberless)

numerous	['nju:mərəs] *a.* 许多的，无数的 (existing in large numbers) 【例】Justin had ***numerous*** books in his bookcase.
copious	['kəupjəs] *a.* 丰富的 (large, or in large amounts) 【例】Lucia found relief at last in a ***copious*** flow of tears.
plentiful	['plentiful] *a.* 大量的 (present or available in large quantities) 【例】Here the hotel rooms were ***plentiful*** and cheap.
considerable	[kən'sidərəbl] *a.* 相当大(或多)的 (large in size, amount, or degree) 【例】Bill earned ***considerable*** amount of money during his lifetime.
myriad	['miriəd] *a.* 无数的 (constituting a countless or extremely great number) 【例】A ***myriad*** of options exists for us.
innumerable	[i'nju:mərəbl] *a.* 无数的 (too many to be counted: used for emphasizing a large amount or number) 【例】There are ***innumerable*** examples of his generous nature.
numberless	['nʌmbəlis] *a.* 无数的 (too many to be counted) 【例】There are ***numberless*** stars in the sky.

叙述 (narrate, relate, recount, recite)

narrate	[nə'reit] *v.* 讲述，叙述 (to tell a story in speech or writing) 【例】Mark ***narrated*** the shocking details of his night in jail.

relate	[ri'leit] *v.* 讲述，叙述 (to tell someone about something that has happened or what someone has said)

【例】 Phillip began to *relate* the horrors of his childhood to friends.

【用】 relate sth. to sb. 将…讲述给…

recount	[ri'kaunt] *v.* 描述，叙述 (to say what happened)

【例】 Michelle *recounted* her conversation with Sam.

【用】 recount sth. to sb. 将…叙述给…

recite	[ri'sait] *v.* 详述 (to give a long detailed spoken description of something)

【例】 Winnie *recited* the entire guest list.

【用】 recite sth. to sb. 将…详述给…

宣布 (announce, declare, proclaim, set forth)

announce	[ə'nauns] *v.* 宣布，宣告 (to make a public or official statement，especially about a plan，decision，etc.)

【例】 The veteran *announced* his retirement.

declare	[di'kleə] *v.* 正式宣布，声明 (to announce officially that something is true or happening)

【例】 Larry's claim to the property was *declared* valid.

【用】 declare sb. sth. 宣布…是…；declare off sth. 宣布取消（婚约等）

proclaim	[prə'kleim] *v.* 陈述，说明 (to state something publicly)

【例】 The two companies *proclaimed* the conclusion of a union contract.

set forth	宣布，提出 (to explain or describe something in a clear way，especially in writing)

【例】 This memorandum *sets forth* basic departmental policies.

宣传 (publicize, promote, hype, advertise, trumpet, promulgate, air)

publicize	['pʌblisaiz] *v.* 宣传 (to publish or broadcast information about a thing or person)

【例】 The author appeared on television to *publicize* her latest book.

promote

[prə'məut] *v.* 宣传，推销 (to support or encourage something)

【例】The company spent 50 thousand dollars making commercials to *promote* a new product.

hype

[haip] *v.* 夸大的广告宣传 (to use a lot of advertisements and other publicity to influence or interest people)

【例】We had to *hype* the film to attract the financiers.

【用】hype sth. up 言过其实地宣传…

advertise

['ædvətaiz] *v.* 为…做广告，宣传 (to try to persuade people to buy a product or service by announcing it on television, on the Internet, in newspapers, etc.)

【例】Religious groups are currently not allowed to *advertise* on television.

【用】advertise for sth. 为…做广告

trumpet

['trʌmpit] *v.* 鼓吹 (to announce something publicly in a way that is intended to make it seem very important)

【例】What Tony only knows is to *trumpet* his praises.

promulgate

['prɔməlgeit; prəu'mʌlgeit] *v.* 宣传，传播 (to make an idea or belief known to as many people as possible)

【例】It *promulgates* a brand of heaven-on-earth religion.

air

[eə] *v.* 广播；公开 (to broadcast something on the radio or on television)

【例】The advertisement was submitted to CBS which accepted and *aired* it.

旋转 (wheel, reel, revolve, rotate, spin, swivel, trundle, whirl)

wheel

[wi:l] *v.* 转动，旋转 (to turn on or as if on an axis)

【例】The nurse *wheeled* the cart up to the bed.

【用】wheel round/around 转身

reel

[ri:l] *v.* 来回旋转 (to wind on or as if on a reel)

【例】Men in wheelchairs *reeled* around the room, shooting and singing.

【用】reel sth. in/out 在卷轴等上缠绕；reel sth. off 一口气说或重复…

revolve
［ri'vɔlv］v.（使）旋转，绕转（to move in a curved path round a center or axis）
【例】The earth *revolves* around the sun.
【用】revolve round/around sb./sth. 绕着…旋转；以…为中心

rotate
［rəu'teit；'rəuteit］v.（使）旋转，（使）转动（to turn round an axis or a center）
【例】The earth *rotates* on its axis while it revolves in its orbit.

spin
［spin］v.（使）旋转（turn or cause to turn or whirl around quickly）
【例】The teacher *spun* round to see who had spoken.
【用】spin sth. round 使…快速旋转

swivel
［'swivəl］v. 旋转（to revolve rapidly）
【例】On hearing the voice，the patient *swiveled* his chair round to see who had come in.
【用】swivel sth. round 使…在旋轴上转动

trundle
［'trʌndl］v. 推动，滚动（to progress by revolving）
【例】The farmer *trundled* a wheelbarrow through the river.

whirl
［wəːl］v. 旋转（to move in a circle or similar curve especially with force or speed）
【例】The letter was picked up by the wind and *whirled* into the air.

询问（query, ask, question, inquire, interrogate, cross-examine）

query
［'kwiəri］v. 质问，质疑（to express doubt or uncertainty；question）
【例】I *queried* whether his words could be relied on.
【用】query sb. about sth. 向…提出关于…的问题

ask
［ɑːsk；æsk］v. 问，询问（try to get information）
【例】You should *ask* if you don't know.
【用】ask after 问候；询问；ask for 请求，要求，寻求；ask over 邀请去（家、办公室等）

question
［'kwestʃən］v. 询问，审问（to put a question to）
【例】The teacher *questioned* the children about what had happened.

inquire [in'kwaiə] *v.* 打听，询问（to ask someone for information about something）

【例】The buyer *inquired* about prices of those cell phones.

【用】inquire into sth. 调查…；inquire of/about sth. 询问…，打听…

interrogate [in'terəgeit] *v.* 审问，询问（to ask someone a lot of questions in order to get information，in an angry or threatening way）

【例】Police had *interrogated* the crime for three times but they still got nothing.

【用】interrogate sb. about sth. 询问…；审问…

cross-examine [ˌkrɔsig'zæmin] *v.* 反复询问；追问（to ask a witness questions during a trial after another lawyer has already asked them questions）

【例】Police *cross-examined* all the suspects.

迅速的（swift, speedy, hasty, winged）

swift [swift] *a.* 快的，敏捷的（happening quickly or immediately）

【例】The communication network was *swift* in operation.

【用】be swift to do sth./in doing sth. 快速地做…

speedy ['spi:di] *a.* 快速的，迅速的（characterized by rapid motion）

【例】Carl finished his work in a *speedy* way.

hasty ['heisti] *a.* 急速的，匆忙的（done in a hurry because you do not have much time）

【例】After the *hasty* meal，men had moved forward to take up their positions.

【用】be hasty in doing/to do sth. 草率或仓促从事…

winged [wiŋd] *a.* 迅速的（moving fast）

【例】Dick was a *winged* messenger.

压制（quell，subdue，crush，conquer，suppress，quash，vanquish，silence，put down，stamp out）

quell ［kwel］ *v.* 镇压，压制（to cause a violent situation to end）
【例】Police *quelled* the riot.

subdue ［səb'dju:］ *v.* 制服，抑制（to hold someone and make them stop behaving in an uncontrolled or violent way）
【例】Police used tear gas to *subdue* the rioters.

crush ［krʌʃ］ *v.* 镇压，制服（to put down；subdue）
【例】The military operation was the first step in a plan to *crush* the uprising.
【用】crush sth. （up）把…捣碎、压碎

conquer ［'kɔŋkə］ *v.* 克服，抑制（to gain or secure control of by or as if by force of arms）
【例】You are the manager，so you have to *conquer* your shyness and your fears.

suppress ［sə'pres］ *v.* 压制，镇压（to stop opposition or protest using military force or strict laws）
【例】All religious activities were *suppressed*.

quash ［kwɔʃ］ *v.* 镇压（to use force or violence to stop the political action taken by a group of people）
【例】Troops were displaying an obvious reluctance to get involved in *quashing* demonstrations.

vanquish ［'væŋkwiʃ］ *v.* 压制，克服（to overcome or subdue，to suppress）
【例】If you want to succeed，firstly you should *vanquish* your fears.
【用】vanquish sb. at sth. 在…（多为比赛）中击败…

silence	['sailəns] *v.* 使沉默；压制（to stop someone or something from speaking or making a sound） 【例】Like other tyrants，he tried to ***silence*** anyone who spoke out against him.
put down	镇压，制止 【例】Government sent troops to ***put down*** the rebellion.
stamp out	扑灭；镇压（暴动等） 【例】The government is determined to ***stamp out*** crime.

淹没（submerge, sink, submerse, plunge, immerse, dunk, dive, swamp, drown）

submerge	[səb'məːdʒ] *v.* 沉没；淹没（to put something under water） 【例】Floods have ***submerged*** parts of the island，killing many people.
sink	[siŋk] *v.* （使）下沉，（使）沉没（to go below water's surface） 【例】They could do nothing but watch the boat fill with water and ***sink*** finally. 【用】be sunk in sth. 陷入或坠入…（某种状态）；sink like a stone 急速下降
submerse	[səb'məːs] *v.* 使沉入水中；淹没（to submerge） 【例】The river overflowed and ***submersed*** the farmland.
plunge	[plʌndʒ] *v.* 把…投入（或刺进）（to cause to penetrate or enter quickly and forcibly into something） 【例】Boys ran fast to the bank of the lake and then ***plunged*** in. 【用】plunge into（使）投入，（使）插进，猛冲
immerse	[i'məːs] *v.* （使）浸没（to plunge into something that surrounds or covers） 【例】The girl ***immersed*** the leek into the boiling water. 【用】immerse in sth. 使陷入…，使沉浸在…
dunk	[dʌŋk] *v.* 泡，浸（to dip (as a piece of bread) into a beverage while eating） 【例】Many people like to ***dunk*** their bread in milk. 【用】dunk sth. /sb. in/into sth. 将…浸入…

— 305 —

dive	[daiv] *v.* 跳水（to jump into water）
	【例】The heart-broken girl was standing by a lake and about to *dive* in to end her life.
	【用】dive into sth. 审入…，潜入…；投入…
swamp	[swɔmp] *v.* 使陷入，淹没（to fill with or as if with water）
	【例】Lots of houses were *swamped* by the flood.
	【用】swamp sb. /sth. with sth. 以…（繁多的事物）压倒…
drown	[draun] *v.* （使）淹死，淹没（to suffocate by submersion especially in water）
	【例】Forty-eight people have *drowned* after their boat capsized.
	【用】drown sth. in sth. 将…浸在…中；drown sb. /sth. （out）（指声音）淹没在（另一声音中）

严格的，严厉的（strict, severe, stern, harsh, rigorous）

strict	[strikt] *a.* 严格的，严厉的（rigorous in the imposition of discipline）
	【例】Dad's very *strict* with us about table manners.
	【用】be strict with sb. 对…非常严厉
severe	[si'viə] *a.* 严厉的，严格的（very or extremely strict）
	【例】Our teacher was equally *severe* on students who were late for class.
	【用】be severe on/with sb. 对…非常严厉
stern	[stə:n] *a.* 严厉的，严格的（serious and severe）
	【例】Frank is much too *stern* with his son.
harsh	[hɑːʃ] *a.* 严厉的，无情的（extremely severe or exacting）
	【例】The law has been *harsher* on soldiers than it has on civilians.
	【用】be harsh on sb. 对…非常严格
rigorous	['rigərəs] *a.* 严格的，严厉的（very strict or severe）
	【例】The training involved *rigorous* exercises.

掩盖（veil, cloak, conceal, cover, disguise, hide, mask, screen, shroud）

veil	[veil] *v.* 遮蔽（to cover, provide, obscure, or conceal with or as if with a veil）

【例】Cindy made no attempt to *veil* the contempt in her voice.

cloak ['kləuk] *v.* 掩盖，掩饰 (to cover or hide with or as if with a cloak)

【例】The appearance of good will *cloaked* a sinister intention.

【用】cloak sth. (in sth.) 掩盖，隐藏…

conceal [kən'si:l] *v.* 隐藏；掩盖 (to prevent disclosure or recognition of)

【例】Why did you decide to *conceal* your true identity?

【用】conceal sth. /sb. (from sb. /sth.) 对…隐藏、掩盖或隐瞒…

cover ['kʌvə] *v.* 盖，覆盖 (to hide from sight or knowledge, to lie over)

【例】The injured man was *covered* with a blanket.

【用】cover over 遮盖；cover up 掩盖，掩饰

disguise [dis'gaiz] *v.* 伪装，掩饰 (to furnish with a false appearance or an assumed identity)

【例】The robber escaped by *disguising* himself as a security guard.

【用】disguise sb. /sth. (with sth.) (用…) 掩盖，隐藏…；disguise sb. /sth. (as sb. /sth.) 假扮成…

hide [haid] *v.* 把…藏起来；遮掩 (to put out of sight)

【例】Dark clouds *hid* the sun.

【用】hide sth. from sb. 对…隐瞒…

mask [ma:sk；mæsk] *v.* 掩饰；遮盖 (to disguise one's true character or intentions)

【例】Undergrowth *masked* the entrance to the cave.

【用】masked ball 化装舞会

screen [skri:n] *v.* 掩蔽，遮蔽 (to give shelter or protection with or as if with a screen)

【例】The thief *screened* himself under a bush and waited.

【用】screen sb. from sth. /sb. 保护… (不受责备等)；包庇

shroud [ʃraud] *v.* 遮蔽；隐藏 (to cut off from view, to veil under another appearance)

【例】The affair was *shrouded* in secrecy.

【用】shroud sth. in sth. 用…覆盖、遮蔽…

厌恶 (hate, detest, loathe, abhor, disgust, abominate)

hate　[heit] *v.* 憎恨，不喜欢 (to dislike someone or something very much)
【例】I *hate* washing dishes especially in winter.
【用】hate doing/to do sth. 讨厌或不喜欢做…；hate sb. /sth. doing sth. 讨厌…做…

detest　[di'test] *v.* 憎恶，憎恨 (to dislike very much)
【例】Many people *detest* having to get up early.
【用】detest doing sth. 讨厌做…；detest sb. /sth. doing sth. 讨厌…做…

loathe　[ləuð] *v.* 憎恨，厌恶 (to dislike someone or something intensely)
【例】Lucy simply *loathes* her ex-husband.
【用】loathe doing sth. 讨厌做…

abhor　[əb'hɔː] *v.* 憎恨，厌恶 (to dislike something very much, especially when you think it is immoral)
【例】Alice *abhors* cruelty and violence.

disgust　[dis'gʌst] *v.* 使厌恶，使反感 (to cause someone to feel revulsion or profound disapproval)
【例】We're all *disgusted* at the way Mary treated her boyfriend.

abominate　[ə'bɔmineit] *v.* 痛恨，厌恶 (to hate something because you think it is extremely offensive, unpleasant, or wrong)
【例】Mr. King *abominates* falsehood.

一群 (flock, school; herd, pack, swarm, mob)

flock　[flɔk] *n.* （鸟、兽等）一群 (a group of animals, etc.)
【例】A *flock* of cattle blocked the road.
【用】a flock of 一群

school　[skuːl] *n.* 一群（鱼）(a large group of aquatic fish, such as dolphins, whales, etc.)
【例】Our small boat was attacked by a *school* of sharks.
【用】a school of 一群

herd　[hə:d] *n.* 兽群（a large group of animals of the same type）

【例】A *herd* of elephants thundered across the plains.

【用】herds of 大量的

pack　[pæk] *n.* 兽群（a group of wild animals that live and hunt together）

【例】Wolves hunt in *packs*.

【用】a pack of sth. = a sth. pack 一群

swarm　[swɔ:m] *n.* 群，一大群（a large group of insects flying or moving together or a large number of people moving together as a group）

【例】*Swarms* of police officers surrounded the building where a bomb exploded.

【用】a swarm of 一大群

mob　[mɔb] *n.* （盗贼等的）一群（a large crowd of people that is dangerous or difficult to control）

【例】A *mob* of reporters was waiting outside the courthouse.

【用】a mob of 一群；mobs of 大量的

依靠（rely, depend, count/on/upon, lie on, sponge on/off, build upon, lean）

rely　[ri'lai] *v.* 依靠，依赖（to be dependent for support，help or supply）

【例】She *relies* on her husband for tuition.

【用】rely on 依靠，依赖

depend　[di'pend] *v.* 依靠，依赖（to be determined，based，or contingent）

【例】Their future *depends* on how well they do in school.

【用】depend on 依靠，依赖

count on/upon　依靠，指望（to depend on someone to do what you want or expect them to do for you）

【例】The whole team was *counting on/upon* me，and I let them down.

lie on　取决于，依赖

【例】The hostage's life *lies on* the negotiations between rebel groups and government.

sponge on/off　依赖 (to ask for money and other things from friends or relatives and make no effort to give anything back or pay for anything yourself)

【例】Louis has been *sponging on/off* us for many years.

build upon　依靠，指望

【例】We need to *build upon* the ideas we have had so far.

lean　[li:n] *v.* 倚靠 (to depend on)

【例】Everybody needs someone to *lean* on in times of trouble.

【用】lean on 依赖，依靠

移居 (migrate, emigrate, immigrate, rove, range, relocate)

migrate　[mai'greit；'maigreit] *v.* 移居 (to move from one country, place, or locality to another)

【例】People *migrate* from rural areas to large cities.

【用】migrate from…to… 从…移居到…

emigrate　['emigreit] *v.* 移居外国（或外地）(to leave one's place of residence or country to live elsewhere)

【例】We're thinking of *emigrating* to New Zealand.

【用】emigrate from…to… 从…移居到…

immigrate　['imigreit] *v.* 移居入境 (to come into a country of which one is not a native for permanent residence)

【例】The war caused a lot of people to *immigrate* from Germany to the United States.

【用】immigrate from…to/into… 从…移入…

rove　[rəuv] *v.* 流浪，漂泊 (to move around an area without a definite direction or purpose)

【例】They could *rove* at will among the stars.

range　[reindʒ] *v.* 漫游 (to move with complete freedom around a large area)

【例】There were buffalo *ranging* the plains of North America.

relocate　[,ri:ləu'keit] *v.* 重新安置 (to move to a different place, or to make someone do this)

【例】The authorities have *relocated* thousands of families from the flooded areas.

【用】relocate the business 重新安置商业活动

以前的 (former, past, preceding, previous, prior)

former　['fɔːmə] *a*. 以前的，前者的 (of an earlier period or time; being the first mentioned of two things or people)

【例】The owner of this castle is Mr. Smith，while the **former** owner was Mr. Johnson.

【用】a shadow of one's former self 已不再有以前的力量或影响

past　[pɑːst; pæst] *a*. 以前的，过去的 (happening or existing at any earlier time)

【例】These old ladies can never forget the **past** sufferings.

preceding　[ˌpriːˈsiːdiŋ] *a*. 在前的，前面的 (existing or coming immediately before someone or something else)

【例】The information we discussed yesterday is located on the **preceding** pages.

previous　['priːviəs] *a*. (时间或顺序上) 先前的，以前的 (coming before in time or order)

【例】I came across Joan the **previous** day.

【用】previous to sth. 在…之前

prior　['praiə] *a*. 在…之前 (happening, existing, or done before a particular time)

【例】We didn't receive any notification **prior** to today's date.

【用】prior to sth. 在…之前

因此，所以 (therefore, accordingly, consequently, hence, thus, thereby, as a result)

therefore　['ðeəfɔː] *ad*. 因此，所以 (as a result of the reason that has just been mentioned)

【例】Bill was ill，and **therefore** could not come on time.

accordingly　[əˈkɔːdiŋli] *ad*. 因此，所以 (as a result of something)

【例】Justin was tired out，**accordingly**，we sent him to bed.

consequently　['kɔnsikwəntli] *ad*. 因此，从而 (as a result, therefore)

【例】Ken works very hard，**consequently**，he did very well in school.

hence	〔hens〕*ad.* 因此，所以 (used for introducing something that is a result of the fact that has just been stated) 【例】This bracelet was handmade and **hence** expensive.
thus	〔ðʌs〕*ad.* 因此 (as a result of the fact that you have just mentioned) 【例】More pupils will attend the schools, and they will **thus** have more teachers.
thereby	〔ˌðeə'bai〕*ad.* 因此，从而 (because of or by means of what has just been mentioned) 【例】Kate is 18 years old now, **thereby** gaining the right to vote.
as a result	因此，作为结果 【例】Man polluted the river, **as a result**, thousands of fish living in it died.

永恒的 (undying, eternal, immortal, unfading, everlasting, imperishable, endless, permanent, ceaseless, constant, infinite)

undying	〔ˌʌn'daiiŋ〕*a.* 不朽的，永恒的 (never ending) 【例】Do you believe the dog's **undying** love for its master?
eternal	〔i'tə:nl〕*a.* 永恒的，永久的 (continuing forever or for a very long time) 【例】The minister spoke of the soul's **eternal** life. 【用】the eternal verities 永恒的真理
immortal	〔i'mɔ:təl〕*a.* 不朽的 (living or existing forever) 【例】Hamlet was one of Shakespeare's **immortal** works.
unfading	〔ʌn'feidiŋ〕*a.* （颜色、光彩、价值等）永不消失的 (not losing color or freshness; not losing value or effectiveness) 【例】The color on this picture was **unfading**.
everlasting	〔ˌevə'lɑ:stiŋ〕*a.* 永恒的，永久的 (lasting or enduring through all time) 【例】The Christian believes the **everlasting** life of the soul. 【用】everlasting life 永生
imperishable	〔im'periʃəbl〕*a.* 不灭的，不朽的 (enduring or occuring forever) 【例】Gray won **imperishable** glory for his bravery.

endless	['endlis] *a.* 无止境的，没完没了的（seeming to have no end or limit） 【例】They asked *endless* questions about my personal matters.
permanent	['pə:mənənt] *a.* 长久的，永久的（happening or existing for a long time or for all time in the future） 【例】Her mother suffered *permanent* brain damage as a result of the stroke.
ceaseless	['si:slis] *a.* 不停的，不断的（continuing without stopping） 【例】I was growing tired of our *ceaseless* quarrel.
constant	['kɔnstənt] *a.* 持续的，不变的（continuous or regular over a long period of time） 【例】The pollution problem has been a *constant* source of concern for us.
infinite	['infinət] *a.* 无限的，无穷的（very great in amount or degree，and seeming to have no limit） 【例】She is a good teacher with *infinite* patience.

勇敢的 (brave, fearless, courageous, heroic, manful, stout-hearted, daring, bold, gallant)

brave	[breiv] *a.* 勇敢的（capable of dealing with danger or pain，without seeming to be frightened） 【例】We all commit *brave* deeds in fantasy sometimes.
fearless	['fiəlis] *a.* 无畏的，勇敢的（not afraid of anyone or anything） 【例】Our *fearless* soldiers were ready to fight the enemy.
courageous	[kə'reidʒəs] *a.* 有胆量的，有勇气的（very brave and determined） 【例】Tom fought a *courageous* campaign against his lung cancer.
heroic	[hi'rəuik] *a.* 英雄的，英勇的（very brave and deserving admiration） 【例】The soldiers made a *heroic* attempt to stop the enemy's advance.
manful	['mænful] *a.* 大丈夫气概的，勇敢的（resolute or brave，especially in the face of adversity） 【例】He suffered from the illness but made a *manful* attempt to smile.

stout-hearted ['staut'hɑ:tid] *a.* 刚毅的，勇敢的（courageous or determined）

【例】They need a ***stout-hearted*** guy to do this hard work.

daring ['deəriŋ] *a.* 大胆的，勇敢的（brave enough to do dangerous things）

【例】His father is a ***daring*** aviator.

bold [bəuld] *a.* 敢做敢为的，大胆的（showing a willingness to take risks）

【例】Sergeant York was definitely a very ***bold*** soldier.

gallant ['gælənt] *a.* 英勇的（unflinching in battle or action）

【例】Chinese people put up a ***gallant*** resistance to the Japanese invaders.

用尽（spend, exhaust, use up, pay out）

spend [spend] *v.* 用尽（exhaust, wear out）

【例】The gas in this car was ***spent***.

exhaust [ig'zɔ:st] *v.* 用尽，耗尽（to consume entirely）

【例】The expedition was forced to turn back when it ***exhausted*** its food supply.

use up 用完，耗尽

【例】Our sugar has been ***used up***.

pay out 花费；支出

【例】My father has ***paid out*** a lot of money on repairing our house.

优雅的（graceful, elegant, refined, polished, cultured, polite）

graceful ['greisful] *a.* 优美的，优雅的（showing good manners and respect for other people）

【例】Shirley was extremely ***graceful*** in defeat.

elegant ['eligənt] *a.* 优美的，文雅的（having the qualities of grace and beauty）

【例】Rose was an ***elegant*** woman with elegant clothes.

【用】elegant manners 优雅的仪态

| refined | [ri'faind] a. (故意显出) 有教养的 (showing or intending to show education, delicate feeling, and gentleness of manners) |

refined
[ri'faind] a. (故意显出) 有教养的 (showing or intending to show education, delicate feeling, and gentleness of manners)
【例】Sophia was so *refined* that she always ate cake with a fork.

polished
['pɔliʃt] a. 雅致大方的 (refined; cultured)
【例】Tim was a gentleman with *polished* manners.
【用】polished manners 优雅的风度

cultured
['kʌltʒəd] a. 有教养的，有修养的 (having or showing good education, manners, and especially an interest in art, music, literature etc.)
【例】*Cultured* minds like good books and painting.

polite
[pə'lait] a. 有礼貌的 (having or showing good manners, sensitivity to other people's feelings, and/or correct social behavior)
【例】Jonathan's refusal was firm but *polite*.
【用】be polite of sb. to do sth. 某人做某事是很有礼貌的；be polite to sb. 对…有礼貌

忧郁的 (somber, gloomy, depressing, bleak, dreary, mournful, funereal, gray)

somber
['sɔmbə] a. 忧郁的 (of a dismal or depressing character)
【例】"I wish he'll come back", Martha said in a *somber* voice.

gloomy
['gluːmi] a. 忧郁的 (low in spirits)
【例】The poor man felt *gloomy* about his future.

depressing
[di'presiŋ] a. 令人忧愁的，令人沮丧的 (causing emotional depression)
【例】The news Maggie brought back was *depressing*.

bleak
[bliːk] a. 阴郁的，无望的 (not hopeful or encouraging)
【例】Our future looks *bleak*.

dreary
['driəri] a. 阴郁的 (having nothing likely to provide cheer, comfort, or interest)
【例】Foreign trade prospects are *dreary*.

mournful
['mɔːnful] a. 悲痛的，悲哀的 (full of sorrow)
【例】Ken looked *mournful*.

funereal	[fju:'niəriəl] *a.* 忧郁的 (gloomy, dismay)
	【例】There was a *funereal* expression on her face.
gray	[grei] *a.* 沮丧的 (lacking cheer or brightness in mood, outlook, style, or flavor)
	【例】Failed in his exams, the little boy was in a *gray* mood.

犹豫，踌躇 (hesitate, waver, dither, hang back)

hesitate	['heziteit] *v.* 犹豫，踌躇 (to be slow to act, speak, or decide)
	【例】The stunned guests *hesitate* a moment, then burst into wild, unrestrained applause!
	【用】hesitate at/over/about sth. 在…上犹豫不决
waver	['weivə] *v.* 犹豫，动摇 (to vacillate irresolutely between choices)
	【例】John *wavered* among the choices on the menu.
	【用】waver sth. between sth. 在…和…之间犹豫不决
dither	['diðə] *v.* 犹豫不决 (to act nervously or indecisively)
	【例】For God's sake, stop *dithering* and make up your mind.
	【用】dither about sth. 为…踌躇，犹豫不决
hang back	畏缩不前，迟疑
	【例】The journalist *hung back* from asking more questions.

有毒的 (poisonous, toxic, venomous, virulent, noxious, pernicious)

poisonous	['pɔizənəs] *a.* 有毒的，有害的 (containing poison)
	【例】The man was bit by a *poisonous* snake and died in five minutes.
toxic	['tɔksik] *a.* 有毒的 (poisonous and harmful to people, animals, or the environment)
	【例】These plants' fruits were *toxic* and inesculent.
venomous	['venəməs] *a.* 有毒的，分泌毒液的 (capable of producing poison)
	【例】The adder is Britain's only *venomous* snake.
virulent	['virjulənt] *a.* 剧毒的，恶毒的 (extremely infectious, malignant, or poisonous)
	【例】A very *virulent* form of the disease appeared in Belgium.

noxious　['nɔkʃəs] *a*. 有害的，有毒的 (harmful or poisonous)

【例】Many household products give off *noxious* fumes.

pernicious　[pə'niʃəs] *a*. 有害的，致命的 (very dangerous or harmful, especially to someone's moral character)

【例】They were infected by a *pernicious* virus.

【用】be pernicious to sb. /sth. 对…有害

有风的 (windy, blustery, breezy, tempestuous, stormy, blowing, windswept, drafty)

windy　['windi] *a*. 有风的，刮风的 (marked by strong wind or by more wind than usual)

【例】The *windy* weather made the winter days even colder.

blustery　['blʌstəri] *a*. 大风的 (very windy)

【例】It's a cold night here, with intermittent rain showers and a *blustery* wind.

breezy　['briːzi] *a*. 有微风的 (pleasantly windy)

【例】These days were *breezy* and warm.

tempestuous　[tem'pestjuəs] *a*. 有暴风雨的 (of, relating to, or resembling a tempest)

【例】The *tempestuous* gales turned over the ship.

stormy　['stɔːmi] *a*. 暴风雨的 (relating to, characterized by, or indicative of a storm)

【例】It had been a night of *stormy* weather, with torrential rain and high winds.

blowing　['bləuiŋ] *a*. 刮风的 (moving with speed or force)

【例】The *blowing* wind made the little girl tremble.

windswept　['windswept] *a*. 风刮的 (exposed to strong winds)

【例】Can you see the remote and *windswept* hillside?

drafty　['drɑːfti; 'dræfti] *a*. 通风的，有穿堂风的 (exposed to or abounding in drafts of air)

【例】The room is terribly *drafty* with the window open.

有气味的 (smelly, odorous, fragrant, stinky, redolent, odoriferous, aromatic, scented)

smelly ['smeli] *a.* 发臭的，有臭味的 (having a bad or strong odor)
【例】Jack's *smelly* and other people avoid him.

odorous ['əudərəs] *a.* 有突出气味的 (with a strong smell)
【例】There was an *odorous* air in the orchard.

fragrant ['freigrənt] *a.* 芳香的，有香味的 (having a nice smell)
【例】The air in the garden was warm and *fragrant*.

stinky ['stiŋki] *a.* 发恶臭的 (with a very unpleasant smell)
【例】Bill needs to get rid of the *stinky* flowers.

redolent ['redəulənt] *a.* 芬芳的，芳香的 (having or emitting fragrance)
【例】The air was *redolent* with the smell of wood smoke.

odoriferous [,əudə'rifərəs] *a.* 有气味的 (having or giving off an odor)
【例】The rose is an *odoriferous* flower.

aromatic [,ærəu'mætik] *a.* 芬芳的，芳香的 (pleasing to smell)
【例】This type of honey is slightly acid, and has an *aromatic* flavour.

scented ['sentid] *a.* 有气味的，有香味的 (having a pleasant smell)
【例】His body was buried in the sweet-*scented* woods.

幼稚的 (naive, uneducated, inexperienced, unseasoned, gullible)

naive [naː'iːv] *a.* 幼稚的 (lacking experience of life and tending to trust other people and believe things too easily)
【例】I've never seen *naive* fools like her.

uneducated [,ʌn'edjukeitid] *a.* 无知的，未受过正规教育的 (not having had much education)
【例】An "idiot" is a stupid or *uneducated* person.

inexperienced [,inik'spiəriənst] *a.* 无经验的 (lacking experience)
【例】Our football team is promising but *inexperienced*.
【用】be inexperienced in sth. 在…方面没有经验

unseasoned	[ˌʌnˈsiːzənd] *a.* 无经验的（not experienced in a particular activity or job） 【例】*Unseasoned* workers would not be given such a job.
gullible	[ˈgʌləbl] *a.* 易受骗的（easy to trick because one trusts and believes people too easily） 【例】You are too *gullible* to see your own danger.

愉快的，高兴的（merry, jovial, cheerful, joyous, glad, gleeful）

merry	[ˈmeri] *a.* 欢乐的，愉快的（happy and lively） 【例】We wish you a *merry* Christmas. 【用】make merry 作乐
jovial	[ˈdʒəuviəl] *a.* 愉快的（markedly good-humored） 【例】Eve's grandfather is a *jovial*，ruddy-faced old gentleman.
cheerful	[ˈtʃiəful] *a.* 快乐的，高兴的（behaving in a happy and friendly way） 【例】When Rory spotted us，he smiled and waved a *cheerful* hello.
joyous	[ˈdʒɔiəs] *a.* 快乐的，高兴的（causing happy feelings） 【例】We are gathered to celebrate here today the *joyous* union of Ross and Emily.
glad	[glæd] *a.* 高兴的（happy and pleased about something） 【例】I'm *glad* you appreciate my film. 【用】be glad about sth. /to do sth. 为…高兴
gleeful	[ˈgliːful] *a.* 极高兴的（happy and excited） 【例】Mary is surrounded by *gleeful* friends who are obviously reacting to her engagement announcement.

与…相当，比得上（parallel, equal, equate, correspond, approximate）

parallel	[ˈpærəlel] *v.* 与…相当，比得上（to be equal to something else） 【例】Your experience *paralleled* mine.
equal	[ˈiːkwəl] *v.* 等于，比得上（to be the same in value or amount as something else） 【例】Jack *equals* me in strength but not in intelligence. 【用】be equal to sth. 等同…，胜任…

equate [i'kweit] *v.* 认为…相等或相仿（to consider something to be the same as something else）
【例】The principle of hierarchy does not *equate* to totalitarian terror.
【用】equate sth. to/with sth. 将…与…等同

correspond [ˌkɔri'spɔnd] *v.* 相当，相应（to be the same as something else, or very much like it）
【例】The U. S. Congress *corresponds* to the British Parliament.
【用】correspond to sth. 与…相当；correspond with sth. 与…相符合，成一致

approximate [ə'prɔksimət] *v.* 几乎相同，接近（be almost the same as）
【例】What you said *approximates* to the facts we already know.
【用】approximate to sth. 近于…，与…接近

预报；预测（forecast, predict, foresee, prophesy, foretell, divine, augur）

forecast ['fɔːkɑːst] *v.* 预报；预测（to calculate (some future event or condition) usually as a result of study and analysis of available pertinent data）
【例】Experts *forecast* that average salary increase will remain around 4 percent.
【用】forecast sth. at sth. 预测

predict [pri'dikt] *v.* 预言，预测（to declare or indicate in advance）
【例】It's hard to *predict* how the jury will react.
【用】predict that 预测…

foresee [fɔː'siː] *v.* 预见，预知（to see (as a development) beforehand）
【例】The author could never have *foreseen* that one day his books would sell in millions.

prophesy ['prɔfisi] *v.* 预言，预告（to describe a future event using religious or magic powers）
【例】The prophet *prophesied* that a war would break out.

foretell [fɔː'tel] *v.* 预言，预示（to tell beforehand）
【例】No one could have *foretold* such a freak accident.

divine [di'vain] *v.* 预言，占卜（to guess something from what you already know）

【例】No one can *divine* the future.

augur 　['ɔːgə] *v.* 预兆，占卜 (to be a sign of what may happen in the future)

【例】This *augurs* well for us.

【用】augur well/ill for sb. 预示…的凶吉

原谅，宽恕 (excuse, pardon, forgive, condone, spare)

excuse 　[ik'skjuːz] *v.* 原谅，宽恕 (to forgive somebody for something bad they have done)

【例】They *excused* Ben's rudeness because they knew he was under a severe strain.

【用】excuse sb. for (doing) sth. 原谅…做了…

pardon 　['pɑːdən] *v.* 饶恕，原谅 (to forgive somebody for doing or saying something bad or unpleasant)

【例】The governor *pardoned* the convicted criminal.

【用】pardon sb for (doing) sth. 原谅…做了…

forgive 　[fə'giv] *v.* 饶恕，原谅 (stop feeling angry or resentful towards (someone) for an offence, flaw, or mistake)

【例】The husband will never *forgive* his unfaithful wife.

【用】forgive sb. for (doing) sth. 原谅…做…

condone 　[kən'dəun] *v.* 宽恕；容忍 (to overlook, forgive, or disregard (an offense) without protest or censure)

【例】Child labour is still *condoned* in some countries.

spare 　[speə] *v.* 饶恕，不伤害 (to not harm or kill somebody or something)

【例】The gunman killed the men but *spared* the children.

【用】spare sb.'s life 饶恕…

远的 (faraway, distant, remote, removed, far-off)

faraway 　['fɑːrəˌwei] *a.* 遥远的，久远的 (far from a particular place; happening a long time before or after the present time)

【例】Dick went to the *faraway* inland where people live on wheat.

distant ['distənt] *a.* 在远处的，久远的（situated at a great distance; far apart in time）

【例】Bill's eyes scanned the ***distant*** hills.

【用】in the distant past/future 在遥远的过去或将来；distant memory 模糊的记忆

remote [ri'məut] *a.* 远的，遥远的（far away in distance or space; far away in the past or future）

【例】My grandparents were from a ***remote*** town in California.

【用】remote from 远离

removed [ri'mu:vd] *a.* 远离的，遥远的（far away in time or space）

【例】The city remained relatively ***removed*** from the worst of the conflict.

【用】removed from 远离

far-off [ˌfɑːr'ɔf] *a.* 遥远的，久远的（far away in space; happening a long time before or after the present time）

【例】In those ***far-off*** days of our youth, we were alway very happy.

约定，保证（promise, engage, contract, appoint, give one's word）

promise ['prɔmis] *v.* 允诺，约定（to tell someone you will definitely do something）

【例】Leo ***promised*** to marry Nancy.

【用】promise to do sth. 许诺做…

engage [in'geidʒ] *v.* 约定，保证（to bind oneself by a promise）

【例】I'm ***engaged*** to dinner at seven o'clock.

【用】engage to do sth. 保证做…

contract ['kɔntrækt] *v.* 约定，订约（to agree to do something or make someone agree to do something by a formal written agreement）

【例】This company has ***contracted*** to supply us with raw materials.

【用】contract to do sth. 签合约保证做…

appoint [ə'pɔint] *v.* 约定（时间，地点）（to choose a time or place for something to happen）

【例】Why not to ***appoint*** a day for dinner together?

【用】appoint sth. for sth. 约定…

give one's word 约定，保证

【例】I *give* you *my word* of honor.

悦耳的 (tuneful, melodious, melodic, musical, harmonious, euphonious, euphonic, symphonic)

tuneful ['tju:nful] *a.* 和谐的，悦耳的 (melodious，musical)

【例】These composers had brains，and they selected grand and *tuneful* words.

melodious [mi'ləudiəs] *a.* 声调优美的，悦耳的 (having a pleasing melody)

【例】Selena puts a small silver whistle to her lips and blows a high，*melodious* note.

melodic [mi'lɔdik] *a.* 音调优美的 (beautiful to listen to)

【例】The song is eerie but quite *melodic*.

musical ['mju:zikəl] *a.* 悦耳的 (having the pleasing relating to or having the character or form of a symphony)

【例】We are all attracted by the *musical* sounds of a child's laughter.

harmonious [hɑː'məunjəs] *a.* 音调和谐的，悦耳的 (musically concordant)

【例】*Harmonious* sounds can produce a calming effect when life brings stress and tension.

euphonious [ju:'fəuniəs] *a.* 悦耳的 (pleasing to the ear)

【例】The singer lent a high *euphonious* tenor to the song.

euphonic [ju:'fɔnik] *a.* 语调好的 (pleasing or sweet sound)

【例】From their first song，they kept up a surging momentum of rolling guitars，*euphonic* melodies and passionate singing.

symphonic [sim'fɔnik] *a.* 交响乐（式）的 (relating to or having the character or form of a symphony)

【例】We were accompanied by *symphonic* orchestras.

允许 (permit, allow, license, consent, entitle, grant)

permit [pə'mit] *v.* 允许，许可 (to allow someone to do something, or something to happen)

【例】Lily's mother wouldn't *permit* her to go.

【用】permit of sth.（尤用于否定句）认可…；容忍… permit sb. to do sth. 允许…做…

allow [ə'lau] *v.* 允许，准许（give permission）

【例】We *allow* smoking only in restricted areas.

【用】allow for sth. 斟酌…，考虑…；allow of 容许，容许有…的可能；allow doing sth. 允许做…；allow sb. to do sth. 允许…做…

license ['laisəns] *v.* 给…发许可证，准许（to give or yield permission to or for）

【例】They're only *licensed* for beer and expensive wine.

consent [kən'sent] *v.* 同意，允许（to give approval for something）

【例】Tony finally *consented* to go.

【用】consent to do sth. 准许做…；同意做…

entitle [in'taitl] *v.* 使有权（做某事）（to give someone the right to do something）

【例】It *entitled* you to withdraw cash at two post office of your choice.

【用】be entitled to/doing sth. 有权利做…

grant [grɑ:nt；grænt] *v.* 允许，同意（to allow someone to have or do what they want）

【例】Mike was finally *granted* an exit visa.

【用】take for granted 认为…是理所当然；（因视作当然而）对…不予重视

运送（send, transport, transfer, mail, ship, relay）

send [send] *v.* 送；发射（to cause to be conveyed by an intermediary to a destination；transmit by radio waves）

【例】These goods will be *sent* to New York by train.

【用】send away 把…打发走；send for 派人去请；send off 邮寄，发送

transport [træns'pɔ:t] *v.* 运输（to move people or things from one place to another，usually in a vehicle）

【例】The last evacuators will be *transported* by plane.

【用】transport sb./sth. from... to... 将…从…运送到…

transfer [træns'fə:] *v.* 转移；调动（to convey or cause to pass from one place, person, or thing to another）

【例】Our luggage will be **transferred** from railway station to our home by truck.

【用】transfer sb. /sth. from... to...　将…从…转移到…；将…从…调任到…

| mail | [meil] v. 邮寄（to send a letter, package, etc. to someone by post） |

【例】Would you mind **mailing** this letter for me?

| ship | [ʃip] v. 用船运；运送（to send goods or people somewhere by ship） |

【例】Fresh supplies were **shipped** by lorry.

【用】ship sb. /sth. off　将…送走

| relay | [ˌriː'lei] v. 传送；转播（to communicate information, news, or a message to someone） |

【例】The pop festival was **relayed** all round the world.

【用】relay sth. from... to...　把…从…传到…；把…从…转播到…

赞美，称赞（acclaim, applaud, hail, commend）

| acclaim | [ə'kleim] v. 欢呼，称赞（to publicly praise someone for a major achievement） |

【例】This champion was **acclaimed** a hero.

【用】acclaim sb. /sth. as sth.　称赞…为…

| applaud | [ə'plɔːd] v. 称赞（to express approval） |

【例】The professor **applauded** her decision to complete her degree.

| hail | [heil] v. 致敬，为…喝彩（to greet with enthusiastic approval） |

【例】They **hailed** this hero as their King.

【用】hail sb. /sth. as sth.　热情地承认…为…

commend [kə'mend] *v.* 称赞，表扬（to praise someone or something formally or publicly）

【例】When I **commended** her performance，she burst into tears.

【用】commend sb. on/for sth. 因为…而称赞某人

责备 (blame, scold, condemn, reprove, reproach, rebuke)

blame [bleim] *v.* 责备，埋怨（to say or think that someone or something is responsible for a bad situation）

【例】Don't **blame** me later if you don't listen to me now.

【用】blame sb. for sth. 因…责备…；blame sth. on sb. 将…怪罪在…

scold [skəuld] *v.* 责骂，训斥（to criticize someone severely and angrily for something they have done wrong）

【例】He never **scolded** others unfairly.

【用】scold sb. for sth. /doing sth. 因…斥责…

condemn [kən'dem] *v.* 声讨，极力谴责（to say publicly that you think someone or something is bad or wrong）

【例】In the past women were **condemned** for wearing short skirts.

【用】condemn sb. /sth. for/as sth. 因…极力谴责…

reprove [ri'pru:v] *v.* 责骂，申斥（to criticize or blame someone for doing something wrong or bad）

【例】"Don't be silly, Tom." his mother **reproved**.

【用】reprove sb. for sth. 因…责备…

reproach [ri'prəutʃ] *v.* 斥责，批评（to criticize and feel disappointed with someone for something they have done）

【例】The little boy was severely **reproached** for his rude behavior.

【用】reproach sb. /oneself for sth. 责备…（尤指未做成某事）；reproach sb. /oneself with sth. 因…而责备…

rebuke [ri'bju:k] *v.* 指责，非难（express sharp disapproval or criticism of (someone) because of their behavior or actions）

【例】The missionaries **rebuked** the natives for lack of mercy.

【用】rebuke sb. for sth. 因…指责或非难…

增大 (magnify, enlarge, increase, expand, amplify, exaggerate, overstate)

magnify ['mægnifai] v. 放大，扩大 (to make something appear bigger, more important, severe, or dangerous than it really is)

【例】Our fear and confusion only **magnified** the problem.

【用】magnify oneself against sb. 抬高自己贬低…

enlarge [in'lɑːdʒ] v. 扩大，放大 (to make something bigger)

【例】We're **enlarging** the production scale to produce more and better products.

【用】enlarge sth. 放大…，开阔…

increase [in'kriːs] v. 增加，增长 (to become larger in amount or number)

【例】The company's costs **increased** dramatically over the last decade.

【用】increase sth. from...to... 使某物从…增加到…

expand [ik'spænd] v. 扩大，扩张 (to become larger in size and filling more space)

【例】The water froze inside the pipe, causing it to **expand** and burst.

【用】expand sth. into sth. 使…扩大为…

amplify ['æmplifai] v. 放大（声音等）；扩大 (to make larger or greater)

【例】The attorney decided to **amplify** the story by talking to a reporter.

exaggerate [ig'zædʒəreit] v. 夸张，夸大 (to describe something in a way that makes it seem better, worse, larger, or more important)

【例】The paper's political influence has been greatly **exaggerated**.

overstate [ˌəuvə'steit] v. 夸张 (to talk about something in a way that makes it seem more important, impressive, or severe than it really is)

【例】He may have **overstated** his ability in the interview.

粘着，附着 (stick, cling, adhere, cleave to, cohere)

stick
［stik］ *v.* 粘贴，粘住（to fasten one thing to another, especially using a sticky substance such as glue）
【例】The broken pieces of the vase were well ***stuck*** together.
【用】stick to sth. 坚持…

cling
［kliŋ］ *v.* 紧紧粘住；缠住（to refuse to go or let go; to stick firmly）
【例】Eva ***clung*** to her husband as he said goodbye.
【用】cling on to sth. 紧抓住…，不放弃…

adhere
［ədˈhiə］ *v.* 粘附，附着（to stick to something）
【例】The two pieces of paper are ***adhering*** and we couldn't get them apart.
【用】adhere to sth. 粘附…；坚持…

cleave to
粘着（to stick close to sth. /sb）
【例】With such a heavy load，Daniel's feet seemed ***cleave to*** the ground.

cohere
［kəuˈhiə］ *v.* 黏合，结合（to hold together firmly as parts of the same mass; to be united）
【例】The movie as a whole failed to ***cohere***.
【用】cohere with sth. 与…符合

战斗，搏斗 (battle, combat, struggle, contend, clash)

battle
［ˈbætl］ *v.* 作战，斗争（to engage in fight）
【例】In a town thousands of people ***battled*** with police and several were reportedly wounded.
【用】battle for 为…斗争

combat
［ˈkɔmbæt］ *v.* 战斗，搏斗（to fight an enemy or opponent）
【例】We must ***combat*** the enemy everywhere until victory is ours.
【用】combat for 为…奋斗

struggle
［ˈstrʌgl］ *v.* 斗争，搏斗（to use your strength to fight against someone or something）

【例】An old man **struggled** with a criminal on the road.

【用】struggle along 挣扎

contend [kən'tend] *v.* 斗争；竞争（to strive or vie in contest or rivalry or against difficulties）

【例】Our armies were **contending** with enemy troops for control of the strategic territory.

【用】contend with sb. /sth. for sth. 和…争夺…

clash [klæʃ] *v.* 发生冲突（to come into conflict）

【例】A group of 400 demonstrators ripped down the state Parliament's front gate and **clashed** with the police.

【用】clash into sth. 猛撞…

战胜，超越 (surpass, excel, outdo, outshine, defeat)

surpass [sə'pɑːs；sə'pæs] *v.* 超越，胜过（to become better, greater, or stronger than）

【例】This chocolate mousse **surpasses** any restaurant dessert I've ever had.

【用】surpass sb. /sth. in 在…（方面）超越

excel [ik'sel] *v.* 胜过（to be superior to）

【例】Tom's meals are always good，but this time he has **excelled** himself.

【用】excel oneself 比以前做得更好

outdo [ˌaut'duː] *v.* 超越，胜过（to be better than someone else at doing something）

【例】No one can **outdo** Susie in stylishness.

【用】not to be outdone（为了）不被超越

outshine [ˌaut'ʃain] *v.* 明显比…更优异；超越（to be much better than someone or something else）

【例】Shirley **outshined** all the other competitors.

defeat [di'fiːt] *v.* 战胜（to win victory over）

【例】Our country has the capability to **defeat** any aggressor.

找到，发现 (find, stumble upon, come upon, chance upon, ferret out)

find
['faind] *v.* 找到，发现 (to discover something or see where it is by searching for it)
【例】The boy *found* his lost key in his bag.
【用】find sb. doing sth. 发现…做…

stumble upon
偶然发现
【例】The urge to wider voyages caused men to *stumble upon* New America.

come upon
偶遇
【例】Fear *came upon* her as she waited.

chance upon
偶然遇见
【例】We *chanced upon* them in the shopping mall yesterday.

ferret out
搜出，发现
【例】It took me three days to *ferret out* the solution to the mystery.

珍爱 (treasure, cherish, adore, idolize, appreciate)

treasure
['treʒə] *v.* 珍爱，珍视 (to take great care of something because it is very valuable or important)
【例】My grandmother *treasured* that piano until the day she died.
【用】treasure sth. up in 将…珍藏在…

cherish
['tʃeriʃ] *v.* 爱护，珍爱 (to think that something is very important and to wish to keep it)
【例】How can a person *cherish* possessions more than friends?

adore
[ə'dɔː] *v.* 崇拜，爱慕 (to love someone very much)
【例】That girl absolutely *adores* her nieces and nephews.

idolize
['aidəlaiz] *v.* 极度喜爱或仰慕 (to think that someone is perfect)
【例】My sister had *idolized* Madonna from the start.

appreciate
[ə'priːʃieit] *v.* 赏识 (to recognize the good or special qualities of a person, place, or thing)
【例】Van Gogh's paintings weren't *appreciated* until after his death.

真诚的，热心的 (wholehearted, earnest, all-out, sincere, fervent, hearty)

wholehearted ['həul'hɑ:tid] *a.* 全心全意的，热心的 (completely and sincerely devoted, determined, or enthusiastic)

【例】 Mary gave her *wholehearted* support to her husband.

earnest ['ə:nist] *a.* 诚挚的 (marked by or showing deep sincerity or seriousness)

【例】 It is my *earnest* wish that you use this money to continue your study.

all-out ['ɔ:l'aut] *a.* 竭力的，全部的 (made with maximum effort)

【例】 The editorial was *all-out* for improving relations with China.

sincere [sin'siə] *a.* 诚挚的，真诚的，诚恳的 (not feigned or affected)

【例】 Tom has a *sincere* admiration of his opponent.

fervent ['fə:vənt] *a.* 热烈的，强烈的 (having or showing great emotion)

【例】 We all have the *fervent* hope that matters will be settled promptly.

hearty ['hɑ:ti] *a.* 亲切友好的，热忱的 (enthusiastically or exuberantly cordial)

【例】 There was a *hearty* applause as soon as he ended his address.

真实的 (honest, veracious, truthful, faithful, straight, factual)

honest ['ɔnist] *a.* 诚实的，正直的 (free from fraud or deception)

【例】 Tom is an *honest* man, you can trust him any time.

【用】 earn/turn an honest penny 以正当的手段凭努力工作挣钱

veracious [və'reiʃəs] *a.* 诚实的；真实的 (truthful, honest)

【例】 His son was *veracious* and kind-hearted.

truthful ['tru:θful] *a.* 诚实的，说实话的 (telling or disposed to tell the truth)

【例】 Most religions teach you to be *truthful*.

faithful ['feiθful] *a.* 忠实的，忠贞的 (loyal)

【例】 Nancy had been *faithful* to her promise to guard this secret.

【用】be faithful to sb. /sth. 对···忠实的

straight [streit] *a.* 正直的 (exhibiting honesty and fairness)

【例】Onscreen，John Wayne was a blunt talker and a *straight* shooter.

【用】as straight as an arrow 正直的

factual ['fæktʃuəl] *a.* 真实的，事实的 (of or relating to facts)

【例】Any comparison that is not strictly *factual* runs the risk of being interpreted as subjective.

争吵，争论 (quarrel, argue, bicker, squabble, wrangle, feud)

quarrel ['kwɔrəl] *v.* 争吵，争论 (to have an argument)

【例】We *quarreled* over something silly yesterday.

【用】quarrel about/over sth. 因为···争吵；quarrel with sb. 和···吵架

argue ['ɑːgjuː] *v.* 争论，争吵 (speak to each other in an angry way because they disagree)

【例】It is time to stop *arguing* tax-rate reductions and to enact them.

【用】argue with sb. 与···争论；argue against sb. on sth. 在···问题上与···争辩

bicker ['bikə] *v.* 争吵，斗嘴 (to argue about things that are not important)

【例】The two women *bickered* constantly.

【用】bicker (with sb.) (over/about sth.) (为···与···) 争吵

squabble ['skwɔbl] *v.* 口角；争吵 (to argue with someone about something that is not important)

【例】The children were *squabbling* over the remote-control gadget for the television.

【用】squabble (with sb.) (over/about sth.) (为···与···) 大声争吵

wrangle ['ræŋgl] *v.* 争吵，争辩 (to argue about something for a long time)

【例】My boyfriend always *wrangles* with me for some tiny things.

【用】wrangle (with sb.) (over/about sth.) (为···与···) 争吵

feud [fjuːd] v. 长期斗争 (to be involved in an angry disagreement that continues for a long time)

【例】The two countries have long **feuded** over that island.

【用】feud with sb. /sth. 与…长期不和

蒸发 (evaporate, vaporize, dehydrate)

evaporate [i'væpəreit] v. 蒸发 (to change into gas or steam)

【例】Alcohol **evaporates** quickly.

vaporize ['veipəraiz] v. (使) 蒸发 (to become a vapor, or to change something into a vapor)

【例】The benzene **vaporized** and formed a huge cloud of gas.

dehydrate [ˌdiːˈhaidreit] v. 除去水分 (to remove water from)

【例】Normally specimens have to be **dehydrated**.

正确无误的；精确的 (accurate, correct, precise, faultless)

accurate ['ækjurət] a. 正确无误的；精确的 (right or true in every detail)

【例】Bruce's very **accurate** in his calculations.

【用】be accurate to 精确到

correct [kə'rekt] a. 正确的，对的 (right according to the facts, with no mistakes)

【例】Columbus was **correct** when he claimed the earth was round.

precise [pri'sais] a. 准确的，精确的 (minutely exact)

【例】The **precise** date and place of his birth are unknown.

【用】to be precise (常放在最后) 更精确地说

faultless ['fɔːltlis] a. 无错误的，无缺点的 (containing no mistakes at all)

【例】Mary went over her homework and found it **faultless**.

正式地辩论，讨论 (debate, argue, dispute, controvert, contest, deliberate, rebut)

debate 〔di'beit〕 v. **正式地辩论，讨论**（to contend in words，to discuss a question by considering opposed arguments）

【例】They *debated* for over an hour on the merits of the different systems.

【用】debate upon/on sth. 讨论…

argue 〔'ɑ:gju:〕 v. **争论，争辩**（to express an opposite opinion，to give reasons for or against something）

【例】Bernie *argued* for the proposed tax cuts.

【用】argue against sb. on sth. 在…问题上与…争辩

dispute 〔dis'pju:t〕 v. **争论，争吵**（to say that something such as a fact is not true or correct，to argue about something）

【例】The two governments *disputed* over the ownership of the territory.

【用】dispute with sb. on sth. 与…争论…

controvert 〔'kɔntrəvə:t〕 v. **议论，辩论**（to argue about something by reasoning）

【例】We have *controverted* the topic for hours.

contest 〔kən'test〕 v. **辩论**（to state formally that you disagree with something or think it is wrong）

【例】Gender discrimination is a hotly *contested* issue.

【用】contest with sb. 与…辩论

deliberate 〔di'libərət〕 v. **商讨**（to think about or discuss something very carefully，especially before you make an important decision）

【例】The jury *deliberated* several hours before bringing in a verdict.

【用】deliberate on 仔细研究，审议

rebut 〔ri'bʌt〕 v. 〔律〕**辩驳，驳斥**（to show or say that something is not true）

【例】The prosecutor's arguments were *rebutted* by the defense lawyer.

证明（prove, confirm, certify, validate, verify, document）

prove ［pruːv］ *v.* 证明，证实（to provide evidence that shows that something is true）
【例】Gordon is still fighting to *prove* his innocence.
【用】prove sb.'s innocence/guilt 证明…的清白或有罪；prove sth. to sb. 向…证明…

confirm ［kənˈfɜːm］ *v.* 证实，确定（to prove that something is true）
【例】The study *confirmed* the findings of earlier research.

certify ［ˈsɜːtifai］ *v.* 证明，证实（to state officially that something is true, accurate, or of a satisfactory standard）
【例】More than two witnesses *certify* that this is your legal signature.
【用】certify sb./sth. as sth. 证明…是…

validate ［ˈvælideit］ *v.* 证实（to officially prove that something is true or correct）
【例】The evidence does seem to *validate* his claim.

verify ［ˈverifai］ *v.* 证明，证实（to say that something is true or correct）
【例】Jerry's story has been *verified* by other witnesses.

document ［ˈdɔkjumənt］ *v.* 用文件（或文献）等证明（to support something with evidence）
【例】Their allegations are very fully *documented*.

支持，赞成（favor, support, back, endorse, advocate, sanction）

favor ［ˈfeivə］ *v.* 支持，赞成（to be or tend to be in support of）
【例】The debater adduced facts to *favor* his contention.
【用】favor with 支持

support ［səˈpɔːt］ *v.* 支持（to approve of an idea or a person or organization and help them to be successful）
【例】People *support* the new political party.
【用】support doing sth. 支持做…；support sb. in (doing) sth. 支持…做…

back ［bæk］ *v.* 支持（to give support to a person, organization, or plan, making them more likely to succeed）

【例】Claude's defense said they had found a witness to **back** his claim that he was not the murderer.

【用】back sb. on sth. 支持…做…

endorse [in'dɔːs] *v.* 支持，赞同（to express support for somebody or something, especially in public）

【例】The company offered a million dollars to **endorse** its political candidate.

advocate ['ædvəkeit] *v.* 提倡，支持（to publicly support a particular policy or way of doing things）

【例】Mr. Williams is a conservative who **advocates** fewer government controls on business.

sanction ['sæŋkʃən] *v.* 批准；支持（to give official approval or permission for an action; to show approval for a particular behavior or belief）

【例】Public opinion **sanctioned** a more liberal view on divorce.

知识；专业技能（ability, know-how, expertise, capability, experience, talent, proficiency, knack, flair, mastery）

ability [ə'biləti] *n.* 能力；才能（the quality of being able to do a particular job or activity well）

【例】**Ability** alone is insufficient to make a fortune; opportunity is essential.

【用】to the best of one's ability 尽其所能

know-how ['nəuhau] *n.* 知识；专业技能（knowledge of how to do something smoothly and efficiently）

【例】We're looking for someone with some **know-how** in computer programming.

expertise [ˌekspə'tiːz] *n.* 专门知识（或技能等）（special skill or knowledge that you get from experience, training, or study）

【例】You must have **expertise** to achieve this goal.

capability [ˌkeipə'biləti] *n.* 能力；潜质（the ability to do something）

【例】The little girl has great **capability** as a dancer and should be trained.

【用】capability to do sth. / of doing sth. 做…的能力

experience　[ik'spiəriəns] *n.* 经历；体验（knowledge and skill gained through time spent doing a job or activity）
【例】Yesterday afternoon Frank told me about his *experiences* in Australia.

talent　['tælənt] *n.* 天资，才能（a natural ability for being good at a particular activity）
【例】My sister has a *talent* for music.
【用】talent for 做…的才干

proficiency　[prə'fiʃənsi] *n.* 熟练，精通（a high degree of ability or skill in something）
【例】Dean has a *proficiency* in martial arts.
【用】proficiency in sth. /doing sth. 精通…

knack　[næk] *n.* 技巧；特殊能力（a clever way of doing something）
【例】Tom has a *knack* of making money.

flair　[fleə] *n.* 本领；天资（a skill or instinctive ability to appreciate or make good use of something）
【例】My little son has no *flair* for complicated calculations.
【用】flair for sth. 在…上的天分

mastery　['mɑːstəri; 'mæstəri] *n.* 精通，熟练（possession of great knowledge or skill）
【例】Cecil's *mastery* of political theories impressed the professors.
【用】mastery of sth. 精通…

直率的，坦白的（frank, square, straightforward, blunt）

frank　[fræŋk] *a.* 坦白的，直率的（honest about the situation, even if this offends people）
【例】She decided to be *frank* in refusing his invitation.
【用】to be frank 老实说，说实话

square　[skweə] *a.* 正直的，公平的（simple and telling only the truth）
【例】I don't need explanation, please just give me a *square* answer to the question.

straightforward　[ˌstreit'fɔːwəd] *a.* 正直的，坦率的（telling what you think is true or right）

【例】She gave a *straightforward* explanation for her mistake.

blunt ［blʌnt］ *a.* 坦率的（saying what is true or what you think, even if this upsets people）

【例】Let's be *blunt*—your products will not attract younger people.

指定（appoint, delegate, designate）

appoint ［əˈpɔint］ *v.* 任命，委任（to choose someone to do a particular job or have a particular position）

【例】We need to *appoint* a new treasurer.

【用】appoint sb.（to/as sth.）任命…担任…

delegate ［ˈdeligeit］ *v.* 委派…为代表（to choose someone to do a job for you or to represent you）

【例】Bill was *delegated* to contact the manager.

【用】delegate sb. to sth. 委派…为…的代表

designate ［ˈdezigneit］ *v.* 任命，指派（to formally choose someone or something for a particular purpose）

【例】Nobody has yet been *designated* as group leader.

指控，控告（accuse, indict, inculpate, impeach, incriminate, impute）

accuse ［əˈkjuːz］ *v.* 指控，控告（to say that someone has done something wrong or committed a crime）

【例】The man was *accused* of killing 10 men.

【用】accuse sb. of (doing) sth. 指责…有错；因…指控…

indict ［inˈdait］ *v.* 控诉，起诉（to charge someone with a fault or offense）

【例】The jury refused to *indict* the man accused of arson.

【用】indict sb. for sth. 因…控告或告发…

inculpate ［ˈinkʌlpeit］ *v.* 控告（to accuse or blame）

【例】Rod *inculpated* both men to the grand jury.

impeach [im'pi:tʃ] *v.* 控告，弹劾 (to officially charge someone with a crime and ask a court of law to judge them)

【例】The parliament decided to ***impeach*** the President.

【用】impeach sb. for sth. 因…控告或弹劾…

incriminate [in'krimi,neit] *v.* 控告…有罪，牵连 (to make someone appear guilty of a crime or wrongdoing)

【例】He refused to answer questions in order not to ***incriminate*** himself.

impute [im'pju:t] *v.* 归咎于 (to put the responsibility or blame on somebody or something, often falsely or unjustly)

【例】They ***imputed*** their defeats in the war to the strategies of the generals.

【用】impute sth. to sb. /sth. 将…的责任加之于…

致命的 (lethal, fatal, deadly, mortal, killing, malignant)

lethal ['li:θəl] *a.* 致命的 (very dangerous and able to kill you)

【例】In their hands, they each have a ***lethal*** weapon.

fatal ['feitəl] *a.* 致命的 (causing someone to die)

【例】It is ***fatal*** to enter any war without the will to win.

【用】be fatal to sb. /sth. 对…致命的

deadly ['dedli] *a.* 致命的 (able or likely to kill people)

【例】Tom sank into the ***deadly*** swamp.

【用】the seven deadly sins 受上帝惩罚的七大重罪

mortal ['mɔ:təl] *a.* 致死的，致命的 (serious enough to cause death)

【例】It was too late to save him, as he had already received a ***mortal*** wound.

killing ['kiliŋ] *a.* 致死的 (causing someone to die)

【例】This crisis was a ***killing*** blow to the economy of the country.

malignant [mə'lignənt] *a.* 恶性的，致命的 (spreading or developing in a way that is not normal and is dangerous)

【例】He had got a ***malignant*** cancer and I had to remove him.

终止，停止 (quit, cease, discontinue, desist, halt, finish, conclude)

quit
[kwit] *v.* 停止，放弃 (to stop doing something)
【例】Jean told me that she had *quitted* her job.
【用】be quit of sb. /sth. 摆脱…

cease
[siːs] *v.* 终止，停止 (to stop happening or continuing; to stop doing something)
【例】Just a few weeks，the magazine *ceased* publication.
【用】cease out 绝迹

discontinue
[ˌdiskən'tinjuː] *v.* 停止；中断 (to stop doing something that someone is doing regularly)
【例】The board of directors have decided to *discontinue* the production of washing machine.

desist
[di'zist] *v.* 终止 (to cease to proceed or act)
【例】I have *desisted* from alcohol.
【用】desist from/in 停止…

halt
[hɔːlt] *v.* （使）停止 (to bring to a stop; to end something)
【例】The carriage was *halted* only at the edge of the cliff.

finish
['finiʃ] *v.* 完成，终止 (to come to an end; to bring to an end)
【例】When will you *finish* your college course?
【用】finish up 彻底完成，结束

conclude
[kən'kluːd] *v.* （使）结束，终止 (to end, especially by someone saying or doing something)
【例】The negotiation was *concluded* at 8 o'clock.
【用】conclude with sth. 以…结束

主要的 (main, principal, chief, central, prime, major, predominant, foremost, crucial)

main
[mein] *a.* 主要的，最重要的 (most important)
【例】The *main* focus of her speech was on the new sales strategy.

principal
['prinsəpəl] *a.* 最重要的，主要的 (most important, consequential, or influential)
【例】The salary is good，but that is not the *principal* reason I accepted the job.

| chief | [tʃiːf] *a.* 主要的，首要的（of greatest importance or influence） |
| | 【例】Unemployment was the ***chief*** cause of poverty during the 1930s. |

central	[ˈsentrəl] *a.* 中心的，主要的（of primary importance）
	【例】They live in ***central*** Boston.
	【用】the central states 中部各州

prime	[praim] *a.* 首要的，主要的（first in rank, authority, or significance）
	【例】Our ***prime*** concern was the safety of our people.
	【用】Prime Minister 首相，总理

major	[ˈmeidʒə] *a.* 重要的，主要的（more important, more serious, larger, or greater than other things）
	【例】Age is a ***major*** factor affecting chances of employment.
	【用】a major problem/obstacle 较大的问题或障碍

| predominant | [priˈdɔminənt] *a.* 占优势的（having superior strength, influence, or authority） |
| | 【例】The ***predominant*** view was that she was guilty. |

| foremost | [ˈfɔːməust] *a.* 最好的；最重要的（most important or most well-known） |
| | 【例】He is one of the ***foremost*** authorities in Chinese culture. |

crucial	[ˈkruːʃəl] *a.* 至关重要的（extremely important）
	【例】Yao Ming played a ***crucial*** role in the team's 98-92 victory on Saturday.
	【用】be crucial to/for sth. 对…至关重要的

著名的（famous, prominent, eminent, renowned, distinguished, celebrated）

famous	[ˈfeiməs] *a.* 著名的（widely known）
	【例】The town of Gouda is ***famous*** for its cheese.
	【用】be famous for 因…而闻名

| prominent | [ˈprɔminənt] *a.* 出名的，杰出的（important and well known） |
| | 【例】The order was given by a ***prominent*** member of the government. |

eminent ['eminənt] *a.* 有名的 (important, respected, and admired)

【例】Bill is one of France's most ***eminent*** scientists.

renowned [ri'naund] *a.* 著名的 (famous and admired for a special skill or achievement)

【例】The program includes a performance by the world-***renowned*** Berlin Philharmonic Orchestra.

distinguished [dis'tiŋgwiʃt] *a.* 著名的 (successful and respected by many people)

【例】The Chinese nation is ***distinguished*** for its diligence and courage.

celebrated ['selibreitid] *a.* 知名的 (famous and praised by many people)

【例】The garden became ***celebrated*** for its exotic plants.

装饰 (decorate, beautify, ornament, garnish, adorn)

decorate ['dekəreit] *v.* 装饰，点缀 (to make something look more attractive by putting nice things on it or in it)

【例】When will you ***decorate*** your Christmas tree?

【用】decorate sth. with sth. 用…装饰…

beautify ['bjuːtifai] *v.* 美化 (to make something look more beautiful)

【例】Merry spent most of her time on ***beautifying*** her home.

ornament ['ɔːnəmənt] *v.* 装饰，点缀 (to add something to something else to make it more beautiful)

【例】The columns are ***ornamented*** with geometric designs.

【用】ornament sth. with sth. 用…装饰…

garnish ['gɑːniʃ] *v.* 装饰 (to enhance in appearance by adding decorative touches)

【例】The chef ***garnished*** the fish with lemon slices.

【用】garnish sth. with sth. 用…点缀…（多用于食物）

adorn [ə'dɔːn] *v.* 装饰，装扮 (to enhance the appearance of, especially with beautiful objects)

【例】The wall was ***adorned*** with several magnificent oil paintings.

【用】adorn sth. with sth. 用…装扮…

装载 (load, fill, stack, stuff, lade, cram, weigh down, saddle, burden)

load
[ləud] *v.* 装，装载 (to put something onto or into something such as a vehicle or container)
【例】We *loaded* the truck with goods.
【用】load up 装载，装满；load down 使负荷，使负荷过重

fill
[fil] *v.* 装满，充满 (to make something full)
【例】Tom *filled* the bucket with water.
【用】fill sth. with sth. 用…将…填满

stack
[stæk] *v.* 堆积 (to arrange things so that they stand one on top of another)
【例】I *stack* all my books in the attic.
【用】stack sth. up 将…堆起

stuff
[stʌf] *v.* 填进，塞满 (to fill a container or space with something, especially something soft)
【例】The quilt was *stuffed* with cotton so it was very soft.
【用】stuff sth. up with sth. 用…将…塞满

lade
[leid] *v.* 装载（货物）(to put cargo on board)
【例】The products must be *laden* on board before noon.

cram
[kræm] *v.* 填塞，塞满 (to put people or things into a space that is too small)
【例】The hall was *crammed* with people.
【用】cram sth. into sth. 将…塞进…里面；cram sth. in 将…塞进去

weigh down
压弯 (to cause to bend down with added weight)
【例】There are so many apples that they *weigh down* the branches.

saddle
['sædl] *v.* 使承担，使负担 (to place under a burden or encumbrance)
【例】He *saddled* himself with debts after buying the new house.
【用】saddle sb. with sth. 让…承担（使人厌恶的责任、任务等）

burden
['bə:dən] *v.* 负重，装载 (to carry something heavy)
【例】The horse was *burdened* with some large parcels.
【用】burden sb. /oneself with sth. 加…负担于某人

自负的 (conceited, self-satisfied, vain, pretentious, smug)

conceited　[kənˈsiːtid] *a.* 自负的，自高自大的 (characteristic of false pride; having an exaggerated sense of self-importance)
【例】*Conceited* girls walk home from school with their noses in the air.

self-satisfied　[ˌselfˈsætisfaid] *a.* 自鸣得意的，自满的 (excessively satisfied with oneself or one's achievements)
【例】The *self-satisfied* smile on Linda's face disgusted me.

vain　[vein] *a.* 自负的，自视过高的 (full of self-admiration; thinking too highly of one's appearance, abilities etc.)
【例】Dirk was *vain* about his looks, spending hours in the gym.

pretentious　[priˈtenʃəs] *a.* 自命不凡的，自负的 (claiming or demanding a position of distinction or merit)
【例】It's so *pretentious* of Jane to greet everyone in French.

smug　[smʌg] *a.* 自满的，自命不凡的 (too satisfied with one's abilities or achievements)
【例】The little boy looked so *smug* about knowing the answer.

阻止 (discourage, prohibit, deter, block, retard, balk, obstruct, hamper)

discourage　[disˈkʌridʒ] *v.* 阻止，阻拦 (to try to prevent something from happening)
【例】The government is taking measures to *discourage* the use of cars in cities.
【用】discourage sb. from doing sth. 阻拦…做…

prohibit　[prəˈhibit] *v.* 禁止，阻止 (to officially stop something from being done, especially by making it illegal)
【例】Smoking is *prohibited* in public.
【用】prohibit sb. from doing sth. 阻止…做…

deter　[diˈtəː] *v.* 阻止 (to make someone decide not to do something)
【例】The bad weather didn't *deter* people from coming to the game.
【用】deter sb. from doing sth. 阻止…做…

block [blɔk] *v.* 阻碍，堵塞 (to use power to stop something from being done or from succeeding)

【例】The plan to build a new shopping mall was *blocked* by local residents.

retard [ri'tɑ:d] *v.* 阻碍（某人或物）的发展；妨碍 (to slow down or delay the development of something)

【例】Lack of vitamin will *retard* children's growth.

balk [bɔːk] *v.* 妨碍；犹豫不前 (to be unwilling to do something or let something happen)

【例】she *balked* at the idea of compromise.

【用】balk at sth. 不愿接受…

obstruct [əb'strʌkt] *v.* 妨碍，阻碍 (to put difficulties in the way of something.)

【例】He disliked the plan but had not actively *obstructed* it.

【用】obstruct sb. in/from doing sth. 阻挠…做…

hamper ['hæmpə] *v.* 妨碍，阻挠 (to prevent something from happening or progressing normally)

【例】Lack of fund is *hampering* our work.

最初的 (initial, original, embryonic, undeveloped, incomplete, rudimentary)

initial [i'niʃəl] *a.* 开始的，最初的 (happening at the beginning of a process, or when someone first sees or hears about something)

【例】The *initial* talks were the base of the later agreement.

original [ə'ridʒənəl] *a.* 最初的，原始的 (existing at the beginning of a period or process, before any changes have been made)

【例】Our *original* plan was to go to Spain, but it was too expensive.

embryonic [,embri'ɔnik] *a.* 开始的 (just beginning to develop and grow)

【例】The project is still in its *embryonic* stage.

undeveloped [,ʌndi'veləpt] *a.* 未充分发育的；未发展的 (not fully grown)

【例】The lungs of the fetus are still *undeveloped*.

incomplete	[ˌinkəmˈpliːt] *a.* 不完善的，不完全的 (lacking one or more parts) 【例】The school building, begun five years ago, is still *incomplete*.
rudimentary	[ˌruːdiˈmentəri] *a.* 未发展的 (not developed) 【例】Further research showed that the right kidney of this animal was *rudimentary*.

最后的 (final, ultimate, terminal, conclusive, eventual)

final	[ˈfainəl] *a.* 最后的，最终的 (last; occuring at the end) 【例】The *final* exam is the student's last hurdle before graduation.
ultimate	[ˈʌltimit] *a.* 最后的，终点的 (happening at the end of a process or activity) 【例】Becoming a super star is his *ultimate* goal.
terminal	[ˈtəːminəl] *a.* 末端的，终点的 (of, relating to, situated at a boundary, an extremity, or an end) 【例】The History Museum is the *terminal* stop for this bus route.
conclusive	[kənˈkluːsiv] *a.* 最后的 (happening at last or in the end of a process) 【例】Are you sure this is the *conclusive* result?
eventual	[iˈventʃuəl] *a.* 最后的，最终的 (happening or existing at the end of a process or period of time) 【例】All the citizens are happy for the killer's *eventual* capture and imprisonment.

最重要的 (uppermost, highest, leading, maximum, superior)

uppermost	[ˈʌpəməust] *a.* 至上的；最重要的 (in or into the highest or most prominent position) 【例】The economy appears to be *uppermost* in people's minds.
highest	[ˈhaiist] *a.* 最高的 (ranking above the others in importance or quality) 【例】It was reported that Mr. Smith had this information on the *highest* authority.

leading ['li:diŋ] *a.* 最重要的，主要的 (coming or ranking first)

【例】Cancer is the *leading* killer among elders in this city.

【用】play a leading role in sth. 在⋯中起主要作用

maximum ['mæksiməm] *a.* 最高的，最大限度的 (being the largest number, amount etc.)

【例】The murderer is expected to be transferred to a *maximum* security prison.

superior [sju:'piəriə] *a.* 优越的 (situated higher up)

【例】Lulu was said to be of very *superior* intelligence.

【用】be superior to sb. /sth. 比⋯优越的，超过⋯的

做，处理 (deal, transact, perform, execute, prosecute, handle, carry out)

deal [di:l] *v.* 处理，对付 (to take action to do something, especially to solve a problem)

【例】The government had taken effective measures to *deal* with drug smuggling.

【用】deal in 经营；deal out 分配，分发；deal with 应对，处理

transact [træn'zækt] *v.* 执行，处理 (to carry on the operation or management of)

【例】Mr. Harrison was on his way to New York to *transact* some business there.

perform [pə'fɔ:m] *v.* 做，履行 (to carry out an action or pattern of behavior)

【例】Several grafts may be *performed* during one operation.

execute ['eksikju:t] *v.* 执行，履行 (to carry out fully)

【例】The landing was skillfully *executed*.

prosecute ['prɔsikju:t] *v.* 彻底进行，执行 (to pursue (an undertaking, for example) until completion; to follow to the very end)

【例】An investigation was *prosecuted* to find out whereabouts of the murderer.

handle ['hændl] *v.* 处理，应付 (to cope with or dispose of)

【例】It was a difficult situation but Rorry *handled* it very well.

carry out 实施，执行

【例】We all have certain jobs to *carry out* , so be alert.

做作的 (affected, contrived, assumed, mannered, stilted)

affected　　［əˈfektid］ *a*. 做作的，假装的（artificial, pretentious and designed to impress）
【例】Bob's ***affected*** manner annoyed her.

contrived　　［kənˈtraivd］ *a*. 不自然的，做作的（obviously planned or calculated; false or artificial）
【例】Emma wrote a novel with a ***contrived*** ending.

assumed　　［əˈsjuːmd］ *a*. 假装的（taken up or used so as to deceive; pretended）
【例】Having released from the prison, Gary had to live by an ***assumed*** name.

mannered　　［ˈmænəd］ *a*. 矫饰的，做作的（behaving, speaking, or writing in a way that is artificially formal and not natural）
【例】The writer's prose was far too ***mannered*** and self-conscious.

stilted　　［ˈstiltid］ *a*. 不自然的，生硬的（stiffly or artificially formal; stiff）
【例】I praised them in my ***stilted*** German.

索　引

backwash	32	battery	8	beverage	26
bacon	81	battle	330	bewail	111
badger	206	bauxite	31	bewilder	214
badminton	100	BBC	68	bewitch	217
baffle	215	beak	17	bias	12
baffling	175	bean	21	bibulous	95
balance	133	bear	248	bicker	334
balanced	80	beatific	89	bighearted	91
balcony	77	beautify	26,344	bikini	74
balk	347	becoming	266	bilateral	50
ballet	65	bedbug	17	bilingual	64
ballpark	100	bedrock	32	bill	82
ballplayer	100	bedside lamp	79	billboard	50
ballroom	66	bedspread	78	billiards	100
ball-point	56	beef up	176	biodegradable	40
balm	93	beef	80	biography	62
bamboo	21	beetle	17	biological	41
ban	245	befall	139	biology	4
bang	239	befoul	47	biosphere	37
bankrupt	47,245	befuddle	214	biscuit	81
banner	70	beg	243	bizarre	234
bar	246	begin	198	blackguard	98
bare	202,213	beguile	233	blackmail	97
bargain	83	behavior	12	blacksmith	15
barometric	35	belch	109	blame	12,327
Baroque	61	belief	295	blandish	149
barren	30	believe	292	blank	202
barrenness	91	belly	16	blanket	78
barrier	48,72	beloved	91	blast	147
basalt	31	bench	78	bleak	316
base	29	bendable	252	bleed	256
baseball	100	beneficent	91	blemish	287
basement	76	beneficial	51	blend	168
bashful	162	bequeath	194	blight	24
basic	156	berth	86	blink	254
basketball	100	beset	106,205	blizzard	34
bass	65	besiege	106	block	347
bassoon	65	bestow	194	blockade	107
bat	17,100	bet	136	bloodthirsty	148
bath towel	78	betray	90	bloom	24
batter	240	better	274	blossom	24

fundamental	156	department	53	goalpost	101
funereal	317	generate	132	gobble up	280
funny	234	generation	88	golden	25
fur	18	generic drug	94	golf	100
furniture	77	generous	124	gorge	280
furrow	14,235	generous	198	gorgeous	74
further	277	genetic	41	gorilla	13
fuse	251	genial	2	Gothic	61
futurism	61	genocidal	96	gown	74
gain	170	gentle	89,286	grab	14
galaxy	26	genuine	258	graceful	315
gale	147	geography	4	gracious	89
gale	35	geology	4	grade	145
gallant	315	geometric	5	gradual	41
gallery	61	geometry	5	graduate	3
gamble	136	germinate	23	graft	23
gamble	95	get	170	grain	80
Gamma rays	9	ghetto	97	granite	32
gang	98	gigantic	225	grant	194,325
gangster	98	gill	18	grape	22
gap	89	give notice	277	grapevine	70
gardener	22	give one's word	324	grasp	218
gardenia	21	glacial	36,211	grassland	18
gargantuan	225	glad	320	grassy	33
garland	26	glamorous	215	gravel	32
garlic	22	glare	222	gravitation	7
garnish	344	glassware	49	gravity	7
gasoline	10	glazing	44	gray	317
gasp	84	gleeful	320	graze	45
gather	267	glint	254	Greece-Roman	
gathering	168	global	34	wrestling	103
GATT	51	globe	30	Greek	63
gauche	90	gloomy	316	green finger	22
gauge	229	glove	74	green industry	40
gavelock	101	glow	254	greenhouse effect	38
gaze	221	gluttony	95	greening	39
gem	32	go on	139	gregarious	19
gene	41	go out	288	grieve	110
general accounting		go to bed	270	gripe	108
department	53	goal	101	grizzle	25
general affairs		goalkeeper	101	grub	271

phrase	64	plastic	11	pond	19
physical	84,255,287	plateau	31	poor	244
physician	93	platform ticket	86	pop	109
physics	3	platform	86	pop	66
physiognomy	30	playwright	63	popcorn	26
pianist	65	plead	244	poppy	95
piano	65	pleasant	34	popularity	50
pick out	250	plentiful	300	porcelain	49
pick	14,276	pliant	251	pork	81
picture	218	plot	63	portable	42
piddling	284	plough	23	portrait	61
pierce	126	pluck	14	portray	179
pigment	61	plug	79	pose	177
pigpen	19	plump	226	positive	247
pigsty	19	plunge	306	possess	216
pile up	267	plus	5	possible	200
pilferage	52	poem	63	poster	50
pill	94	poet	63	postgraduate	3
pilot	45,87	poetry	63	postpone	131
pine	21,201	poison	287	posture	243
pineapple	22	poisonous	317	potato	22
pink	25	poke	271	potent	95
pinkeye	92	polar	34	potential	12,200
pinpoint	192	polarization	98	poultry	14
pioneer	14	pole-vault	101	pound	239
pious	91	policy	50	powder	94
pirate	98	polish	115	power	5
pirated	73	polished	316	powerless	299
pitch	7	polite	316	practical	58
pizza	81	politics	4	practiced	189
placid	104,286	pollen	24	prairie	31
plague	205	pollutant	38	praise	3,204
plain	125	pollute	38,286	prawn	17
plain	31,71,220	pollution	38	pray	243
planet	27	pollution-free	38	preceding	312
planetarium	29	polychrome	28	precious	106
planetary	27	polygon	6	precise	335
planning department		polymer	11	predict	34,321
	53	polymerization	11	predominant	343
planter	22	pommel	103	preeminent	174
plaster	62	pommelled horse	103	preface	73

splurge	166	stateroom	85	storm	159
spoil	89	static	7	stormy	318
sponge on/off	311	static electricity	7	stout	226
sponge	78	static	160	stout-hearted	315
sponsor	99	stationary	160	straight	333
spore	21	stationery	49	straightforward	339
sportsmanship	47	statistic	55	strangle	253
sportswear	73	statistics	6	strategy	50
spot	249	statue	62	straw	21
spotlight	67,192	stature	84	strawberry	22
spout	109	status	243	stream	226
spray	227	steak	81	streetcar	85
spread	252	stealthy	217	strengthen	175
spring	227	steamer	84	stress	64,236
springboard	102	steel	176	stressed	188
sprint	101	steerage	85	strict	89,307
sprout	23	stellar	27	stride	130
spur	197	stem	24	strike out	254
spurn	193	step	130	strike	159
squabble	334	step	65	stringer	69
squall	35	stepfather	90	strip	295
squander	166	stepmother	90	stripe	75
square	5,339	stepson	90	stroll	213
stab	127	stern	307	strong	238
stable	160	stew	82	struggle	330
stack up	267	steward	87	strut	131
stack	72,345	stewardess	87	stub	95
staff	55	stick	126	studio	67
stagehand	66	stick	329	stuff	345
stagger	224	still	105	stumble on	141
stalk	24	stilted	350	stumble upon	331
stall	131	stimulate	12,172	stunt man	67
stall	283	stinky	319	stunt	67
stamp out	306	stint	183	stupendous	225
stand for	211	stir	172	stylish	77
stand-in	67	stock	83,88	subdue	305
stare	221	stomach	16	sublime	174
starlet	27	Stone Age	14	submerge	306
start	197	stool	77	submerse	306
startle	190	stopping train	86	submit	149
state	243	storage battery	8	subscribe	72

substance	9	surcharge	52	tablet	94
substantial	287	surface	290	tack	56
substantiate	115	surgeon	93	tackle	15
substitute	43	surgery	93	tactful	58
subtract	179	surmise	293	taint	154
subtraction	5	surpass	331	take advantage of	265
subtropical	33	surprise	190	take on	162
subtropics	33	surround	106	take place	139
suburb	76	survey	222	takeoff	87
suburban train	86	survive	122	talent	339
subway	86	survive	41	talkative	68
subzero	35	suspend	132	talon	18
sufficient	124	suspicious	118	tame	15
suit	73	sustain	285	tangible	287
suitable	266	sustainable	40	tangle	170
sulfur	10	swagger	130	tanker	85
sultry	36	swallow up	279	tapestry	78
sum	5	swallow	17	target	49
summarize	154	swamp	307	tariff	48
summon	166	swarm	310	tarmac	87
sundial	30	sweat	84	tasteless	80
sunglow	28	sweater	73	taunt	120
sunny	207	swift	304	tax	60
sunset	28	swindle	98	taxi rank	85
sunspot	28	switch	79	taxi stand	85
sunstroke	92	swivel	303	taxi	85
superexcellent	174	swordsman	67	taxicab	85
superior	349	swordsmen film	68	tea table	78
supermarket	83	symbolism	61	team spirit	59
supernova	27	symbolize	211	team work	58
supersede	41	sympathetic	164	teamwork	53
supervise	2	symphonic	325	tear	143
supervisor	54	symphony	65	tease	120
supple	252	symptom	94	technical school	2
supplement	70	synchronous	29	technical	2
supplicated	3	synopsize	154	technician	54
support	337	synthesize	183	technology	43
supporting role	66	synthetic fiber	11	tedious	261
suppose	293	synthetic	11	teetotal	95
supposing	176	table of contents	73	telecommunication	49
suppress	305	tableland	31	telescope	9